# GOING EXPAT
# MEXICO

Cover designed by Mark Cameron
Cover photo of Olas Altas beach, Mazatlán, Sinaloa, by Janet Blaser
Interior designed by Iris Cameron

Janet Blaser
Visit the author's website at JanetBlaser.com
and on Facebook and Instagram @TheJanetBlaser

Printed in the United States of America
First Printing: December 2024

*To all those who show me what love is*

"What's important is that you make the leap. Jump high and hard with intention and heart. It's up to you to make your life. Take what you have and stack it up like a tower of teetering blocks. Build your dream around that."

- Cheryl Strayed
*Tiny Beautiful Things*

# Table of Contents

# GOING EXPAT
# MEXICO

## Americans share their lives south of the border

Compiled by Janet Blaser

# Introduction

Lots of people fantasize about moving to Mexico. What's not to like? Sunny beaches, affordable health care, an easy visa process, tacos for breakfast, lunch and dinner, an amazing, vibrant culture, and of course, a lower cost of living. All of this points to a less stressful life that's filled with more happiness.

I've been in Mexico almost 20 years now, living my little life as best I can, striving for all those things and more: more happiness, more community, more loving relationships, more joy. Is it easier to live like that here in Mexico, to create that kind of a life? It certainly seems to be. And for the last year, as I've compiled this book, what people wrote in their chapters validated that even more.

My first book, *Why We Left: An Anthology of American Women Expats*, was written with the goal of inspiring others who might be thinking about living abroad, but didn't know how to start or what to do, or were filled with doubts and fears about what their new lives would look like. It was a simple, straightforward idea borne of gratitude and appreciation for how Mexico had welcomed me and allowed me to become the best version of myself while living so happily within her borders. I'd also been inspired by the stories of so many expat women I'd met through the years who'd had the courage to follow their hearts and think outside the box.

That was in 2019. *Why We Left* was, and still is, quite successful and still selling well. I didn't plan on writing another book; it wasn't on my radar at all.

Then the political landscape in America took, shall we say, a turn for the worse. Now, people are leaving the US, or thinking about it, for very different reasons. As I watched what was happening—and what was looming ever larger on the horizon—I began receiving worried messages from folks asking for advice and help in leaving the US and moving to Mexico. They have a completely different mood than the past, a startling and sad change to see. Instead of moving happily toward a more positive lifestyle, the priority for many people nowadays is how to get out of a bad situation that looks to get even worse.

So that's basically how this book came about. *Going Expat Mexico* is my way of trying to help, to use my experience and skill set to provide a possible alternative to what feels like a very broken American Dream. That said, many of you are just looking, like I was, for a better way to live that also includes a bit of an adventure. Whoever you are, I salute you for having the courage to step outside the box and see what else is out there!

*Going Expat Mexico* is the first in a new series of anthologies I'm compiling written by Americans who've moved abroad to a variety of countries: Mexico, Italy, Portugal, Costa Rica, and maybe Spain too. The contributors who've shared their stories in these pages are a diverse group. While *Why We Left* was only women, this book includes men and couples too. Some I know personally; a few wrote for my first book and have shared an update on their lives since then. Most are just regular folks excited and happy to share their new lives abroad, what they did and how they did it. As I read and re-read their chapters, I found myself smiling a lot and often laughing out loud. I feel like they're all my friends now, and it makes me happy that they're so happy.

And that's the kicker: All of them are happy they did what they did. No one regrets their decision to move to Mexico.

What's also striking is everyone's willingness, time and time again, to move forward into the unknown, and their thoughtful observation as they do so. They write of learning to be humble and humbled; of laughing often, smiling more, and waking up every day with a renewed sense of self and a deeper appreciation for life. The joy of getting up each morning and "doing your day" the way you really, really want to. The satisfaction of doing something really good for yourself, of following your heart and being deeply at peace.

Yet change is scary; we all know that. Sometimes, though, it's necessary, or it's going to happen anyway. If you can move through it, little by little, the "new" becomes familiar and then it's not so scary anymore. This, after all, is just one step on a long path of many, and it's a path that you want to take. And if you've picked up this book, chances are there's a little voice in your heart that's whispering, "Do it! Just do it!"

I hope that you'll enjoy reading this book as much as I've delighted in putting it together, and that you'll find it a fun and valuable resource to create the future you want to have. My intention for *Going Expat Mexico*—and all the books in this series—is to inspire and encourage you, to allay the fears and worries preventing you from moving forward with your adventurous, brave, and wonderful expat dream. Happy travels!

# 1. From the Concrete Jungle to the Yucatán Jungle

Joey McCune & Mitch Moore

Xpu Há, Quintana Roo

As I write this, a gentle jungle breeze is moving through my home. All the doors are open and the scent of our night-blooming garden is starting to float in after the afternoon sun warmed the flowers all day. We have a family of monkeys outside in the trees, swinging and playing as they end their day. It's 7 p.m., the last of the sunset is disappearing, and it's just beginning to get dark. Soon the cricket song will start.

I love the evenings in the jungle. During the days there's a sound that emanates from the immense amount of wildlife, and it's a peaceful rhythm, but at night everything quiets down and the cricket song ignites with a sound that sinks into my soul.

I read recently that a scientist discovered that when the audio file of cricket song is slowed down, they sing in perfect harmony, much like an angelic choir. It sounds like human voices singing, with four-part harmony and a swaying choral panorama. This enchanting sound is one of the reasons why I love the jungle in the evening; it's pure magic. It's a special way to end the day and always rocks me to sleep at bedtime.

We never considered moving to the jungle, though. In fact, we envisioned moving to the beach and swaying in a hammock overlooking the sea. The jungle was never something that was on our radar.

I'm a small-town girl from Sequim, Washington. My husband is a California boy who spent summers at his grandparent's farm in

Montana. We raised our family in Seattle, but both of us yearned for a slower pace of life and more sunshine.

We lived a good life in Seattle. We had a beautiful home, two successful careers, a vacation home, and some investment properties. One daughter was fully launched post-college, and our son was in his junior year of university.

I'd worked more than 20 years in real estate, with my own firm in Seattle, and had been a sound healer for several years as a side gig and hobby. My husband, Mitch, was a design/build contractor specializing in remodel, and owned his own well-respected company.

From the outside looking in, most would say we'd made it. We did all the things you're supposed to do in life. We saved our money, took special family vacations, and invested in a strong real estate portfolio for our future. But we were unhappy. We worked tireless hours and didn't feel fulfilled. We felt like we were on an endless hamster wheel and couldn't get off. I was 45 and Mitch was 53.

We often talked about making a move internationally, but the timing was never right—we had a lot of excuses. But let's rephrase that! Is the timing ever right? Aren't there always excuses?

After watching endless episodes of House Hunters International, Mexico Life, and Buying Beachfront with the attitude of "We will do it someday!" I finally decided it was time. I woke up one morning after a long night of contemplation, rolled over and asked Mitch if he was ready to get the hell out and make a big move.

His response was, "If my company magically sells, (who buys a remodel company?) that will be our answer, and we should go." We listed his design/build firm and—bam! We sold it. The Universe answered. It was happening!

At that point there was no looking back. We listed our properties, including our main home, and moved through the process of liquidating our assets. We didn't really have a plan other than to downsize and find an area that fit our current and future needs and that would also offer the possibility to make money somehow.

We considered Belize, Bali, Thailand, Guatemala, Ecuador, Peru, and Mexico. After all was said and done, we decided on Mexico, which made the most sense for many reasons. Its proximity and ease of getting to and from the US, future grandkids, the expat community, cost of living, as well as a relatively easy process to become an expat and permanent resident. Our focus became set on Mexico. Neither of us spoke Spanish.

We meet a lot of people in life that say they want to do something adventurous or make a change. Many have grown tired of the hamster wheel; they dislike their jobs and feel burned out. But few people actually make a change, do anything about it, or put their words into action. The truth is, it's scary to jump off a ledge into the unknown. It's scary to make a change! Most people are stopped by this fear.

Well, this is a tale of two people who woke up one morning and said, "Let's sell it all and move to Mexico!" Which is exactly what we did! Some may say that's crazy, but we've enjoyed the journey and are happy to share the magic that has unfolded.

So many of us find ourselves not happy in our lives. Something is missing. We aren't happy with our jobs, with our pace of life, with our perceived outcome. We realize we were born, worked our entire life, didn't enjoy ourselves as much as we should have, and then we die. We're looking for a purpose or more meaning to fulfil us.

Finding purpose, or living a purposeful life, is important. When our focus is on "finding" something, we treat it like it's outside of us, and that's where we look. Our truth though, is ours to create and choose. When we expand our conscious awareness about the currents that move us, when we get in touch with our heart's true desires and develop a sensitivity to pick up the "impulse," we gain clarity and see aligned action ahead. This is what leads us to a purposeful life. Most of the time it's fear that holds us back from trying something new or from taking a leap into the unknown.

Seven years ago, my husband Mitch and I decided to find our purpose and take that leap. Because sometimes it's impossible to have a plan, we trusted that without a plan, we would find the right situation that fit our needs. We were open to what felt right, and we tried not to have expectations.

We traveled around Mexico until we found a spot that felt perfectly aligned for us, five kilometers into the jungle on the Yucatán Peninsula in Xpu Há. In our wildest dreams, we never thought that we would move to the jungle. As I mentioned earlier, we'd envisioned a hammock on a beach, yet we ended up with something completely unexpected. A great lesson in being open to what comes next.

Xpu Há is one of the best-kept secrets around and we really lucked out with the location. While we may live deep in the jungle, we're also only five kilometers from one of the best beaches in the Riviera Maya. Tulum and Playa del Carmen are the cities that flank us. We're 25 minutes from either one, yet live in a peaceful part of the area that's quiet, tranquil, and magical.

We fell in love with an off-grid home, but don't let that fool you—we're not living in a tree house like Swiss Family Robinson! We're not Tarzan and Jane, although it does feel that way some-times with all of the wildlife around. We live in a state-of-the-art, off-grid, luxury home with all the amenities you'd expect from any luxury home anywhere, with floor-to-ceiling walls of windows that showcase the jungle that's all around us. The overall aesthetic mar-ries indoor/outdoor living well, and we appreciate the openness to the outdoors, the natural light, the fresh air, and the privacy.

We live with an incredible amount of wildlife. We have fam-ilies of monkeys, toucans, parrots, and yes, even jaguars. We fall asleep to cricket song and wake up to birdsong from at least 50 species. It's an exciting adventure each day. I never knew I would become obsessed with birds and wildlife; I'm truly a birdwatcher these days. We even have a pet wild bird, Pedro, that taps on our bedroom window every morning to wake us up. Because our home is all glass, he likes to follow me around and watch me in the living room. I keep him very busy. He and his mate sleep in a tree, cud-dled up each night near our front door. They hum and snore and cuddle together. Each day, Pedro is our alarm clock. I have no idea what his partner Ermita does. Apparently, she's the one that goes off to work.

We also have five jungle cats, regular house cats that bred with wild cats and were born in the jungle. These cats live outdoors and rarely let us pet them, but we feed them and care for them, and in return, they care for us by catching snakes and scorpions.

Life is incredible here. The peace and tranquility are unmatchable. We love our home, we love the setting, we love the warm, embracing culture, we love the incredible food from the Yucatan, we love the lower cost of living and lower cost of fantastic healthcare, and we love all of the beautiful sunshine. I don't think I can ever move back to a place without sunshine after living in Mexico. Coming from Seattle, I didn't realize how much I needed it.

We left a fast-paced lifestyle with a lot of hustle and are deeply appreciative of how relaxing the reset to our nervous system has been. This was one of the most important aspects in our transition for us and a big reason we made an international move.

But the most incredible part of our story is that on our property there's a 65-million-year-old cave and *cenote*. Whenever friends visit, they can't believe that this is our house and that we own a *cenote*. Honestly, we feel the same way. Sometimes I just want to pinch myself. When we bought the property, we didn't know we had one—no one did.

*Cenotes* are crystal-clear swimming holes connected to an underwater river system throughout the Yucatán Peninsula. The ancient Mayans believed that the *cenote* water was sacred, and that the *cenotes* were the entrance to the underworld, their heaven.

Sixty-five million years ago, a meteor hit the earth, causing the ice age; that's when the dinosaurs went extinct. Well, that meteor hit just outside of Tulum, in what is now called the Chicxulub crater. When it made impact, it broke into thousands of pieces around the Yucatán Peninsula, and each piece created a sink hole. These sink holes are the iconic *cenotes* that have made the area so popular.

There's a magical story about how we realized we had a *cenote* on our land, and it's all because of the Mayan Toh bird. The Toh are considered to be the guardian birds of the *cenotes*. They look like Dr. Seuss characters, with two floofy cobalt-blue tail feathers. They only live in *cenotes*, where there's water.

At the beginning of Covid, my husband's mother became ill and died from what we realize now was probably the coronavirus. Mitch was devastated and was spending time in the cave.

Several families of Toh lived in our cave, which was strange because it didn't have water.

One day, Mitch noticed a hole in the rock floor of the cave, about a foot in diameter. When he looked inside, he saw a small fish swim by—which meant we were connected to the underground river system.

With the world shut down, Mitch decided to get to work, to explore more and open up this incredible find. Since we're off-grid with only solar power, and the rock is very hard limestone, it was hard work.

Together with five men, Mitch worked tirelessly to break through the limestone, repurposing everything they pulled out, even using trees that had naturally fallen after a hurricane to build stairs. For a while we thought perhaps it was just a giant mud puddle.

Mitch would put on kid-size swimming goggles he'd bought at a local grocery store, and I'd tie a rope around his waist as he dropped into the hole to see where it went and how far it would go. I would tug on the rope so he wouldn't get lost and would know which direction was up. The water was so muddy it was easy for him to lose track of where he was. He held his breath and explored. He was trying to find out how large the hole was. It turned out to be a second cave under the original cave—but underwater.

A *cenote* is not a real *cenote* unless it has an inflow and an outflow from the underground river system to keep it clean and clear. After months of work, one morning the water was crystal clear, and a beautiful turquoise color, and we knew we had a *cenote*. The natural river system filtered the water with the inflow and outflow. The sun's rays shown in through the open cave and it looked like heaven's rays dancing on the water. We couldn't believe it.

We feel blessed to be the guardians and stewards of such an incredible and magical wonder, and we're honored to share this magical sanctuary with those who feel called to visit. Our *cenote* is unlike others because it has only been used in ceremony. It's very special and very private, and we feel it is a portal.

It's our water temple, and we named it Cenote Sagrado. We host weddings and private events and also offer private "Sound Journeys" and traditional Cacao Ceremonies, as well as other holistic services. We enjoy meeting guests who come to visit us from all over the world.

When we made the move, we couldn't afford to retire; we were too young for that. We didn't have jobs that could transfer with us. We had enough money to buy a home and get creative in some fashion, but we needed to trust that we would find a way— and we did! We followed our hearts and didn't allow our heads to get in the way.

It has been a magical fun ride, one that we do not regret. One that has been meaningful and fulfilling and we hope inspiring to others. Every day we're thankful we made the decision we did. We honored that decision, we believed in ourselves and the unknown, and we're grateful that we did.

If you find yourself in the Riviera Maya, come visit! Join us in the jungle. We love to share our story, and we love to share the magic of Mexico and our very special piece of Paradise. Our *casa* is your *casa*.

⌒

*Since 2017, Joey McCune and Mitch Moore have lived off-grid in the jungle near Tulum, in Xpu Há, Quintana Roo. On the property they bought, they unexpectedly unearthed a cenote and have since created a sacred space where they do sound healings, offer holistic services, and host weddings and other private events, as well as international and "stay with me" retreats in their jungle home. For more information: SoundHealingTulum, @CenoteSagradoEvents and www.SakredJourneys.com. Joey also runs www.MayaEliteProperties.com, a real estate company serving the Riviera Maya.*

# 2. The Messy, Complicated, Privileged Life of an Expat

## Kelsey Erin Shipman

## San Miguel de Allende, Guanajuato

"They fired me," my husband said, his eyes filling with tears. We were less than a year into the mortgage on our first home, had just enrolled our daughter in a preschool with a two-year wait-list, and were balancing credit card payments to make ends meet each month. I was the primary caregiver to our toddler, Hazel, and was only able to work part-time.

"They're giving me one more month of health insurance—that's it," he said between shallow breaths.

That was October 12, 2023. It was in the middle of massive tech-industry layoffs and 10 days before my 38th birthday. We agonized for a few months over what we were going to do. We emptied our savings account. We borrowed money from friends. We sold both of our cars. We cried in bed at night.

By Christmas, we had decided to move to Mexico.

There's no perfect way to be an expat. It is an inherently complicated position in a world forever marked by colonization, racial discrimination, and globalization. Americans, in particular, show up in Mexico with a unique mix of cultural myopia and entitlement. They can't stop talking about how cheap everything is—from taxis to groceries to doctor appointments—and yet, they still resent the "gringo tax" often added on to their purchases. They tend to get mired in the ever-growing and easily accessible bubble of other expats, and sometimes forget they're guests in someone else's country.

Believe me, I understand. I've lived, studied, and worked in seven different countries and made a lot of mistakes. I balked at the cans of horse meat in the neighborhood markets of Uzbekistan. I took photos of the waiting crowd the moment I stepped off the plane in Ghana. I gave coins to homeless children in Bolivia until a crowd of dozens followed me back to my hostel. I mispronounced "bus stop" in France over and over again to many rolled eyes.

As Americans, our passport privilege can take us virtually anywhere. We rarely have to think beyond hotel rooms and plane tickets when pondering a trip abroad. US passport holders can travel to over 180 destinations without a visa for short-term trips. In contrast, citizens of Afghanistan can only access 26 countries without a visa. Applying for a visa to visit another country means a lot of money, time, and paperwork, often to be denied without reason. This ease with which Americans travel can lend itself to a sense of entitlement. Because we can go anywhere, we deserve to go anywhere.

I remember being 19 years old and pursuing my university's study abroad office brochures. It seemed like the choices were endless: Africa, Asia, South America. Nowhere was off-limits to my American passport or American dollars. Now close to 40 years old, I know that there's a price to this disposition. Entitlement cheapens your experience. You forget that travel is a privilege.

There were a lot of reasons why moving to Mexico felt like the wrong choice. Our family was in Austin. Our friends from Mexico reminded us of all the reasons why they'd left. We hadn't even lived in our house for a year. Above all, we felt like we were using our passport privilege to escape the bleak economic realities of our country and exploit those same realities abroad.

Personally, politically, morally, we weren't sure we were doing the right thing. We were moving to a town in Central Mexico with an exploding expat population which was driving up home and commodity prices, making it hard for Mexicans there to make ends meet. This, in particular, felt painfully familiar.

Our home, Austin, Texas, used to be a sleepy town that attracted artists, progressives, and "weirdos" in the middle of the Bible Belt South. It used to be a cheap city where you could live in a garage apartment in the middle of a funky neighborhood for a few hundred dollars a month. Now it's a magnet city for technocrats fleeing the out-of-control housing prices on the coasts. The result? All of the middle- and working-class people we knew growing up are being pushed out of the city, fundamentally changing the culture we love.

Would we be doing the same thing to the people in San Miguel de Allende who are struggling to afford to live in their homes? I can't ignore that the answer, whichever way you look at it, is yes. Would our arrival contribute to the cultural losses of an economy increasingly reliant on tourism? Yes. These are the imperfect choices we make for survival.

When my husband was laid off, we were terrified. After two years abroad in Asia, we had moved back to Austin to have a baby, but the city was unrecognizable. Housing prices had skyrocketed after the pandemic. Californians had been moving to the city at an incredible rate—300 a day by some estimates—and driving up the price of almost everything. To those burdened by a high cost of living on the West Coast, Texas is appealing because it has large homes, a warm climate, and a familiar mix of cultures. But, for two public school teachers with a newborn, the "Texodus" was financially devastating.

So we moved to Mexico. Why? We were looking for a lower cost of living, a temperate climate, and a familiar cultural environment. Sound familiar? San Miguel de Allende has had a substantial community of American expats since 1937, when Stirling Dickinson recruited hundreds of American veterans to study at his art institute in the heart of the city. Today, around 10% of the population is American, with another 60 nationalities represented in this small, Central Mexican town.

There are a lot of things to love about San Miguel: its gorgeous colonial architecture, its seemingly perfect climate, its friendly people and luscious gardens. But Americans have forever changed the cultural fabric. We are still changing it. I have no doubt many "Sanmiguelenses" share the same sadness and resentment I feel towards the Californians that have forever changed my hometown. Even though I love Mexico and have studied Spanish all my life, I'm doing the same kind of damage here.

And that's a large part of what it means to be an expat in Mexico. Contradictions. I have a deep respect for Mexican culture. I've been listening to its music, eating its food, and learning its language all of my life. I enrolled my daughter in a Spanish immersion school at 18 months old. I have many close friends whose families immigrated to the US from Mexico. When I lived in West Africa and Central Asia, I literally dreamed about salsa and tortillas. But none of that changes the fact that I live here as a privileged outsider.

I can't say we were economic refugees when we left the US for Mexico, though we were middle-class public-school teachers drowning in debt and priced out of our home. Though we had no plans to move back to Texas, I'm not even sure we were immigrants because we struggled to imagine ourselves living abroad forever. The controversial word "expat" is the only label that really fit because it acknowledges our privileged status as Americans abroad.

We arrived in Mexico a favored minority. It was easy to get our temporary residency—there was no visa lottery, dreary asylum application process, or dangerous trek across the desert. We were not detained in the airport or questioned invasively. I did have a teary run-in with an immigration officer while getting my photo taken for my temporary residency card. But that just resulted in a bunch of stunned officers sharing confused looks at the babbling gringa who couldn't get her prohibited earring out of her ear while her toddler slapped bits of pancakes against the second-story window.

Because my husband and I are both able to work remotely, we continue to earn US dollars while living in Mexico. Our money goes much farther than at home, and we're able to have an admittedly beautiful life here. We live in a gorgeous neighborhood with cobblestone streets and landscaped plazas. We walk our two-year-old daughter to school every day among bougainvillea, hummingbirds, and butterflies. And, for the first time ever, we have ample and affordable childcare.

But we will always be outsiders.

There's no amount of time or language proficiency that will make us Mexican. My daughter, though growing up bilingual and multicultural, has the passport privilege to travel virtually anywhere unimpeded. But she will also grow up a racial minority, which I hope will help her gain awareness of her whiteness in a way that's more difficult in the US

But. And. But. And. But. This could be our mantra living in Mexico.

We love it here, but there are days when I long for the ease and comfort of home. I've never felt so welcomed in a foreign country, and I know there are painful realities of life in Mexico that I am largely shielded from. My life is so much easier here, but I know my presence is changing this city in ways that I can't fully understand. I speak the language, respect local culture, and revel in my friendships with Mexican women. But I get frustrated when the taxi driver has no change or the plumber is four hours late.

But. And. But. And. But.

So much of our life is an imperfect mishmash of privilege and cultural awareness and alienness and compromise. There's no way to avoid the history of colonization that underlies the ease of expat travel. I can't ignore the train of migrants perpetually seeking safety and employment in my home country. And yet, we've learned so much by moving here.

In the States, I often felt that my daughter was a menace in public. Restaurant patrons would roll their eyes when she would send a sippy cup flying through the air or stuff her mouth with cheesy pasta. I've changed more than a few diapers tucked away on a park bench, hiding behind her overstuffed backpack. I always felt that we were a messy, unwelcome burden anywhere not explicitly for kids.

But in Mexico, children are an integral part of everyday life. Men in three-piece suits stop and wave to my daughter though café windows. Old women in the market hand her fresh tortillas to snack on. Even if she cries on the bus, hurls a bowl of rice on the floor, or runs barefoot through the plaza, people smile.

It's not perfect. I've received more than a few finger wags when my daughter suddenly undresses in public and runs away with her underwear at her ankles. The first preschool she attended had a complaint for me every day at pick-up. She doesn't listen. She won't keep her shoes on. She won't walk in a straight line.

*"Bien hippie,"* is what our housekeeper calls her—another gift of living in Mexico. Affordable domestic help. Without it, we'd be struggling to work, care for our young daughter, maintain our

household, and navigate the ways of a foreign country. You know, the way it was back in the US Tired, stressed, and perpetually busy.

And frankly, that is how our housekeeper's life is—she cleans our house all day, then goes home and cleans hers. Her help allows me to work and spend more time with my daughter. But she has no one at home to help her with her young son. She often arrives exhausted, and we share stories of tantrums and late-night feedings.

But. And. But. And. But.

And then, there's the other Americans. Loud, entitled, and often "helping" by imposing their own cultural norms. I don't want to be like them, and of course, I am. They chastise Mexicans for letting their dogs roam the neighborhood unattended while walking their own dogs off leash. They market themselves as experts on living in Mexico, but never learn to speak more than a few words of Spanish. They hang Mexican flags above their front doors but become incensed when things don't operate like they do in the States.

There's also an abundance of NGOs started and supported by Americans. They rescue dogs, raise money for school supplies for local children, and invest in native gardens for the public. They employ many local people in their homes repairing, gardening, cooking, and cleaning. Many pay rent to Mexican landlords and patronize local language schools. There are cases of multi-generational families being lifted out of poverty because of American support.

But. And. But. And. But.

There's a lot of English in the town we live in, and in any other time in my life, I would think of that as a bad thing. In my early 20s, I was caught in the trap of perpetually seeking the authentic. I wanted to see places without tourists, without travel guides, without English translations. Now I understand that my simple presence changes places. Nothing is authentic with an American watching and recording with their phone.

I'll admit, in the midst of a lay-off with a toddler and two elderly dogs, I was looking for something easy: a familiar culture, an accessible language, somewhere with a short flight home. My favorite parts of Texas come from Mexico—the food, the music, the people. Even though Central Mexico is very different from Central Texas, we kept waiting for the culture shock to arrive.

Instead, we felt comfortable in a multicultural city where we could meet both expats and Mexicans with young children. Perhaps it is because I was a Spanish teacher for many years, or because my husband grew up on enchiladas and breakfast tacos, or because we both have many friends at home whose families are from Mexico, but our transition here was the easiest we've ever experienced abroad.

It feels easy to meet people here. Our dogs play with our Mexican neighbors' Pomeranians and my husband plays pool with a mix of locals and expats. There are a lot of marriages here between Mexicans and Americans, and our daughter fits in seamlessly with the intercultural group of kids in our neighborhood. Our daughter is so comfortable with the fruit vendors at our local market that she draws them pictures and brings them flowers. They hand her endless mango and watermelon slices.

There's also a thriving community here of Americans with young children. All of us moms are looking for things to do after school, and the abundance of children's activities, often run by Mexicans, is impressive. Musical theater summer camp. Children's rock-climbing clubs. Trampoline parks. Cafés with playscapes, monkey bars, and treehouses. There are endless clothing swaps, mother's groups, and music classes for all ages.

Out of all five members of our family, our two-year-old daughter is most certainly the happiest in Mexico. A little bundle of endless energy, her active brain thrives in a bilingual environment. As the one who has to chase her around, I'm particularly gratified that she has an added layer of challenge to her days. She moves fluidly between Spanish and English, and confidently corrects her father's latent pronunciations.

The purple public buses thrill her with every ride, and she finds no lack of friends at the local playgrounds. It is beautiful to watch slightly older girls take her by the hand and lead her to the top of the slide. They offer to push her on the swing and effortlessly share their snacks. I've never seen an American child do that, here or at home.

My daughter wakes up so darn happy every day. She picks flowers on the way to school, waves at passing taxis, and begs to go to the market first thing Saturday morning. We are hardly ever in a car here, unlike at home, and I think she thrives in this smaller world. There are so many people here to love her, both friends and strangers, and she's unburdened by the cultural complexities we wrestle with each day. She is truly free.

Still, it's complicated.

Mexicans suffer under a constantly fluctuating currency exchange rate that generally favors the US dollar. Although improving, more than one-third of the country lives below the official poverty line. In San Miguel de Allende, close to half the population live in moderate or extreme poverty. No matter how bad our financial circumstances are, we have more than most people here.

And yet, we arrived in San Miguel de Allende with nearly empty bank accounts, very few household items, and both of us only working part time. Before deciding to move to Mexico, we seriously considered moving into my in-law's attic with two dogs and a toddler. Things were dire and we didn't know how to survive. So, we used our passport privilege, our ability to work remotely, and our previous experiences abroad, to move to Mexico. We made an imperfect choice.

Mexico has given us so much in return. A culture where children are adored. A thriving community of artists and musicians. A comfortable house in a beautiful neighborhood. Loving adults who help us care for our home, our daughter, and our pets. A place where we can recover, regroup, and restabilize. The question is, of course, what will we give in return.

But. And. But. And. But.

❦

*Kelsey Erin Shipman is a writer based in San Miguel de Allende, Mexico. She writes articles on food and culture and ghostwrites books for creative professionals on doing what you love. Her work has appeared in USA Today and The Austin Chronicle, as well as numerous literary journals, and she served as the Writer-In-Residence at the Katherine Anne Porter Literary Center. Mother of a Chihuahua, Anatolian Shepherd, and two-year-old girl, she's always out of coffee and sunscreen. Follow Kelsey on Instagram @kelseyerinshipman and on her website (kelseyshipman.com).*

# 3. Feeling Happiness Every Second of Every Day

Amy Jones

Merida, Yucatán

I wake up every morning with a smile on my face and gratitude in my heart. I look out my second-floor bedroom window at rooftops with water and gas tanks, oddly positioned PVC pipes, and the occasional watchdog. Across the street, neighbors remodel an old house. Their workers play old-style *bachata* music late into the night. School kids walk down the street to school. Ladies wait to take the bus to work. Old men gather at the local coffee shop every morning. I smell freshly baked bread from the market. Every single person is happy no matter where I look. This is my daily life.

This neighborhood where we live and work brings so much joy, I feel my heart will burst. When I first moved, I wasn't ready for this kind of local life. I needed to bridge the gap slowly. It's taken time to learn the culture, the language, the nuances, the do's and don'ts, and ease into it. This culture forces you to slow down, to enjoy life, to not take yourself so seriously, and most importantly, to live for today. I've learned to let go of expectations and to be in the moment. Being on time isn't a deal breaker. I've turned down many work opportunities because life isn't only about making money. Enjoying life is my first priority.

Small things make me incredibly happy. One is learning Yucatecan Spanish from my husband, Angel. Communicating with locals is a game-changer. I'll never forget the day of "the shift." Deciding to practice my Spanish, I visited a local restaurant. The waiter, an elderly man, timidly approached my table. I could tell by his demeanor he didn't know any English. I greeted him in my best Yucatecan Spanish. I asked him about his day and thanked him in advance for his attention. Meeting my eyes, he audibly gasped. His trepidation turned into a big smile. It was a memorable day, to say the least. It was the first time, without Angel, that I was able to communicate effectively. My heart filled with joy recognizing my progress.

Looking back over the last five years, I want to share how my life has changed deeply, profoundly, and radically. I know happiness and I feel it every second of every day.

In September of 2019, my research started with a trip to Mérida. Driving in the Centro Historico and seeing the pastel-colored colonial houses in person was breathtaking. Everything looked just like it did on the internet! A feeling of pure joy washed over me as I began to explore.

One day, I visited gorgeous Santa Lucia Park. Full of history, it was the location of the Yucatecan Serenata, a weekly performance of song and dance. It's no wonder the charm and allure attracted me—there are two things that I love: music and dancing. The magnificent trees in the middle of the park beckoned me. As I stood beneath them, I felt a peace pass over me. I closed my eyes and took a deep breath. My feet began to grow roots, deep into the ground. Deeply connected with the imagery, my intuition said, "Move, move, as fast as you can." I hesitated. It screamed, "Move, move, move, NOW!"

Never do I question when my intuition is so strong. I returned to Dallas and sold everything. I wanted a new life and only brought items that fit in suitcases. Just three months later, on Christmas Day, I moved to Mérida—the best present ever!

This was the day living began. There's an enormous difference between being alive and living. The Maya believe that when a person reaches 52 years of age, they attain the special wisdom of an elder. In their calendar system, two cycles come together every 52 years, and the celebration of the cycles is called the New Fire Ceremony, *El Fuego Nuevo,* a time of new beginnings. The celebration is also called, "Binding Up of the Years." Discovering this was profoundly and deeply impactful. How I love the name, "Binding Up of the Years!" In June of 2019, I celebrated my 52nd birthday. Finishing the first cycle of life, I was ready to step into new beginnings.

The excitement of this newfound information created an energetic and emotional response. I was like the proverbial kid in the candy store. My daily outings were glorious adventures. Smells tempted me down a variety of streets. Beautiful colonial houses fascinated me. Music enticed me into unfamiliar areas. It was all I could do to stop exploring and return to my Airbnb to rest for the following day.

## Year One: 2020

This was the year that: (1) I learned to accept help from others, and (2) I didn't need to understand everything.

During Covid, I leaned on Angel. The Universe had put him in my path the first week after I moved. I didn't know this man but I believed in the process. I learned to trust. I learned what a healthy relationship looked like and felt like. I learned that allowing someone to help me was not a sign of weakness but instead was a gift for myself and the person helping me. I learned to stay out of judgment and allow things to take their own course. I couldn't control anything during this time, which was scary and a huge lesson. I recognized I had the strength and determination to wait out this unknown time with compassion.

One time Angel told me, "*Mi amor*, you don't have to understand everything. Trying to understand causes more stress and anxiety. I've lived here my entire life and I still don't understand everything. Just accept that's the way it is and move on. You'll be happier." I took his advice to heart, and he was right. I was happier with letting things flow, accepting that things are the way they are.

Angel showed me a different side of life and of myself. When the student is ready, the teacher will appear. Every day is a learning experience about the culture, the food, and the Yucatecan way of life. The people are beautiful, and their happiness is apparent, engaging, and contagious. I waited so long for happiness that I feel like I'm still dreaming.

## Year Two: 2021

This was the year I fell deeply in love. Before leaving Dallas, I resigned myself to being single the rest of my life and made peace with it. Post-divorce, like we're supposed to do, I made my list of wants/needs/dealbreakers.

One day, I looked at Angel and realized that he had, without exception, every single dealbreaker quality on my list. He was too young, with two young children by two different women, he smoked, he didn't meet my minimum height requirement, he didn't have a car, etc., etc., blah, blah, blah. Yet, here was this amazing, gorgeous, sweet man ready to help me with every request. Literally, he would tell me, "*Mi amor*, I'm just waiting for instructions. What do you need? Tell me and I'll get it for you." (Now what woman doesn't want that?!)

Over time, we fell into a graceful partnership. In October, we decided to get married, more out of necessity than anything else. This was something we had both said we'd never do. He had never been married and didn't plan on it. I had been married before and didn't want to do it again. A major shift happened to both of us. We committed to each other and it felt different. We went through some incredibly tough times and stood by each other. Using the imagery of my feet growing roots, it felt like we were now entwined; roots, trunk, branches, and leaves. We joined together in an amazing way that felt good, right, nourishing, and supportive for both of us.

## Year Three: 2022

This was the year I began my mourning process. I'd lived in Mérida for a little more than two years at this point. My life was falling into place. Angel and I were married. We had a gorgeous home. My business, LifeinMerida.com, was flourishing, and with Angel by my side, we were ready to take it to the next level.

As everything fell into place, I recognized the need to mourn the "old me," the person I no longer was. I needed to mourn the little girl who didn't get her needs met. I needed to mourn the teenager who couldn't be herself. I needed to mourn the wife who couldn't make her marriage work. I needed to mourn the divorcee who'd had unrealized dreams. And in mourning all these multifaceted people, I gained an appreciation for all the lessons that had brought me from there to here.

I spent the better part of the year going back in time, and exchanged mourning for celebrating. The little girl learned to be self-reliant. The teenager learned to express herself through writing.

The wife learned that it takes two committed people to make a relationship work. And, finally, the divorcee learned that when she just lets go and allows the Universe to bring her what she needs in the right time, right circumstances, and right place, her life can radically change.

## Year Four: 2023

This was the year when I truly integrated. Remember the elderly waiter I spoke Spanish with? This is the year that happened. After that situation, I created a little checklist of things I wanted to accomplish speaking in Spanish:

- Order at the drive-through at Carl's Jr.
- Give my Amazon delivery driver instructions over the phone
- Go to a doctor who didn't speak English
- Move around the city without using Google Maps
- Communicate effectively with locals
- Compliment people on the street and in shops
- Negotiate with local vendors for touristy items (when appropriate)
- Ask questions when I needed help in the grocery store

Angel and I created a rule to help with my Spanish. Inside the house was English. However, outside the house, I was on my own and spoke in Spanish only. He stood close to listen and assist, if needed. But otherwise I had to do it all by myself. It's one of the greatest gifts he's given me. Ready to help at any given moment while allowing me the opportunity to do it on my own.

## Year Five: 2024

This was the year when I began to thrive and felt totally in my element. Interestingly, 50% of expats who move here decide that Mérida is not for them. Unmet expectations, the heat, culture, language, slower pace, and other factors cause them to move either back to their home country or to another destination, within Mexico or in another country altogether. Not me! This year I feel more alive, completely settled, and utterly successful. Our business continues to grow and blossom. Our marriage is strong and stable. Our circle of friends—locals, expats, and clients-turned-friends—is expanding. I look at my life and feel like I'm the luckiest person in the world. This is my spot. I found my place. I experience happiness every single second.

My biggest secret? Staying in gratitude 100% of the time. I don't take anything for granted. I accept the inconsistencies in electricity, water pressure, trash pickup, rules, regulations, and all the other differences of living in a foreign country. I look at my life, the people around me, the experiences I've had, and the lessons I've learned, and I'm grateful for all of it, because without it I wouldn't be where I am today. I finally know the definition of happiness, and I feel it constantly every day. There's no turning back.

⁓

*Amy Jones is a dynamic lifestyle writer and passionate educator whose blog, LifeinMérida.com, captures the essence of life in the culturally rich city of Mérida, Mexico. With a keen eye for detail and a genuine love for her surroundings, Amy shares personal experiences, useful tips, and advice about a variety of topics, making her blog a go-to resource and inspiring others to embark on their own adventures. Her honesty, transparency, and willingness to share challenges sheds much-needed light on the realities of expatriate life.*

*One of her unique attributes is being married to a local. She and her husband, Angel Rodriguez, offer little-known insights to bring awareness to cultural differences for a better understanding of local life. Her background includes real estate, international moving assistance, and education; an inspiring voice for those seeking adventure and connection in a new place.*

*She is the owner of Life in Mérida™, Mérida Retirement Tours™ and Life in Mérida™ Real Estate, and offers consultations, informative guides, research tours, and real estate representation. Often referred to as the Mérida Ambassador, Amy invites her audience to explore the beauty and diversity of Mérida.*

# 4. A Good Run

### Lina Weismann
### Sayulita, Nayarit

"Can I pet your dogs? How old are they?"

"Sure! They're both about 17 years old."

"Wow, that's crazy! What do you feed them?"

"I make their food, but they're Mexican mutts and get to run every day. It keeps them young."

"Where do you live?"

"Mexico."

"Oh, New Mexico?"

"Nope, old Mexico, real Mexico, you know, where Mexicans live."

I think I've had some version of the above conversation about a million times. Yes, we live in REAL Mexico; yes, we raised our son there; no, it's not dangerous. In fact, it's safer than the open-carry state that we're currently visiting in the United States.

Now that our son has graduated from college and is living on his own, we're no longer restricted to spending long summer months at home in Mexico and can travel a bit. A few years ago, we purchased a camper van, which we leave with family in the US, and have spent summers exploring Bureau of Land Management land. It's interesting to be in the country where I was born and raised but that is clearly not my home. Everywhere I go, I compare the stores, the sounds (or lack of them), the scenery, and the people to my real home, about 1,600 miles south.

I wrote about my choice to leave the great old United States for a quick bout with Mexico in 2008 in another book, "Why We Left: An Anthology of American Women Expats," also compiled by Janet Blaser. My chapter, "Exit Strategy," explained how I, along with my family, decided to move permanently to Mexico. Now, 17ish years after relocating, it feels like it's time to write about what's happened since then.

When I look back at what I've shared in the past, so much of it still seems valid, and yet so much has changed. The world has changed, our town has changed, Mexico has changed, and I've gotten older—oh my! As I write this, AI is everywhere, critical elections are happening around the world, the Mexican economy is booming, and American immigration to Mexico has gone up about 80%.

What does all this mean? What is my role in this quickly changing place that is my community— which happens to be in another country? Am I an expat, an immigrant, a resident, or just nuts? So many folks we've known over the years have had their "Mexico experience," and, for valid reasons, have called it a day and left. We remain. While this version of my story will still involve some much-needed anecdotes, it might be more introspective and reflective than my previous telling. I think that comes with age!

Between 2008 (the year I moved to Mexico), and 2024, there have been a lot of changes worth noting. When we first moved to Sayulita, internet was a rarity and not expected or promised. Certainly, we did not have it at our home. Now, one can assume that every rental in town has it and there's a service in town that one can connect to. Since whatever you need is just a click away, expectations for information, conveniences, and communication are radically different. As part of our global economy, commercialism and convenience abound. Small-town Mexico is no exception.

With Mexico being Mexico, and the rise of both immigration and tourism, our sleepy town, and all towns along the Nayarit and Jalisco coast, have had to adjust. Referencing his own small town, a friend recently told me, "Paradise is no longer Paradise." I have a slightly different take: Paradise sometimes needs to be managed. With increased tourism and a stronger economic base, folks with money have arrived. While that totally makes it easier for me to raise funds for needed local programs, it also changes expectations for services, life, and infrastructure.

Years ago, when we had an electrical outage, we'd be grateful to get services back within three days. Now, if a part of town goes without electric or Wi-Fi for three hours, folks freak out. People actually ask and complain about Wi-Fi speed and water pressure and expect food allergies to be attended to. What have we become? Don't get me wrong, improved economic conditions in Mexico and in our area have led to better employment opportunities for locals, a growth in the Mexican middle-class, and amenities for all. Soy milk is now a thing, *motos* are everywhere, and people can buy appliances easily. About two months ago, I was shopping at a large grocery store in Bucerias and almost fell over when I saw a roasting pan! However, I'll say this now: If I get one more invitation to a WhatsApp group, my head will simply explode.

Given all this, I get asked all the time, "So, has Sayulita changed?" Yes, all small towns change, especially those that you want to go to. However, what most tourists experience is a three-day wild ride in the four blocks around the plaza, where they believe everything is located. To get to the soul of our town, you must scratch the surface. While that doesn't take much, most do not bother.

How do you get off Mr. Toad's wild ride? It's pretty easy: Stay sober, speak a little Spanish, get outside of the four-block tourist area, volunteer, ask meaningful questions. You get the point. Have you ever been to Disneyland? Do you know how when you walk around everything seems perfect and easy, kind of like it was meant for you to enjoy? Well, it is. Talk to someone who works at Disneyland, and they will tell you about all the underground tunnels where hard-working people sweat every day to make Cinderella smile and provide you with cold beverages. We're not so different. Want to know the real town? Take a walk through Centro between 6 a.m. and 7 a.m. See all the workers washing down the streets, sweeping and setting up their businesses. Watch how the garbage truck and our local not-for-profit recycle program do their morning pick-ups. See the delivery trucks unloading. It takes work to manage "Paradise."

In the last year or so, there has been an emergence of a new bi-cultural and bi-lingual younger generation that somehow "gets" our community in a way that many do not. Some of these folks were born and raised here, and some, like me, have immigrated and have a true interest in preserving what they've found. As I go around town talking about recycling, infrastructure, etc., I'm noticing a new awareness of folks who understand that they have to take responsibility for the world, and particularly our town. This new generation is choosing to see the challenges facing our fragile community, and, more importantly, they're choosing to take responsibility to help manage our local resources. They come with new ideas, talents, and initiatives.

This new generation also gets a critical point in small town Mexico: What needs to be done, needs to be done by you. There is simply no "they." Garbage on the beach? Pick it up. Hurt animal? Your responsibility. Natural disaster? Get together with friends and make a difference. Remember that 100-year flood that happened in Sayulita about a decade ago? Well, it happened again several years ago. Similar to last time, the riverbank simply gave way after a series of major storms, and, of course, the poorest communities were affected the most. It didn't affect the four-block tourist area, and I swear tourists were in town at the time having brunch and sipping mimosas while the rest of us were assessing the damage. Then the Marines showed up to help. Let me say that again: The Marines showed up, as did the county *presidenta*, or mayor. We were shocked.

The Marines worked on digging out the banks of the main river for a few hours until the media miraculously appeared to take photos. After that, they disappeared, never to return. (That part did not shock us.) Many of us worked for the next few months to clean up affected areas and raise funds to replace homes and belongings lost in the disaster, with help from this new generation of doers.

Let me say it again, there is no "they." You want something done? Get off your sofa, gather other concerned individuals, and get to work. So many more people understand this now than 20 years ago. You can feel the energy in town; it makes my heart sing.

I was at home on March 11, 2020 when an international pandemic was declared and travel everywhere halted. My 20-year-old son was on his college spring break in Paris with friends. Life as we knew it immediately and drastically changed.

The president of the United States announced that all flights to the US were cancelled and that no one could enter the country.

In the few hours it took him to clarify that what he meant to say was that only US citizens could arrive on US soil, there was quite a whirlwind in our home. Luckily, my brother and his family live in France, so we thought, well, he can stay there for the next week or two until this blows over. As we all soon found out, that was not what would happen.

On March 12, 2020, Sayulita closed. For real. For the next 10 weeks, it was a ghost town. The Mexican government was clearly taking this pandemic seriously. Non-essential businesses were not allowed to open, and we were all supposed to "shelter in place." The police were actually in town arresting folks for being on the beach and surfing—I kid you not. Within a week, a group of locals called the "*vigilantes*" were guarding both entrances to town, only letting in people that lived here. Similar groups of local men did the same thing in most of the coastal towns in our area. These men were protecting their families and took their jobs seriously.

Being the Jewish mom that I am, I joined a group of locals and helped provide and deliver meals to them three times a day during their 24-hour shifts. I also organized with friends to create and fund a local food bank where *canastas* (food boxes filled with basic essential items) were distributed to families in town and in neighboring communities. Hotels, restaurants, etc., all closed and fired staff in droves. People were in need.

The next month was Semana Santa. If you've never been in a Latin American country, you may not know that Semana Santa is kind of sacred. It's the week around Easter when workers get time off, and everyone—I mean everyone—goes to the beach. If you live in a Mexican beach town, it's easily the busiest time of the year. But hold on to your hats: the Mexican government actually cancelled Semana Santa. Not only did they cancel it, but the ban was also successful. While most chose to respect the government orders and not travel, official sanctioned and unofficial *vigilantes* were stationed all along the coast to turn back those who thought these rules did not apply to them. Who knew? The Mexican government also laid out a fairly well-thought-out and organized vaccination plan, with vaccines mostly donated from Russia, China, and Europe. Honestly, it was impressive!

Now, I understand that getting the vaccine was somehow politically charged in the US Trust me, it wasn't in Mexico. Let me set the stage.

The public health care system in Mexico is very lacking. Most people do not have private care and those that have public care often do not access it due to long waiting lists, lack of transportation, and lack of trust in the system. While I can't give you statistics on how many folks in Mexico, or even just in our area, died due to Covid, I can say this: People died, and more than you think. Accurate statistics simply do not exist. Folks died of respiratory illnesses before the pandemic was announced, and once we understood what was going on, more folks died. Folks who had diabetes died. Folks that had heart conditions died. Folks that could not or did not seek treatment died. The cute *joven* (young man) who always helped direct traffic during holidays? He died. Folks that had private health care and went to the hospital died. Yes, folks in our town died. A friend of mine who lives in a rural community about 30 minutes north of us said that she was going to about four funerals a week. Let that sink in. Trust me, offering a free vaccine that could stop you from dying was not political.

About 10 weeks into this international event, Mexico decided to put its economy first and welcome tourism back. Mexico became one of the few countries in the world to welcome tourists without a testing program for entry. And come they did. Within two weeks of this decision, we all learned what the term "digital nomad" was.

Markets were considered "essential businesses," so the farmer's market I managed was able to reopen again, with restrictions. We changed the customer flow so it was "one way;" vendors had to be separated by two meters; both vendors and customers had to wear masks at all times; and we had to have antiseptic hand wash on every table. No worries; vendors were happy to come back to work and shoppers were happy to have local produce and natural medicines.

However, I will never forget the cute blond from Canada who showed up and refused to put on a mask, saying, "We're in Mexico, there are no rules here."

I held my tongue and did not say, "Actually, there are lots of rules here, but you don't seem to know or respect them, as you don't speak the language, and you're clearly too privileged to care."

I also didn't say, "Oh, and, by the way, the person you want to buy lettuce from over there just lost her brother to Covid and is here working alone because her 70-year-old mother doesn't want to be exposed to foreigners who carry germs."

After taking a few deep breaths, what I did say was, "We have about 70 families working in this market who are trying to support our community with healthy products and provide their families with an income. If customers don't follow the regulations, then we'll be shut down and these families will lose their income. I know none of us wants that!"

She turned around and left.

When we first moved to Sayulita, I was working remotely for my old position in San Francsico. (I think I was the town's first digital nomad. Actually, the term didn't even exist then.) Mind you, I agreed to work remotely, and they agreed to have me work remotely, without me even having Wi-Fi at my house. Like all newbies coming to Mexico, I just figured, how hard can it be to get Wi-Fi? Turns out it was a lot harder than any of us thought.

We went to the Telmex office in nearby Bucerias to sign up for their internet service. Silly us, we didn't even have a phone line. That had to come first. They politely took all our information and said it would take 3-4 weeks. According to our neighbors, the wait would be more like six months, if it happened at all. In the meantime, I walked every day to a friend's house down the street, as she graciously let me sit out on the patio to use their Wi-Fi. Sometimes it even worked.

For the first several years of my remote work in Sayulita, I had an "Out of Office" message on my email that said something like, "If you don't hear back from me in an efficient manner, no worries, I'm fine. I am in Mexico with faulty Wi-Fi, electricity, and water. I will respond the second I can!" In those days, one could get away with a message like that.

While I was attempting to work, my husband was going to the Telmex office every other day, starting about a month after our original service order. One day, he was determined to make it happen. He went into the Telmex office with cash in hand. While we thought we now had this Mexico thing wired, he came home with his tail between his legs. Apparently, there was a gringo in line in front of him, in a similar situation, who tried to bribe the Telmex worker. The worker proceeded to tell the guy off—not a common occurrence in these parts. He was properly chewed out for asking for special treatment with a bribe and chastised in advance for probably then complaining about Mexicans taking bribes. Oops.

We were at a loss until I had an idea. I baked some banana bread and sent my lovely husband back to the office the next day with instructions to thank the Telmex worker profusely for all his help. Boom. That weekend, we got Wi-Fi and a private message from the worker with an invitation to lunch! We had set a record: a Wi-Fi connection in five weeks!

Living in Mexico for this many years has certainly changed our knowledge and experience of life here. As a bucket list trip last year, my husband and I went with friends to a huge hot spring destination about a two-hour drive outside Mexico City in the middle of nowhere. We rented a car and prepared our nerves to drive through the crazy traffic of the world's largest city in the western hemisphere and eventually found the hot springs. No reservations; old school. We stayed in the "fancy" hotel, which actually had Wi-Fi, as some of us had to work. We'd all lived in Mexico long enough to know that the food would suck but that we wouldn't starve. We were also smart enough to bring our own drinking water and wine. That night and the next day, we floated in the mineral-rich river, explored the cave with its hidden springs and waterfalls, lost our flip-flops in the current, and simply enjoyed the trees, mountains, and other folks enjoying a well-deserved holiday. No white faces around.

On the way back to Mexico City, we stopped at one of the many circus tents dotting the road. On the way there, we'd figured out they were roadside restaurants, set up with no electricity or running water. If you've never stopped at a random restaurant along the highways and streets of Mexico, you're missing out! My first time was about 18 years ago; I had the best *birria* I've ever had, even though I didn't know what it was.

The four of us sat down among what appeared to be local cow hands amidst the questioning looks of the restaurant owners and ordered. Places like this have no menus; someone comes to tell you what they have, and you make a choice on the spot. Pulling into a roadside stand, you kind of never know. This one had two things on the "menu" so we ordered two of each, figuring we would see what showed up. It smelled good so what could go wrong? We had a lovely lunch and then headed back to the city. Along the way, we pulled over as I had my eye on a cow hide that I just could not resist buying. (Such are the roadside attractions of Mexico.)

After we got back, I realized that we were able to go on and enjoy the trip the way we did because Mexico is our home. I don't think someone living in another country and/or not speaking Spanish would have felt comfortable doing what we did. Although totally objectively safe, it would have been too out of their comfort zone. These are the kinds of privileges we've been able to experience living a true existence in another country. Mexico promotes a sense of adventure that we've come to count on and appreciate.

When we first moved to Mexico, I was in my early 40s. I've now completed my 60th year around the sun. While I still feel younger than my age, age and time on this earth make a difference. I'm not sure if I've become more introspective or have just accumulated more knowledge and perspective as the years go by. I mean, wrinkles are the payment for wisdom, right?

While everything seemed new and different 20 years ago, things now seem more predictable. Government not doing anything? Yep. Surprise rain in January? Yep. Building codes being ignored? Yep. There are things that just go with the territory when you're living in a small town in Mexico. If you let it upset you, you do not last.

That doesn't mean there's nothing one can do to improve things; there are. But actions here need to be informed by history, culture, and relationships. Doing things the "American" way will simply not work.

After all these years, am I an expat, a resident, an immigrant, or something else? I would like to officially distance myself from the term "expat." Moving to Mexico has absolutely nothing to do with me being a patriot or not. I chose to leave my home country for many reasons and then chose to stay in Mexico, again for many reasons. The fact that Americans use the term "expats" for themselves, and somehow individuals from other countries are referred to as "immigrants" feels very privileged to me. Call me resident or immigrant any day.

As I get older, like most, I'm starting to look back at legacies, memories, and pinpoints in my life. I spent close to 20 years in the mental health field in the US before changing my country of residence. I worked hard, alongside dedicated individuals, to try to make life better for some. I showed up in hospital emergency rooms to talk with teenagers who wanted to die. I responded to community crisis; I wrote white papers on change. However, as I sit here in my early 60s, the greatest impact I feel I've had is in this crazy little town.

About 16 years ago, a small group of women and I started a local farmers' market. We began with half a dozen vendors on an abandoned dirt lot. Now it's a not-for-profit organization that provides 75 vendors with a way to support their families, and also provides healthy, local food products to our community. Some of our vendors have been with us for many years, and I've had the privilege to see their children born and their pride in supporting their family from products they grow or make.

Almost 10 years ago, I participated in water quality improvement projects here, and about six years ago, I was part of creating a not-for-profit recycling program aimed at reducing trash in town. I know, none of these projects or accomplishments are rocket science. They exist all over the world. But the impact of making concrete changes in a small, tight community brings an incredible amount of satisfaction. If I'm only remembered for these things, I'm good.

I just got back from walking with my 17-year-old dogs. They don't go far, but they do still run every day. While Mexican mutts are a tough breed, I truly think that things like growing up without leashes, being able to run on the beach, adventure in the jungle, chase things, eat weird crap, and make their own friends are a direct result of their quality of life and longevity. They get to explore and have a sense of freedom. I know that their time is coming, but they've had a good run.

Last year, we decided it was time to do a bucket list trip with them. They've now seen snow and hail, swam in rivers, chased deer, and cuddled with kittens. I'm inspired by them. The life we have chosen here and chosen to share with our son and many animals is easily inspired by curiosity and adventure. Embracing the uncomfortable can take years off your life and round out the edges a bit. Sometimes bushwacking is just what the doctor calls for.

$$\backsim$$

*Lina Weissman lives in Sayulita with her husband and many animals—both domestic and jungle friends. Her son grew up in town and is now living and working in the US. When not actually traveling, Lina plans her next adventure. She also spends way too much time volunteering. Lina's hobbies include reading, cooking and anything crafty.*

# 5. Transitions

Jovonna Gonzalez

Mexico City, Mexico City

Tears blurred the screen in front of me as I searched for the right words. The cursor blinked in the empty subject line, taunting me with the blank body of text. I wanted to be brief. Concise. I'd agonized over this decision and now that I'd made it, I wanted to be swift so I didn't leave the door open to talk myself out of it all over again.

"Dear Joel..." I started. In retrospect, I don't know exactly what I wrote but I used the word resignation, I talked about my kids, now former students, and once satisfied, quickly hit "Send."

With the ease of a click, I quit my job. I left a career and closed a massive chapter in my life. I shed the identity I'd grown into adulthood with and steeled myself to embrace a season of uncertainty and instability. But I was not well-prepared for how heartbreaking it would be. Even after more than a year and a half of wrestling with the decision, quitting teaching took the wind out of me. No one warned me that I would need to grieve the loss. That although it was the right decision, it would be crippling, and I would be paralyzed for a season as I tried to chart a new course I never really anticipated needing. The goal was to make decisions rooted in love rather than allow fear to determine what would come next.

And like any good unemployed millennial, my first step on that new path was to move back home with my parents, where I nursed my broken heart back to health with matcha lattes, endless job applications, and time spent deepening the well-worn couch cushions in my family living room. Ironically, I started to feel better than I had in years, but it wasn't a singular or stable feeling. Instead, it was full of contradictions, where peace met frustration, where confusion met excitement, and where determination met desperation. Desperate for some kind of answer, some understanding of how you trade in a once soul-filling, now soul-crushing, calling for something else. But I was eager to move on, to start the next chapter, to accept the good with the bad, and reclaim some part of myself. And for me, that ultimately meant reclaiming a life outside of the United States.

By the time I reached the age of 33, I'd lived in three different countries and spent summers traveling through many more. My life had tethers that pulled me to various corners of the globe, but I hadn't found my place yet. I hadn't stumbled into a city that felt livable, that felt like there was space for me. That felt like a place I could flourish, not simply exist.

So when the idea of a Thanksgiving trip to Mexico City was suggested by my dad, I was an immediate "yes." With a surplus of time and the gusto of someone unencumbered, a solo trip seemed justified. I went to Oaxaca for the week prior and sat in cafés, tried every *mole* available, and sought out a highly recommended *temazcal* ceremony. One morning I hopped in a taxi, which took me into the neighboring hills before delivering me to a quiet homestead where I was served hot tea and given instructions about how the *temazcal* would work. I sheepishly made my way into a mud hut, somewhat nervous that there wouldn't be others joining me in the ceremony. I sat and attempted to open myself up to the entirety of the experience.

My *guardiana* began by talking about the cyclical nature of life, our relationship with death, and the peace we should find in the connection between the living and the dead. At that moment, I thought of my aging grandmothers.

First, my Nani, my maternal grandmother, whose face is so clearly seen in mine. Arguably a vain woman who wore high heels to my college graduation with a sprained ankle, but also a woman who seeks joy. She wants to be surrounded by friends and family, full of laughter and booze. I know my desire to present myself in a certain way must come from her.

My Grammy, my biological father's mom, is a tough woman. She's proud and deeply dedicated to her family, traits I think I carry too. Honestly though, I grew up feeling slightly out of place in her house.

Finally, my Grandma Connie, now a skeletal shell of her old self. With her buttery soft skin and tender disposition, she's the embodiment of compassion and generosity. Dementia has plagued her brain and robbed us of her wisdom and grace. Meanwhile, we have struggled watching her journey through this slow, painful process of death. And we have had to live in this in-between as we wait for death to fully claim her.

I gasped as the *guardiana* poured cold water over me at the end of the ceremony. I felt refreshed. Reborn. Renewed. At peace. Content that my grandmothers had passed on the gifts I was destined to inherit from them, I prayed for their peace and eventual release. I also prayed for my family in general, specifically for my dad and his brothers, so that they would be ready.

After a bumpy ride home back down the hill, E.'s name flashed on my phone. the screen. I answered giddily. A friend in another part of the world—I was unburdened and eager to connect.

Quickly that was shattered by her tone. She delivered the news swiftly.

"J. died."

Gasping yet again, I was confused. This was not the death I imagined just hours before. Not the death I prepared myself for and accepted. It was one that felt unfair. It wasn't a life well and fully lived but one tragically cut short. I hung up the phone, made my way to a café, and wrote. Quietly and peacefully, tears rolled down my face. I watched a hearse roll by, accompanied by musicians, in this mystical city that seemed to dance between the living and the dead.

A few days later, I arrived in Mexico City and met my family at my *tia's* house. In the week we spent together, we ate our way through the city, went to museums, and aimlessly wandered through different neighborhoods with no set agenda. Our conversations drifted from the frivolous to the monumental, and I continued to find grace, comfort, and encouragement in their company.

Memory is a funny thing; mine is poor and relies heavily on my own ability to craft a narrative around a moment or a fleeting scene and cement it as reality. Still, I think it was my dad who suggested it: "Why not Mexico City?" Aware that I was keen to leave the US, we sat together in a city he called home in his youth and planted a seed.

This seedling of an idea, of yet another move, was treated with the same pragmatic, rational approach I've always used to tackle life's big choices. On the outside I'm an adventurous wanderer, but on the inside I'm a detailed-oriented, spreadsheet-loving planner who keeps countless lists so I can come back and compare how reality aligned with that original vision.

However, this was all secondary to the very real, full-time work of looking for a new job. One of my biggest concerns when leaving education was how it might jeopardize my ability to live outside the United States. This quirky fun fact about me had become part of my identity in the same way this title of a teacher had. I reveled when my mom would report how someone from church, the grocery store, or an old friend from high school would ask, "Where's Jo now?" I loved the idea that I was this kind of explorer, putting down (temporary) roots in different places, and forging a new life every few years.

Once luck struck and I found myself with a job offer in January 2023, I felt free to really start planning and imagining. I started a spreadsheet titled "Relocation Logistics 2023," with places like Mexico City, Buenos Aires, and Lisbon on the list. The columns listed visa requirements, length of stay, costs, and general pros and cons. Mexico seemed like an obvious choice, but I grappled with the allure of Europe, or the Paris of South America. So often frozen by decision paralysis, and healing from a deep distrust in my own ability to make decisions for myself, I shared the spreadsheet with others, only to quickly ignore their opinions and challenge myself to follow the intuition I'd once trusted and now almost villainized.

The reality was that I felt good in Mexico City; I felt like myself. I thrived in the noise, in the chaotic busy streets, with a language that was familiar yet distant filling my ears. At some point, April became a deadline I set for myself that no one was holding me accountable to and it became a solidified date of departure. I spent much of February and March onboarding for that new job, and in the afternoons, I'd sort through the boxes that still lived rent-free in my dad's garage. The number of boxes dwindled as I ruthlessly purged items that once had sentimental value but no longer held the same luster. I boarded a one-way flight on April 30 with two checked bags and an unfamiliar sense of calm.

From everything I read online, gaining temporary residency in Mexico was easy—time-consuming but easy. The crucial step was on arrival. It was critical that my passport not be stamped as a visitor. I needed to notify the agent that I was pre-approved for temporary residency, show them the fancy visa sticker I'd gotten only a few days before, and have them mark my passport for *canje*.

As someone who has been held at immigration in Turkmenistan, Russia, and even Canada, I was not surprised when the immigration officer accidentally stamped my passport anyway. He quickly realized his mistake, but nevertheless I landed in an uninviting room with rough metal chairs and other worried-looking passengers for an hour. I could see the confusion wash over the immigration officer's faces as they read "Gonzalez" on my passport but saw that my language skills didn't match their expectations. Eventually the error was corrected. I called an Uber to the Airbnb I'd booked for six weeks and ordered McDonald's on the way.

Just two weeks after I touched down, a group of rowdy friends arrived for a week-long takeover of the city. They rented a beautiful mansion in Condesa and commenced what felt like an episode of "The Real World" from its late '90s glory days. We bounced around the town recklessly, running on limited sleep, ample tacos, and pounding music. We salsa danced, drank with the rain pouring down around us in Xochimilco, and apologetically spoke Spanglish at every turn.

Even after they left, I squeezed out every ounce of available energy and continued to lean in. I attended every event that sounded remotely interesting: sound baths, storytelling events, beach volleyball, dance classes, weekly Spanish lessons. For the first year, I juggled a busy travel schedule that pulled me out of Mexico every month. I bore the weight of learning a new language as an adult, a language I'd heard from my grandmother and father, but never mastered myself. Often I felt like I was carrying the weight of generations and a language and culture nearly lost by my family back home. Living in Roma Norte, now flooded with gringos like me, occupying cafés with laptops and oversized headphones, I questioned how I'd gain fluency. I listened, observed, and so often compared. I envied the confidence with which so many white men fumbled shamelessly through their broken Spanish.

But I continued to say "Yes." Yes, to every invitation, event, class, or opportunity. I was set up on friend dates and my community began to form.

"Why do Americans talk about community so much? I've never heard this word so much until I started hanging out with gringos," P. lamented, almost accusatory and clearly annoyed.

Of our many unfortunate qualities, Americans are often guilty of roaming the planet, leaving one bad impression after another, so often in search of community, and ironically so often missing it. Why?

"It's because we don't have it," I explained. "We have a culture built on individualism. Capitalism. On the pursuit of our own happiness. We don't have the benefit of being taught, or arguably expected, to care about the people around us. Instead we have the privilege or misfortune to really only think about ourselves."

And damn, that's lonely. This isolation epidemic, this growing problem of people just so sad in their aloneness, is the fruit of years of that ripening culture. I often seek solitude in my life, and have needed it, to balance the incessantly present nature of my family and friends. But with time and age, I see how fortunate I was to grow up deeply engrossed in community. My Mexican American family fulfilled the stereotypes of largess. We rolled deep and loud—birthdays, anniversaries, and holidays included four uncles, three aunts, eight cousins, my two siblings, parents, and our beloved matriarch.

Now, admittedly, my adult choices have pulled me pretty far from that network, from that well-established routine of togetherness, from the all-too-small living room of Grandma's house. While the rest of the clan stayed close, my life blossomed in faraway places where I was met with the challenge of rebuilding, of establishing some kind of other "family." I loathe the phrase "chosen family" because that word feels sacred for me; reserved only for those who shaped me in my youth. At the same time, the communities I built around me as an adult helped me refine that once introverted, uncertain little girl.

In different places this has been easier than others. Turkmenistan, a small, unknown, insular country made it easy: Community was assumed. My village thrived on our awareness of each other. We didn't just know our neighbors, we spent time in each other's homes. We sat together in the afternoons to drink tea and trekked to the bazaar to buy material for new dresses. During the heat of the summer, we ate watermelon together.

London offered up strong, diverse women who shaped me as a professional. San Francisco gave me an outlet to give in the way that always felt most fulfilling, of my time and effort.

But Tanzania was different. I don't know if it was stubbornness, a wrong fit, or simply the fact that I was dead tired of building, but the clear community, the clear web of interconnectedness that existed there seemed to miss me. I had no thread in that net that tethered the others together. So I was unmoored. Adrift.

An unexpected lifesaver found me in the form of a global pandemic, which allowed me to go back to a familiar city in an unfamiliar time and reconnect, even virtually, in the communities I'd just vacated. I was reminded of belonging even when I knew it was fleeting. Eventually, I'd end up on the beaches of San Juan, Puerto Rico, with a silly poodle named Cha Cha, two years before my move to Mexico. I spent the summer in the waves, letting the water wash over me, a cathartic, baptismal experience. That brief summer was rich with connection, growth, and contentment, and gave me a feeling to chase that would center me for the turbulent months ahead.

As I rang in 2024, Mexico City was the calm, with no storms on the horizon. I took stock of the community I'd already built here. The Pilates studio where they knew my name, the barista who knew my order, the writing club friends that had evolved into actual friends. With these threads of a life coming together, I committed to start dating too. At the bare minimum, it would be an opportunity to speak more Spanish and try out some of the many starred cafés and restaurants cluttering my Google maps.

Of all the ways I'd imagined I would possibly meet "my person," I never thought it would be on an app. Nevertheless, there I was, swiping with the rest of them because I was in a new country, a new city, scraping together a life. It was just another tool to try and bridge the lonely gap we're all navigating in a more connected, yet painfully isolated, world.

My brief time on Bumble started very pragmatically; I committed to going on two dates a month. But in the back of my mind, I hoped I was priming myself for someone in real life. That all this practice would leave me energetically open and that I'd draw the right person to me, like moths to a flame or mosquitos to my legs.

In a little restaurant I knew from a previous blind date I met Troll, a welcome nickname. He's kind, generous, and funny. He's thoughtful and loving, a committed man, with self-awareness and a clear desire to be engaged fully in partnership, not just a passenger. He embodies so much of what I'd hoped to find. I feel grateful we were so lucky to both swipe right; to say yes to that date. To show up and now to continue to show up for each other.

It's more than a year later and life in Mexico City is still life. I still go to the dentist, pay my water bill, take out the trash. I don't think life outside the United States is an obligatory part of a life well-lived. I'm mindful that my being here shouldn't be extractive, and aware, too, that it can even be damaging.

In reality, when life is approached with curiosity and patience, the same contentment and joy that's so rich in my current reality can be found in many corners of the world. But for now and for the foreseeable future, Mexico is my home. It's where I met my partner. Where I have a chance to learn more about a rich, complex history on a daily basis. Where I take pride in sharing what I've come to understand. Still, I give myself permission and the grace to change my mind at some point about where I call home.

⌒

*As a kid, I was an introvert, a stark contrast to the gregarious adult I have become. Still, back then, I was often lost in a book or in an imagined world only accompanied by my Barbies and beanie babies.*

*My love of stories continued to grow as I pursued a degree in English and found myself standing in front of a room of high school students, armed with nothing more than a ragged dog-eared copy of a book, and the hope that those kids would appreciate the stories I sought comfort in my whole life.*

*Unexpectedly, my own story took me from California to Turkmenistan, England, and Tanzania, and led to a career navigating both the sloppily lined desks of my classroom and diverse cultural backgrounds, languages, and cities. After more than a decade debating the meaning of the green light at the end of Gatsby, I made my way out of the classroom, having served my community with a booming voice, sarcasm, wit, and the desire to make things better.*

*With a new job title and renewed energy, I moved to Mexico City in April 2023, and started the process of building a home all over again. Another test or testament to my ability to grow and foster community, sometimes with grace but so often without. A rough and tumble approach that has fortunately yielded rich friendships, a broadened definition of home, and a deep appreciation for my roots.*

# 6. Going the Distance

## Jeanne Carr

## San Miguel de Allende, Guanajuato

Going the distance? How many times in my life have I tried to do that and failed? Going the distance to many places is something my husband and I both desired; our first port of call was Mexico. Yes, sunny beaches. Hell, just SUN in particular was calling to us, that and a different culture, language, traditions, celebrations, and lifestyle. We were both tired of the cold, dark, depressing winter weather in Oregon, tired of Covid, but mostly tired of the fractious, destructive politics of our country that insinuated itself into every corner of our lives.

Our first Mexican adventure was to Puerto Vallarta at the end of December 2021. Two weeks on sandy beaches where warm water lapped against our skin and delicious drinks greeted us under whispering palapas—heaven! After that, we headed to San Miguel de Allende, a UNESCO World Heritage Site, a town set in the high plateau region northwest of Mexico City and known for its art, music, architecture, and food.

Why San Miguel? More than 20 years ago, my husband had a colleague that was battling cancer. He said that if he beat it, he and his wife were going to move there when they retired. My husband had no idea where this was or anything about the city. When we met, he began talking about traveling when he retired, and the first place he wanted to visit was San Miguel. He told me the story about his friend, who unfortunately, did not survive to realize his dream.

We subscribed to International Living and began reading about all the places in the world that expats had traveled and moved to, including (over and over again) San Miguel. Each article gave information about the quality of medical care, internet speed and availability, cost of living (housing, groceries), climate, and the unique activities of each place in countries around the world. Focusing on the Western Hemisphere because of its proximity to the United States and the cheaper cost of living put San Miguel at the top of our list.

Preparing to be gone for four months was scary for me. Traveling meant nothing would be predictable: I was excited and a wee bit apprehensive. I felt like a senior in high school: excited about finally "getting out" and anxious about the unknown. Telling people our plans took on a whole new dimension because we would be gone for some time. People's reactions varied. Some were openly envious: "OMG! Four months in Mexico?!" Others were sad that we would not be available; some were afraid of the possibly dangerous circumstances we might encounter.

Heading into San Miguel, which is 6,200 feet above sea level, reminded me of the Palouse and Horse Heaven Hills around Sunnyside, Washington, where I spent seven glorious years as a child, with the exception that cactus replaced the sage. You know you've reached San Miguel when the vehicle slows and your body starts to vibrate as it rumbles over 300- to 500-year-old cobblestone streets. It's amazing that these stones, placed hundreds of years ago, endure better than most Pacific Northwest roads. San Miguel is a bustling city of about 175,000; approximately 10% of those are expats.

I wasn't sure that I would like or even be able to adjust to living in a city, but it seemed to suit me. I found that I appreciated what city life had to offer: world-class restaurants, parks to promenade, amazing architectural sites, moving music, history oozing out of every cobblestone, and people that looked and spoke differently. During the first week in San Miguel, we noticed marked differences between there and the United States:

1. *Agua* (**Water**). In much of Mexico, water is precious and at a premium. The same was true for our *casita*. Water pressure was also almost non-existent, especially in the *baño* (bathroom). Because the plumbing is antiquated (200+ years old), all toilet paper went in a basket next to the toilet. A little gross, but typical for much of Mexico

2. *Caminando* (**Walking**). Many people here walk. Cars, gas, and transportation are expensive compared to wages, so you walk: to the grocery store (although we cheated the first day and cabbed back because we had a lot of items), to dinner, to *el mercado* (market), to El Centro (the central plaza where everyone goes on Sundays to linger, laugh, and loiter with family and friends). Not having a car, we were definitely getting our exercise: three to six miles a day! And when tired of walking, we found buses to be inexpensive ($8 pesos or about 40 cents) and cabs, ubiquitous (about $4 dollars a fare).

3. *Policía* (**Police**). It was a bit disconcerting to see police (and men in military garb) everywhere, even outside the grocery store! I asked our driver, Pedro, why there were so many police everywhere. Was it unsafe here? His explanation was that the military presence made San Miguel (and other places in Mexico) safe. Don't get me wrong; they're not omnipresent, but seeing men in military camouflage with bullet-proof vests and machine guns is disconcerting.

4. *Celebraciónes* (**Celebrations**). I'd read to expect loud celebrations, fireworks, partying and music in Mexico, and there are many things to celebrate in San Miguel. Since religion here is a blend of indigenous traditions and Catholicism, holidays for saints and most holy days are a combination of loud drumming and dancing by people in native garb combined with fireworks that can begin at 5 a.m. and last late into the night. It's actually life-affirming and joyous, so I found that I didn't mind.

5. *Perros* (**Dogs**). And finally, there are lots of dogs in Mexico, and many of them spend their days on rooftop terraces or as strays, barking constantly. What else do they have to do? Many people don't view dogs as pets; they're more like security systems. I've "met" the dog on the terrace outside our back door, and after speaking nicely to him, I think we've reached an understanding.

The thing is, all of these are just differences. There are plenty of cultural annoyances in the United States, too. As each day passed, I felt more at peace and at ease.

Everywhere we walked in San Miguel was beautiful, especially the ornate doors made of every material, size, and shape. We walked to a Newcomers Breakfast and all I wanted to do was take pictures of all the unique doors. It got me thinking: What do doors symbolize? Doors are a transition and a passageway from one "existence" to another. The Roman god Janus was the god of doors and doorways and also the god of beginnings, endings, transitions, gates, gateways, and time. Well, we certainly were at a new beginning and a time of transition.

The courtyard where we enjoyed our *desayuno* (breakfast) was stunning, but the most gratifying part of the morning were the people we met. One woman, who lives in the small northern California town of Rough and Ready (yes, that's the real name), spends every October leading tours to elephant refuges and rehabilitation centers in Kenya. A couple from upstate Michigan sold everything and are traveling the world until the grandchildren start to show up. Another couple had lived in eight different countries. Born in Scotland, she's lived in places including Dubai, Saudi Arabia, and Japan. A woman from Vancouver Island, BC fell in love with Hispanic culture and architecture while owning and running more than 30 stores, some of which were in LA. Her home is now like a Mexican hacienda.

All these people were doorways to new friendships, adventures, information, and creativity. They don't let others define what their world will be but instead make their own agreements about what their lives are going to be like. All the expats (as well as Mexicans) that we met were intelligent, adventurous, kind, and thoughtful. Lesson: Reach out to others wherever you are. You never know who you might meet.

Being fluid and flexible is an ongoing theme of Mexican culture. While walking in Centro, I noticed a tree growing outside a *casa* (house). The owners had allowed the tree to flow into their home, not cutting it down. They even opened a place for it to grow through their wrought iron fence. Remarkable! Just go with the flow! Can't afford a new-fangled, hi-tech security system? No problem—use what you have! In this case (and in several others), shards from broken bottles., cemented on top of walls, made the perfect deterrent.

Old structures here are revered and honored for their history, function, and unique beauty. At one of our favorite restaurants, old shutters adorn a stucco wall while new vines hold it in place. The new supports the old, a stark contrast to many places in the world where youth is venerated and age is scorned. We drove past a bank where there was a long line. A white-haired, older woman got in the line to wait, but the security guard motioned and led her up to the front where she could sit in the shade and wait. Lovely.

My old habits were slowly slipping away. My husband said one morning, "Mexico is like its bougainvillea—it finds the cracks in your walls and grows there." It certainly was growing in me. I'd spent all my life laboring under the agreements that my parents taught me, mostly that you were supposed to be busy and productive at all times. In Mexico, however, I found that I rarely made plans for more than a day. I woke up each morning refreshed, then lay in bed, drank coffee, and read the morning news until 10. I was finally relaxing into the rhythms of the culture.

I watched a video one afternoon on the history of Mexico. The three core Mexican values are (1) respect and dignity, (2) trust of family and friends, and (3) free time. The United States' core cultural values, on the other hand, are (1) time and control of time, (2) freedom of self, and (3) being able to create your own prosperity, all of which, in my opinion, lead to workaholism. I like the idea of "free time" being a value here. Mexicans use their unscheduled hours for celebrating with family and friends.

After a month in San Miguel, we celebrated my birthday. This birthday was particularly significant because Mexico was changing me and helping me to see myself with different eyes. I woke up, turned to my husband and said, "I like who I am here so much more."

Why Mexico? Easy. It's because people love and accept everyone. Speak Spanish at a two-year-old level, like me? Mexicans are very gracious and accepting. We attended a musical fiesta at a venue out in the country. In talking with another expat couple who'd lived in Mexico for several years, one of the first questions we asked was, "What did you do to earn a living before?" We found out that no one cared. They wanted to know about family and friends. They wanted to hear, "*Buenos días!*" (Good morning!) and "*C"omo estás?*" (How are you?) and "*Cuántos hijos tienes?*" (How many children do you have?) Your bank account makes no difference to anyone, nor what you "do." What matters is who you are, which, of course, begs the question, "Who am I?" especially since I no longer identified myself with a job.

I decided that I didn't have to live with anyone else's expectations anymore, which is much easier to do in a foreign country where you can make your own rules. That day I was "*la mujer del sombrero*" ("the hat woman") after buying a beautiful hat at a local artisan market. Tomorrow, who knows? But this I do know: Mexico was teaching me how to be: to be myself, to release old expectations that no longer served me, to focus on being each day rather than doing, and to learn to love and value myself (and others) more.

After four months of exhilarating life in San Miguel, we reluctantly headed back to Oregon to purge our possessions, sell our house, start on our Permanent Residency visa in Portland, and then fly back to Mexico. Yes, we'd made the decision to live in San Miguel and use that as a base to travel.

We soon found out that there's a lot of emotional baggage attached to one's stuff. For me, it was going back through journals I'd kept since college. Some pride accompanied my skimming through those monologues. Realizing how much I'd grown was heartening; realizing how unconscious I was then was eye-opening.

In Swedish culture, cleaning out in preparation for our move (and for death) is called *döstädning*—a combination of the word "*dö*," which means death, and "*standing*," which means cleaning. In her book "The Gentle Art of Swedish Death Cleaning," Margareta Magnusson writes, "Death cleaning is not about dusting or mopping up; it is about a permanent form of organization that makes your everyday life run more smoothly. It is a delight to go through things and remember their worth." That's the process we embarked on—kids, you can thank us now—getting rid of all our accumulated stuff that we don't need any more (the practical part) and "remembering their worth" (the emotional part). We lovingly blew our things out into the world, like seeds from a dandelion. May they find good homes.

Being back in the States meant telling our families our decision and seeing our newest granddaughter. Many expats we met in Mexico said they were only there temporarily "until the grandchildren start arriving." It made me wonder if I would be thought of as a bad grandparent, not living in the same state or even the same country as our grandchildren. I have fond memories of my grandparents and great grandparents. I loved all my grandparents, and I loved the time I spent with them, even though I didn't see them every week, month, or even every year. Why? Because they included me in their lives. I felt important and cared for. I think the most important thing about being a grandparent is just the love we give our grandchildren during the times we *do* see them. After all, isn't that what matters?

After purging our personal belongings, storing what would be shipped, and selling our house, we headed north to Portland and our appointment at the Mexican consulate. The appointment was simple (we'd already emailed our financials): fingerprints, photos, a new holograph Mexican stamp in our passports, payment, and out the door. The last step in the official process would be at the consulate in San Miguel. Getting permanent residency status would allow us to stay as long as we wanted and come and go as often as we pleased. We were not becoming Mexican citizens; that's a whole other legal process that we weren't interested in.

Next step? North to Washington to get our driver's licenses. Our official US address would be our daughter's house in Washington, which saves us a lot of money in taxes every year. This would also be where we stored our car so that when we did visit, we could get around without having to rent one. Many expats have a mailbox somewhere in the States, which becomes their official tax address. Some use a friend's or family member's address and, like us, store things that they're not ready to ship to a new country.

I found it very fitting that all these changes were happening in the fall. Fall is the slow ending of a year, of a summer, and for us, of a way of life.

Have I been anxious? At times, but usually because some past change that was traumatic was triggered for me. I found that now I had the opportunity to fully feel what I couldn't then, and I'm able to see these things in a new, healed light. Endings and beginnings! You can't have one without the other.

And now for the great unknown! Was I afraid? Sometimes, but mostly I was excited to meet the new "me" that Mexico would unearth. I found it very fitting that we arrived just before *Dia de Los Muertos* (Day of the Dead). This is not the American Halloween, filled with horror and humor. It's about honoring and acknowledging one's ancestors: what they've given to you, the family, and the world, who you are because of them. In Celtic tradition it's called Samhain; it's about seeing, listening, and connecting to those on the other side of the veil, as well as the spiritual end of the year. Endings and beginnings: these are the constants in life. My life's lesson has been about heading into (and accepting) change. As Eckhart Tolle so aptly says, "Embrace it like you chose it because you did." And we definitely chose this change, embracing its joys along with its sorrows.

We arrived in Mexico on October 16, 2022. I began reading a book about retirement, since both of us were in its early stages. Stage two of retirement, according to Dr. Riley Moynes in his book "The Four Phases of Retirement," is "Loss and Feeling Lost." For many of our friends, this change seemed like an adventurous vacation, but, like all life, it has its ups and downs. The first week I felt lost and sad. I found comfort in the Daily Word from Unity: "The love I shared in relationships remains, even after form has changed. My ancestors live on through me, as do all the people I have loved. I carry within myself their wisdom, strength, and energy. An invisible cord connects us like a precious keepsake passed down from generation to generation." This is the true purpose and meaning of Dia de los Muertos: remembering and honoring those whom we love that are no longer physically with us. I found this so comforting since family and friends were now far away, although we do have occasional FaceTime calls.

We finally got into the immigration office on November 12 and became permanent residents! We'd hired a legal expert to assist us and felt this was a wise decision, since all documents must be done exactingly in Spanish, or they'll be rejected. It was well worth the money.

Doctors were next. An important task in moving anywhere is finding good medical care. In San Miguel, doctors are your first call in an emergency. They even make house calls. Doctors call an ambulance (if needed), then meet you at the hospital and direct your care among specialists. Our medical insurance would cover emergencies, but not standard care visits. Since medical costs are so much less here and I have such a high deductible through my Cobra insurance in the States, I decided to do a lot of my basic medical care in Mexico and pay out-of-pocket. The same was true for dental and vision. Along with a G.P., I saw a dermatologist. She took one look at my varicose-veined legs and began to lecture me about the possibility of blood clots, ulcerations, sepsis, etc. if I didn't get them taken care of. That night, we got together with a good friend who was friends with a vascular surgeon. She immediately texted him and by the following afternoon, we were at the hospital seeing him. The next day I had tests done, and by Friday, I was seeing an internist who approved me for surgery. The following Thursday, I had an ultrasound done and surgery scheduled for the next week. In three weeks' time, it was all said and done for $2,825 dollars with no insurance. Mexico has excellent medical care!

The great thing about Mexico (and San Miguel) is that there are surprises and discoveries around every corner. We got tickets to see the Whitney Shay Blues Band, part of the weeklong Jazz/Blues Festival in San Miguel. The following night, we headed to see Herbie Hancock for free in the Jardin. For free! It's amazing what's available here that would cost hundreds of dollars in the States, if you could even get tickets. We've also attended two world-class operas in box seats for $60 dollars apiece. We shop at a weekly local organic market, attend art walks every month, and listen to local musicians. Kissed by the air, hugged by the sun, meeting wonderful people, eating delicious food, and experiencing exciting cultural opportunities are all a part of our new home.

By Dec. 12, holiday festivities were in full swing and wouldn't end until Jan. 6. *Posadas* are one of the most joyous celebrations we've experienced. Every night between Dec. 16 and Christmas Eve, a procession of carolers, led by a small child dressed as an angel, heads to a different house in the neighborhood where food and warm drinks are shared, and carols are sung. It replicates the journey of Mary and Joseph going from inn to inn, trying to find a place to stay. By Christmas Eve, we were hosting a dinner for several new friends. The season ended on Jan. 6, or *Dia de los Tres Reyes* (Three Kings' Day, or Epiphany). House parties are thrown and whoever gets the little plastic baby Jesus in the *Rosca de Reyes* (a round, crown-like cake) has to host a tamale party on Candelaria (Feb. 2, representing when Jesus is presented to the priests at the temple). Our good friend got the baby for the second year in a row. Fortunately, she's a good sport and a good cook.

On Oct. 16, 2024, we will have lived in Mexico for two years. We've never regretted moving here and are always relieved and excited to be "home." We've traveled each year to different places within Mexico, including Oaxaca, Puerto Vallarta, Guadalajara, Lake Chapala, and Ajijic. We've found the buses here to be excellent, luxurious, clean, and a very affordable way to travel. Each summer, we head back to the Pacific Northwest to visit friends and family and get medical care for my husband. We relish our short, intense visits with everyone and always have bittersweet feelings when we leave.

Will we live here until we die? We'll see. Mexico now has a new (woman) president, and we're wondering if this will change the presence of the cartel and violence in the country. We'll see. Is San Miguel a dangerous place? No, we've never felt in danger here. Is the cartel a presence here? Of course, but it's a very quiet one. I feel more ill at ease in public in the United States than I do watching a parade or celebration here. Will we move to a different country and live there? We'll see. There are many other countries in Latin America, Europe, and Asia that we'd love to visit and maybe live in.

Do I ever regret taking this plunge? Never! I love everything about living here: the culture, the people, the language (which I'm still learning), the weather, the cost of living, the never-ending discoveries about myself and the country we now call home. What helped me the most was my husband telling me that if we didn't like it after a year, we could always decide again where we wanted to be.

I grew up believing that once I made a decision, I had to stick with it forever. Now I know that there are endless possibilities in life. You can decide and decide and decide again. If we had stayed in Oregon, I feel sure that I would have slowly diminished and died an early death. Here, I feel vibrant and alive, like my life has just begun. Living in another country is the best decision (other than marrying my husband) that I've ever made.

～

*Graduating with a Bachelor's Degree in English and an Elementary Education minor from Western Washington University, Jeanne Carr has been a writer all her life. She has published short stories in "Jaree-da," a Northwest dance magazine, "The Mysterious Magical Cat," by D.J. Conway, and "Belly Dance Transformations," by M. Bliss. Retired from a 35-year career in public education, which included teaching elementary gifted education through high school English, she currently lives in San Miguel de Allende, Mexico, with her husband.*

# 7. The Non-Plan Plan

Amanda Turner

Ajijic, Jalisco

I've always had the travel bug, ever since I was a young girl; Disney trips with my paternal grandparents, summer road trips from Florida to Missouri to spend a couple weeks on the farm with my maternal grandfather. They all had their specific smells and feelings. To this day, when I catch a whiff in the wind of those familiar scents, it takes me back to a place and time of pure 5 a.m. punctual grandparent bliss.

My parents were both in the Marine Corps. I was born in Kansas City, Missouri in May 1986. From there we moved to Camp Pendleton, California, and on to several bases in Okinawa, Japan where I spent all of my elementary school years. To me, Japan was home. It was what I knew well and it shaped my formative years. We were in school on an American base with other children just like myself and my sister—military brats. School consisted of what you would typically find in the American school system, except our education came with Japanese lessons. We learned the alphabet, the language, and other cultural qualities of the Japanese. When we weren't in school, most of our time was spent off-base in the hustle and bustle of Japanese life.

My mom has always been the adventurous sort, and she threw herself into any event or sightseeing trip she was invited on. We reaped the benefits of it. What I remember the most are the tiny but extremely well-organized apartments, traditional Japanese homes with the Shoji sliding doors, where we would sit on the floor to enjoy an intricately curated meal, sake always flowing around the adults, and little tinker shops hidden away in alleys. Those were my favorite. There was a specific store that I can still picture clearly to this day. My sister and I would walk out the base gates, across the highway, and into an alley where there was a tiny candy store, jam-packed with the most unique and flavorful sweets I've ever seen, even to this day. This place was kind of a dump but it was like a gold mine to us. Okinawa was an experience I will never forget and have always longed to return to.

I was 12 when we moved back to the US. It was like entering a foreign country: seeing road signs in English, hearing English spoken everywhere, how differently life was lived, including infrastructure and architecture. It was an extreme change going from Japan to the USA, but, to me, it felt like an adventure awaiting. We landed in Dunedin, Florida, where my grandparents lived. Both of my parents exited the armed services, and we began life as civilians in the Sunshine State. I attended middle school, high school, and college in Florida, and by the end of it I was feverously itching to get out and explore. I spent my 20s in downtown St. Petersburg as a bartender and server, and went on to become a certified SCUBA Dive Master, taking students out on various dives around the state, from beautiful fresh water cold springs with manatees to shipwreck dives off the Florida Keys.

I also had a love of art. I left the SCUBA world to become a full-time artist, starting first with refurbishing furniture under the business name of Paint That Ugly Thing, which turned out to be too much furniture hauling for my taste. I moved on to murals, which also proved to be very labor-intensive in the Florida heat, but hey, I was in my 20s and gaining quite a bit of notoriety under the business name of Ugly Illustration. I created many murals for downtown St. Petersburg businesses, and also hosted several successful art shows in the area, including being asked to showcase at the newly renovated Salvador Dali Museum. But all the while I was dying to explore new lands.

During my time as a full-time artist, I also had another full-time job: researching how to exit the USA and build a life of constant travel until I reached the place I didn't want to leave. For several years I endlessly hunted down the answers for how to work online while traveling the world. Finally, I came to the conclusion that there's no one-word answer, or step-by-step directions, or any one person that can say, "Do this and you'll be fine." The answer was to just go. My dad thought it was great, my mom worried about my safety as a single woman going to South America, and my extended family thought I was crazy. They had so many questions about logistics that I just knew were not important, mainly because I'd done so much research and knew so many others had already paved the path.

I joined several house-sitting websites and Facebook groups, started developing relationships with like-minded people who'd already made that leap, and began selling all my things. I bought a one-way ticket to Costa Rica (because it was the cheapest), packed a backpack and hopped on the flight. I had zero plan for anything, and still to this day I have zero plan when I travel. I have yet to discover if this is a good thing or a bad thing, but it is what it is, which is odd because in every other aspect of my life, I'm a serious planner.

In July of 2017, I landed in San Jose, Costa Rica, and decided I would do the hostel life for a while. This ended up working quite well as I would exchange murals for stays, and when I completed a mural, I would hop over to the next "hot" town everyone was talking about. I met some interesting people along the way and saw stunningly beautiful beaches and wildlife. (Side note: Believe everything you see and hear about monkeys in Costa Rica; they're wild and they want to know everything about you.)

As I was trekking through this tropical climate, I came to realize that what I was really craving were mountains, cooler weather, historic architecture, and a little more culture. I had heard really great things about Costa Rica, but it just wasn't doing the trick for me. I found that while it didn't lack scenery or outdoor adventure, it did lack in culture and historic architecture. Eventually I heard about Monteverde, a town where the mountains meet the clouds. Two days later I found myself in a small tour van on one of the most treacherous, cliffhanging, mountain-climbing adventures I've ever been on. But let me tell ya, I've never seen more breathtaking views in all my life!

I reached the town of Monteverde and fell in LOVE! There was a small café that I would frequent to do all my online work, and it reminded me of the endless hours I used to spend in the cozy, quaint cafes in St. Petersburg. Unfortunately though, this town was very small. There was one café, one paint store to stock up on supplies for my mural/hostel trade work, and one nice restaurant. I quickly realized that I couldn't spend any more than a couple of weeks there or I'd die of boredom. It was also very transient, which all of Costa Rica was, really, as it's a country known for tourism. I decided to complete my murals for the hostel and beat feet to the next location.

Now I knew what I needed, and I was on a mission to find it. Some great folks I met along the way mentioned that I could possibly find what I was looking for in Guatemala. It's a small country with a whole lot of culture, a rich history, and an excellent climate. I took a short flight and when I landed, went straight to Antigua, Guatemala. I was not let down in the least.

Antigua sits in the central highlands of Guatemala, and from 1543 to 1773 was the capital of the country. (Guatemala City has since become the capital.) The streets are cobblestone and lined with Baroque-style architecture. The town sits in a valley surrounded by four volcanos, two of them active. It's sweater weather every day of the year and I was in heaven! I once again exchanged murals for hostel stays and was able to live in one the entire month and a half that I was in Antigua. It was comfortable and centrally located, and they wanted a lot of art, so I had an indefinite contract of stay, although I realized I was growing tired of the hostel life.

I began researching rentals in the area as I'd pretty much decided I wanted to settle down for a while in this beautiful place. That was until I received a call from back home from a client requesting a mural—a big job, paying thousands of dollars. I couldn't turn it down. I was living on my savings and had yet to find that digital nomad dream job. So I packed up my things and booked a round-trip flight from Guatemala to Florida, with every intention of returning to Antigua when the mural job was completed.

During my time using house-sitting websites and Facebook groups, I realized how saturated and competitive the house-sitting market was. Some of the people in the groups had been doing it for years, with 30+ years under their belt traveling and house-/pet-sitting. It had kind of taken the wind out of my sails in my hopes of exploring other lands while having the comfort of a private home for a bit of stability. But while I was in Florida working on my big mural job, I received a message from a woman living in Ajijic, Mexico. She had plans to go toEurope for a month and needed a housesitter to look after her two cats and her plants. She told me the historic town was located in the Sierra Madre Mountain range on Lake Chapala, the largest lake in Mexico, and was heavily populated with English-speaking expats. I jumped on it, cancelling my flight back to Guatemala. I made one last visit with family and friends and booked a new flight for Mexico—again, having done zero research.

I landed in Guadalajara, Mexico on Oct. 31, 2017, took a 30-minute taxi ride to this woman's home and met her and her cats. She left the next day, and I had her house and her felines all to myself for the next month. Nearly everything I needed was within walking distance and easy to find. There was a small corner store about four doors down that I would walk to every other day to get eggs and whatever else I needed. The streets were cobblestone, the mountains were majestic, the weather was perfect, the lake was beautiful, the architecture even more stunning, and she was right—there were quite a few English-speaking expats. This small Mexican town was bustling, and I immediately saw opportunity.

Walking through town one day, I decided I wanted to do a large public mural somewhere that would sort of kickstart my being able to fund my new life in Mexico. I started asking local business owners with big empty walls if they'd be interested in a free mural. Finally a woman who owned a local spa bit. I drew up my mural idea, she approved, and I got to work.

One thing that's very prevalent in Ajijic are Facebook groups; there's one for nearly every interest under the sun. Knowing this, I blasted that mural all over social media during the two weeks it took me to complete it. I became quite well-known, which led to my receiving back-to-back mural jobs for the better part of a year. During this time, I'd left the house-sit and moved in with a friend, helping with rent and watching her dogs when she was out of town, with the intention of picking up more housesits.

One thing I missed dearly from back home was the coziness of a local café, somewhere I could sit for hours and work online, a place that had excellent coffee, great Wi-Fi, friendly staff, and comfortable seating. Ajijic didn't lack in terms of having coffee, but there wasn't an establishment offering all of those things in one place. So in 2018, I did what any sane person would do and opened one, having only been in the country for nine months and knowing only very basic Spanish.

If my family thought I was crazy for open-ended travel, imagine their reaction when I said I was going to open a business. It was actually fairly easy. I'd already received temporary residency, which is a requirement for opening a business in Mexico. I went down to the municipality offices, paid my $1,500 peso annual fee, found an adorable (and inexpensive) rental in Ajijic Centro, received the "ok" from the fire department that I was up to code, and got to work.

I officially opened El Gato Feo Café (The Ugly Cat) in February of 2019, and it quickly became popular. We were the only business in town that had reliable fiber-optic internet, excellent coffee sourced from many different regions of Mexico, in-house baked pastries, comfortable seating, open mic poetry readings and various other monthly gatherings like the local author's group. I created the place I'd yearned for.

While I'm making this sound so easy, it wasn't. It wasn't the hardest thing I'd ever done, but it came close. One thing you need to know about Mexico is that Mexicans are on their own time, especially in a small town. They can't say no when you ask them for something. Half the time they don't show up when you ask them to, but they might come a few days later when you're unavailable for them. The thing is, you need them to do whatever it is, and who knows when they might show up again.

This was my biggest frustration in running the business, mainly because I had not yet figured out how to let go of the capitalistic American way of living. This might sound like I'm insulting the Mexican people, but I most certainly am not. Their way of life is about people; they love parties, they love a good time, they're incredibly welcoming, kind, hardworking, and resourceful, but they're on small Mexican town time. I've learned to not only accept that, but to take advantage of it as well.

About six months after opening my business, I met my now life partner and his mother, who ventured in for a coffee. They were originally from California, and now own Estrellita's, a bed and breakfast about a block down from my café. We began helping each other with our businesses and incorporating them into each other's business plans. A short time later we decided to move the café to the bed and breakfast, and we became a family-owned establishment all in one building. We've become the best of the best in Ajijic, winning awards for "Best of Lake Chapala" for Best Coffee and Best B&B for three years running. Unfortunately, my mother-in-law, Lorraine Pasini, passed away recently. She was very well-known throughout Ajijic and I truly miss her so very much. To say I'm grateful for what she's given me, including her son, is an understatement.

I can't say this journey has been easy, but it has been immensely fulfilling. I also can't say that I never plan on returning to my home country. I miss the USA; the ease of everything, the perfect infrastructure, the patriotism, the beautiful beaches, friends and family in St. Petersburg, Florida, my mom and the farm, family, and the salt-of-the-earth humans that live in Essex, Missouri.

But in the seven years I've been here, Mexico has done something for me that I could never repay. It has nurtured self-interests I never knew I had, like gardening, cooking, baking, and living a healthy lifestyle. The best thing is that my anxiety has mostly disappeared, which was one of my goals in moving to a Latin American country. What I thought was a frightening place actually turned out to be one filled with people who instantly treat you like family. When they say, "Love thy neighbor," in Mexico it's truly a way of life.

Mexico is a very proud nation, with an unfathomable amount of history and culture, and its people have hearts of gold. Here I found the love of my life, a Mexican/American walking encyclopedia who's always reaching higher and can solve any problem put in front of him. He loves me more than anyone ever has in my life. We live in a beautiful home in a gorgeous, botanically lush landscape in the incredible Sierra Madre mountains. I've found and continue to find everything I've ever dreamed of, and I'm eternally grateful to this gracious country for this once-in-a-lifetime experience.

⤳

*Hailing from St. Peterburg, Florida, Amanda Turner has been a permanent resident of Ajijic, Jalisco, Mexico, since Halloween of 2017. Along with her life partner, she owns the award-winning businesses El Gato Feo Café & Roastery (elgatofeocafe.com) and Estrellita's Bed & Breakfast (estrellitasinnajijic.com). Amanda is also a full-time licensed real estate agent specializing in buying and selling in the Lake Chapala area. Her YouTube channel (@TheRealAmandaTurner) showcases homes for sale in Lake Chapala, Mexico.*

# 8. Yellow Brick Road

## Tom & Heidi Lonsdale

## Mazatlán

Heidi and I got together when I was 19 and she was 17, while living in Lake Tahoe, California. Even as teenagers, we always liked to travel. Back in the mid-70s, one of our first adventures was when we were invited to go to the Okanagan Valley in Canada and pick fruit. The VW bus we were in blew up, so we hopped out and hitchhiked the rest of the way. We stayed a couple of months, then returned to California the same way, hitchhiking down the Oregon coast, stopping in the redwoods, sleeping on the beach, and meeting people along the way.

We continued our adventure by loading up our stuff in an old Ford truck and heading to Colorado, hoping to work in the ski areas. Heidi snagged a great job at a tiny ski area, and of all things, I ended up working underground in a mine, in Leadville, Colorado. We lasted about six months and then headed back to California, with the thought of saving money and traveling to Europe.

Well, we couldn't wait out the time it took to save the money, so we ended up going on a trip to Baja California instead. This is when our love affair for Mexico began. Warm water, awesome beaches, great spicy food, and warm and welcoming people, we loved it all! We headed back home and soon after got married, at the tender ages of 19 and 20.

We ended up settling in Mammoth Lakes, California. We both felt like this place fit our personalities, with adventure at every turn: hiking, climbing, skiing, etc. We loved the heavy snow, big winters, and small-town living. I became a contractor and tire chain installer, and Heidi worked as a preschool teacher, house cleaner, and swim instructor, while we raised our four kids.

During our time in Mammoth, we became Christians and God really began to change our lives. We started going on short-term mission trips, first to Mexico and then to other countries. We loved the adventure and being able to help others in need. We no longer traveled just to travel; we began to travel with a purpose. I'm sure we got more out of those trips than we ever gave.

As much as possible, we always brought our kids on these trips. Some people would say that it's hard to travel with kids, but the reality is that kids really help to connect you with a foreign culture and the local community by immersing you in the schools, families, parks, sports, etc. It always helps to have something in common with others. Not only that, but our own kids came back with a broader perspective on life. Our children learned to love other cultures and experienced other ways to do things.

Mexico was always luring us back in different ways. We went from one-week trips to month-long trips, always to Baja. Then we were invited by another family to go with them on an eight-week trip to mainland Mexico, traveling in our motorhome with our four kids. We traveled the whole Pacific coastline, driving down Highway 200 all the way to Guatemala and back. We loved the country and saw incredible scenery. We learned to surf and practiced Spanish along the way. Our mission included things like handing out baseball uniforms in a rural pueblo and feeding the hungry.

Next we went to Ecuador to visit friends who'd moved there and opened three orphanages. By this time, we were in our mid-30s, and our children were aged four, eight, 10, and 12. During our month-long trip, we were extremely moved by what our friends were doing. We met amazing people and heard many amazing stories. When they invited us to stay and help, we saw it as a wonderful opportunity. Believing that God works in mysterious ways, we sold our home, shipped everything we owned, and off we went to Ecuador.

As usual, we didn't do anything in a traditional way, and we got more negative feedback than positive. We owned a business and a home, and our children were settled in school. People couldn't understand why we would rock that boat. They encouraged us to wait until our kids grew up. That kind of feedback made it difficult for us to move forward. After lots of talking and much prayer, though, we knew we wanted this experience for our kids as well as ourselves.

We immersed ourselves in language school, worked with teens and in prison ministries, taught street kids building trades, and cared for orphaned babies. We thought we'd be in Ecuador forever, but after about three years we decided to move back to Mammoth.

Once again, we followed the "yellow brick road," and found ourselves resetting up a home and business, getting our kids enrolled in school, etc. We were all definitely changed people, though, and after a few years, we knew that normal life in the United States wasn't for us. So off we went again, this time to help the needy in the Philippines and build homes in Honduras.

After a year away, we settled back in Mammoth for seven years, working with our church doing three-month mission trips with young adults. The biggest highlight during this time was adopting our two beautiful girls from China. Our older children were almost grown-up.

We traveled to Mexico each year, and also spent time doing relief work around the world: in Thailand after the tsunami, in China, where we taught English and worked in an orphanage, and in the US, helping after Hurricane Katrina and working with feeding programs in various cities.

Then it felt like it was time again to leave the US and be untraditional. After much prayer, we decided to move to Mazatlán, Mexico and start a coffee shop. The intention was to build a community, where young people could experience cross-cultural work, do community outreach projects, and learn work ethics, while being part of a practical language exchange atmosphere. We sold our home—again risking everything—and moved to Mazatlán to begin this next chapter.

During this time, we'd spent three months a year in Mazatlán working alongside a local, radical, and very adventurous pastor who was also a professional surfer. He became a close friend and was instrumental in helping us make this move and get settled.

Once again, we moved or sold everything we owned. We obtained the visas we needed to open a business, bought a home that we turned into a Christian youth hostel, and worked as hard as we possibly could to make our vision happen. We tried hard to help where we could, building homes for the poor, holding community projects parties for families living in the city dump, and giving free surf lessons. Using the proceeds from the coffee shop, we helped pay for weddings, schooling, anything that was presented to us. We tried to just shower love on the people of the community, both locals and expats.

Our vision became a reality, and eventually we owned two coffee shops with 75 employees. We loved our work and community! The other business owners around us became good friends, and our employees became family. We rode our scooters to work and surfed in the afternoons before picking our daughters up from school. It was a beautiful lifestyle full of many positive experiences. Our two youngest daughters were raised in Mazatlán, and they had an awesome upbringing.

Since it's an important part of settling into a new country, we want to share about our housing in Mexico. We started out by renting for a few months at a time in all different areas in Mazatlán. After doing this for about three years, we decided what part of town we wanted to live in and began to look for a house to buy.

We ended up choosing a home that was "For Sale By Owner." They had moved away, and it was pretty much abandoned. The kids had all grown up and the house had sat empty for some time. A few windows were blown out, the pool had mud in it, and the house itself was in pretty bad shape. We could see, though, that in no time at all, it could be up and working. It had three bedrooms, a room for an office downstairs, and was in a great area—which was what really counted for us.

Another big plus was that compared to what we were used to in California, the price was really low.

We began remodeling and fixing up our new home, asking friends for names of good, trusted construction workers. For us, this part was actually enjoyable, except that you have to get used to things never quite coming out as planned. Sometimes we would explain exactly what we wanted, and the workers would say they understood. They would even repeat it back. So we're good, right? That is, until it's done and it's not quite what you wanted. If you can go with the flow and learn to enjoy your "new creations" it can be a great experience.

Eventually we built our home into a youth hostel with five bedrooms, seven bathrooms, three kitchens, and two cabanas near the pool. Seven years later, we sold it as a fully operating and successful hostel.

Next we rented a townhouse on the beach while looking for a good deal on our next home to buy. We thought that with all the people we knew, we would surely find someone who had what we wanted. We made a couple of offers that weren't accepted, so after about a year and a half we decided to buy a lot in a really nice, gated beachfront community in a quiet area in the north of Mazatlán. This lot was also for sale by owner.

While we waited to begin construction, Heidi had the idea to build a duplex instead of a single-family home, renting one out to help pay the construction costs. We ended up building two, three-bedroom units, not knowing at the time that it would turn into an income for our retirement. In the beginning, one of our daughters, her husband and their growing family lived below us, and it was wonderful to be a part of our grandchildren's daily lives.

We had a really good experience building our house. Our construction team was a family; the father was a great builder and had worked as a superintendent builder in Mexico City. He had trained his sons well, and they followed through with the construction on our home in a timely and professional manner.

Our next project was building a little office on the top floor or roof, depending on how you look at it! We needed a place to take care of all the administrative work for the coffee shops, which were incredibly busy. It was an amazing, adorable little space that overlooked the ocean and was also a place for guests to stay.

Looking back on it now, this was such a rich time in our lives. We'd developed such a great community in Mazatlán; not just our family, but our extended family of both Mexicans and expats. I'd have to say this is one of our favorite parts of life. We have no regrets.

Our five-year plan turned into 15 years of amazing, hard, exhausting, fun—a completely worthwhile adventure. To be sure, there were many challenges, but it's been our experience that the hardest things in life are always the most rewarding.

We've seen that it's often hard to make a change, or a move, because we're influenced by the people around us and the culture we live in. When you first start to dream or plan something out of the norm, everybody and his brother will tell you it's not a good idea, that it makes no sense, is foolish, and you shouldn't do it. I suppose they have their reasons. But when you feel like it would be a failure to look back and wonder how something would've turned out, we say you have to do it! It's better to suffer the consequences than to never have found out where that road would've taken you. If you're 100% wholeheartedly focused on doing something, just keep going—against all odds, you'll always win! People will jump in to help and see you succeed.

During our 15 years of living in Mazatlán full-time, we always watched the snowbirds and their excitement as they adjusted to the new culture. They appeared to have the best of both lifestyles. First they would stay two months, then six months, and then longer if they could. Mazatlán offered culture, amazing food, new friend-ships, community outreach, a myriad of volunteer opportunities in schools, orphanages, rescue animal programs, and building proj-ects, and much more.

My favorite saying was, "Yes, you can teach old dogs new tricks." We saw the snowbirds' excitement for both lifestyles. They'd return home with renewed enthusiasm and energy to en-joy their families, grandchildren, and communities all over again. When they would return to Mazatlán each year there would always be a sense of excitement and happy anticipation in that air—the same as when they got ready to leave. We began to see that living in Mazatlán full-time or as snowbirds both had advantages, and that both could be amazing.

After everybody grew up and the kids moved away, we sold the businesses and turned the office into a studio apartment. The ocean views are amazing and it's just a few minutes' walk until you're on the beach with sand in your toes. There's a great surf spot in walking distance, too, and we often meet up with our son and his family, who also live in Mazatlán, or friends for a beach day. A couple of years ago we added another little bedroom and bath-room. Both units walk out onto a big patio, with a covered, comfy seating area and another open area filled with plants and a big table for eating. Slowly but surely, following our hearts, we ended up with a peaceful, beautiful place to come and spend the winters.

We've now moved into the snowbird lifestyle, spending summers in Mammoth Lakes working as camp hosts, and loving on our grandkids and community there. When the snow flies, so do we. We return to Mazatlán, with its warm beaches and loving people.

The US and Mexico are now an integral part of who we are. We have family in both countries. Our children followed us to Mazatlán, and some of our grandkids are being raised in Mexico. (Three were born there.) We're thankful to have passed on this multicultural heritage to our children and grandchildren. We loved having our kids grow up in Mexico. The schools were amazing, and they met such neat friends and families, who they still stay in touch with today.

There's no right or wrong decision about moving overseas; it's not for everybody. But if you're reading this book, chances are you're interested in a radical lifestyle change. We want to encourage you to not let fear or other people's opinions stop you from following your dream. It's been our experience that you'll meet a lot of people who'll be glad that you moved to their country to be part of their community. All you have to do is step out of your comfort zone and be open to coming alive in a new way. Good luck and God bless!

~

*Tom and Heidi Lonsdale began traveling in and out of the US more than 45 years ago. They felt it was God's calling for them to do good works and help others, especially orphans, and devoted themselves to relief work in places like Ecuador, Thailand, the Philippines, Honduras, and Mexico.*

*After multiple trips to Mazatlán, Mexico, with their family in tow, Heidi and Tom moved there full-time. They opened a hostel and then two coffee shops, employing local youth and mentoring the principle of loving others through your work as well as life skills that could be carried over to their own families and children. (Making someone's coffee can be the best part of their day!)*

*Heidi and Tom have family in both countries and are happy to have passed on a multicultural heritage to them. Their two youngest daughters were raised in Mazatlán, and some of their grandkids are being raised in Mexico. (Three were born there.) They're now embracing the snowbird life, spending half the year in Mazatlán and the other half in northern California.*

# 9. Embracing the Unknown

## Nancy Swan

## Loreto, Baja California Sur

My husband always said the house we owned in Sonoma County, California, would be the house he died in. We lived 90 minutes north of San Francisco, in what's known as wine country, in a small town called Windsor.

We met later in life, in our 40s, and married a couple of years later. He was a manufacturing project manager, and I had a career in "tech," that ubiquitous word that encompasses many types of work. I had a thirteen-year-old son I brought to the marriage, and we easily became a family unit. I'm the first to admit how blessed and lucky we are. As Gen X, we were both on the tail end of being able to purchase an affordable house and take advantage of rising house prices. Our home was our nest egg.

When my son moved out on his own, I recall a good six- to nine-month period where I felt a sense of loss, at odds and out of sync. I was at the end of a chapter. A large part of my identity had ended and was no longer needed: the role of "mother." Sure, I was still his mom, but now he was out in the world, making his way. With that no longer defining me, what was I supposed to do? How would I redefine myself? Did I need to find something else?

I still had my career. I'd done very well in my field, advancing and being promoted, and my husband had done the same. We wanted for nothing. I admit my career was a large part of my identity and where I derived self-esteem and value. I took pride in doing a good job, earning the respect of colleagues, and constantly pushing myself to do better.

Over time, I started noticing a shift in my attitude towards work. I started to pull back, not as invested as I once was. Sure, I was still doing a great job, but I started to hold on to that "extra" I always gave to use for myself. It became more important to me what I did when I wasn't at work than what I did at work. And when I went on vacation and turned on my out-of-office message, I left my work phone at home and never checked my email.

In January of 2023, my company laid off a large group of friends and colleagues I'd worked with for years. It perfectly illustrated to me why work and career had taken a backseat in my life. Your company may call you "family," but really all we are is an employee number. And, at the end of my life, I will never regret not turning in that TPS report.

By this time, I was 50. Life was good and I was happy, but I couldn't help wondering what else was out there. Seeing your mom and other adults at 50 and being 50 are two completely different experiences. They seemed old, at the end of something. But when I turned 50, I felt different. Instead of an ending, it felt like the beginning of something. Doing the math, I realized I still had about 30 years ahead of me, definitely the start of a new chapter. So what was I going to do with it?

I'd always had that fantasy of living in another country—if I was a different person, in a different lifetime. Now when I wondered what it would be like, I explored the idea a bit more. After years of thinking I was too valuable to my employer to use all my vacation days, I fully embraced and took advantage of it, chastising my younger self for believing that using my vacation time would portray me as not committed to my job. We traveled to Spain, Portugal, Canada, and Hawaii. During those trips, I'd imagine what it would be like to live there full-time. I even got my husband to go along with the conversation, listing the pros and cons. Spain and Portugal were beautiful but too far from friends and family. Western Canada was breathtaking, but I was surprised at the cost of housing. Hawaii, being a series of islands, felt like another country, but we both admitted to feeling island fever after our two-week vacation. The thought of moving to another country stayed with me, but I moved it to the back of my mind. It was one of those fantasies, but not something we would ever do.

In the fall of 2022, we spent a week in Cancún at an all-inclusive resort. It was the first time I'd been to Mexico, and I loved it. We had an incredible week doing absolutely nothing. I surprised myself by embracing it. My typical vacation style was to pack my itinerary full. If I didn't, I was filled with anxiety that I hadn't taken advantage of the opportunities in front of me. It was that FOMO (fear of missing out) feeling—I had to have stories to tell about vacation when I got home. What would people think if I told them I did nothing?

Doing "nothing" on vacation was new to both of us. We talked about the difference between the words "travel" and "vacation." When we traveled to Portugal and Spain, we spent a lot of time sightseeing, out and about, making sure we saw all the historical sites. What we were doing here in Cancún was vacation. The act of doing nothing, or rather, of being at rest and being okay with it. Rather than keeping track of every landmark we saw, we measured how many books we'd read.

When we got home, we immediately went online to book our next trip to Mexico. This time we chose Puerto Vallarta, primarily because it was only a three-hour flight from San Francisco. This time I was prepared to embrace the idea of doing nothing. Our itinerary rarely deviated from sleeping in, having breakfast, heading to our cabana at the pool, reading, eating lunch in the cabana, cooling off in the pool, heading back to the room, showering, napping, having dinner, and doing it all over again the next day. I had gotten over the FOMO. I became okay with telling people that we spent most of the week in our cabana by the pool. This was a new version of me, and I liked it.

I'd been doing a lot of work to get to this version of myself. Back in April 2020, I'd gotten sober and joined Alcoholics Anonymous (AA), finally admitting alcohol wasn't my friend and that I needed help. I embraced the program and did a lot of much-needed work on myself, letting go of resentments and anger, owning and making amends for my mistakes, doing what I could to make things right, and focusing on the present. One of the biggest changes was learning to give myself grace and compassion. I forgave the younger version of myself for all the mistakes and missteps and gave her a big hug, telling her I knew she'd done the best she could.

In October of 2023, we were flying home from Puerto Vallarta and my husband sat next to a middle-aged lady. They started chatting and she told him she split her time between Puerto Vallarta and Los Angeles. I was listening and watching the exchange. I remember with picture-perfect clarity the moment the idea of moving abroad became a reality for him. She'd just explained her six-month here, six-month there, strategy and I saw a light go on in my husband's eyes.

When we got home, he pursued the conversation, wondering aloud if we shouldn't look at some homes in Puerto Vallarta. I didn't need any other encouragement and started searching. We'd send each other listings. We didn't know if we would sell our home, keep it, or live there full-time or part-time. There were so many questions, but we had the bug and were going with it.

One night he asked, "Would you ever consider moving to a place like Loreto? It's a small town on the Baja peninsula." It turned out Loreto was a place he'd visited a few times in his 20s with his father for fishing vacations

I'm embarrassed to admit, but up until then, I'd thought the Baja California peninsula was part of California. I'd never heard of a town called Loreto. Back to Google I went. Loreto is a small town of about 20,000, a little more than halfway down the Baja peninsula on the Sea of Cortez, in the state of Baja California Sur. I started searching and found some fantastic homes.

Within a week we'd identified a list of homes, found a real estate agent, and booked a flight. We got there on a Friday, looked at homes on Saturday, and made an offer on Sunday that was accepted. It all happened so fast! In the list of houses we looked at, there was one I'd kept coming back to over and over again, looking at the photos. Have you ever had a moment where you get that feeling of absolute certainty about something or a situation? When we walked into that house, that happened to me. It was the one.

Before we wrote the offer we went downtown for lunch and then walked along the *malecón* (the esplanade on the waterfront). We discussed whether we could trade in our life in the States for a small fishing town where life moved so much slower. What about the language? My husband was pretty fluent, but I was not, falling back on high school Spanish for the basics. We had family near us where we lived, as well as friends. My husband had spent most of his life and I had spent the past 25+ years in that part of California. He'd been able to quit working back in July of 2022, so we discussed my job. Would I be able to work remotely in Mexico?

We were in uncharted waters, but we knew enough to know we could figure out the rest as we went along. We weren't able to answer all the questions we had, but it felt right. The old me would have feared all the unknowns, but now I was able to embrace it and just focus on today. We moved ahead, committed to taking control of what we could and trusting the rest would work out the way it was supposed to. We went home and had our house listed within a week. On the first day of the listing, we got an offer and went into escrow.

At this point, we knew we were moving to Loreto full time. We'd thought of buying a smaller place in California, but for the time being put that on hold. We'd both come to the marriage owning our own homes and had turned those into rentals. We eventually sold both houses, which let us pay off the mortgage on our home. This meant we were able to buy the house in Mexico outright and have about half the proceeds still available to us. It was a nice cushion that helped curb my financial fears, which were unfortunately a constant companion in my life.

In 30 days, we sold everything, packed up our dogs, hired a moving company for items we wanted to bring, and by November 18, 2023, were officially in Loreto. It stunned our family and friends because it happened so quickly, catching them off-guard and causing a lot of turmoil. Sure, I had talked in passing once in a blue moon about the "fantasy" of moving abroad, but nothing close to a reality. I do regret that when we left some folks were hurt and confused. It's taken time and patience to make peace and restore those relationships.

The house we bought came fully furnished, and had everything, down to linens, kitchen utensils, and wall art. This meant we sold or gave away pretty much all that we owned, including all of our furniture save for a few key pieces. The act of ridding myself of most of the possessions I'd accumulated in my adult life has been freeing. I thought I'd have regrets, but I have yet to regret getting rid of something and wishing I still had it.

We found a company in San Diego to ship what we were taking with us down to Loreto. They came and picked up our things along with our Toyota 4Runner. It took a couple of months for everything to show up at our new home. The dogs were pretty easy. We got all their vet records and they flew down to Loreto with us. We asked the vet for some relaxers to make it easier for them to fly.

We hadn't closed on our house yet, so we rented another house for a month and also rented a car. The first three to four weeks were rough. We were here but we weren't. We'd severed ties with our old home but weren't in a new home. We'd left all our friends and family behind. We were living out of our suitcases because the rest of our things were about six weeks away from arriving.

I fell into a low-grade depression. I recall taking a walk, looking around me, and being overwhelmed with a feeling of panic. I would go into a coffee shop and be intimidated by everyone speaking Spanish. When I went to the grocery store, I was sure the locals were making fun of me. I was 100% positive we'd made a mistake. The dogs weren't settling very well either. Whenever we left, they would bark, making us hostage or forced to take them with us everywhere. Luckily Mexico is very dog friendly.

I was an absolute mess of anxiety. I felt trapped in our rental and I was afraid to go out and explore. At night I'd lay in bed and my mind would spin. I started beating myself up for making such a humongous mistake. Sure, we could move back, but we wouldn't be able to live the life we'd had before.

I hadn't been able to keep my job so both of us were unemployed. We had enough money to get us through the year, but I found myself in financial fear. I questioned every expense, petrified we would suddenly be broke. I was spinning out on the future: What kind of jobs would we get? Could we get a job? Would a US company hire us? Looking back, I find it funny that after a more than 25-year career, and all of my experience across many different industries, I was somehow positive that no one would ever hire me again.

Ever so slowly, things started to shift. Escrow closed and we moved into our house. The dogs started to relax, and we were able to curb their barking. I took them out for walks every day, which helped me get comfortable with exploring our new home. When I went out, I made it a point to engage and talk with others to practice my Spanish. One of my must-haves in moving here was having some type of AA community and local meetings I could get to. There's a pretty solid group of expats here which means there's a decent-sized, English-speaking AA community. I went to meetings and made new friends.

By New Year's I'd started to hit my stride. Financially we realized we didn't have to work full-time, and I knew I didn't want to go back to the work I'd been doing before. I found some online courses and started to pursue a certificate program in editing.

Looking back, I can see that my husband embraced our new life much sooner than I did. While I started to enjoy living here, I also felt that I constantly had to be doing something. Because of my financial fears, I was always taking courses, studying, and building up new skills to make me employable. I'd wake in the morning, walk the dogs, come back, and spend the rest of the day relentlessly searching for jobs.

At some point, though, the magic of Mexico started to seep in. I started meeting new people and trying new things. One friend invited me on a catamaran day trip on the Sea of Cortez with a group of ladies. New friendships were born. That led to another friend asking me to go snorkeling, which led to borrowing a friend's paddleboard and another friend's kayak and even more snorkeling, both by boat and from the beach in front of my house.

Now I find myself in or on the water four to five times a week. Some of the tour shops give a local's discount on day trips on the Sea of Cortez, and I've started taking advantage of that. I bought myself a beginner underwater camera and soon graduated to a GoPro. I posted a video of my snorkeling adventures which led to other videos. Now when I run into folks, they always ask after the latest video I've posted. I'm having so much fun! I did a scuba dive trip, and at some point, I'm sure I'll get certified, but for now, I'm finding snorkeling, paddleboarding, and kayaking so easy. Have mask and fins, will snorkel! I'm working on my lung capacity so I can continue to freedive and stay underwater longer and longer, exploring the incredible sea life.

Footage from a recent day of snorkeling along the coast of Carmen Island included pods of dolphins, mobula rays, whales, and more fish than I can count. My motto is, "Any day on the Sea of Cortez is a good day," and it's true.

I've stopped obsessively taking courses to learn new skills. At some point, I may pick up some part-time work, but I have no idea what type of work that will be. I'm feeling okay to trust the process, that the right answer will present itself when it's time.

At 55 and 57, we're too young to draw on our retirement accounts, but the proceeds from the sale of our house have provided us with enough income if we live on a budget. We've become very thoughtful about what we buy and use Apple Note on our phones to share our "wants" and "needs." It gives us pause to figure out if something is really a "want" or a "need." For instance, I'd like to buy a used kayak, but for now, that's in the "want" column. Friends let me borrow theirs, and when it's the right time I know I'll be able to find the perfect one to buy.

In the States, two-day shipping and one-click checkout was pretty much a daily habit. There's no such thing as two-day shipping here. That means I'm much more thoughtful on what I do buy online. When I add something to my cart, I wait a day or two before I order. When I come back to it, many times I realize it's something I didn't really need, just a knee-jerk "want"—a behavior that was second nature in the States.

Because we enjoy being in the water so much, a priority is to set aside money every month so I can go out on boats with friends a few times and my husband can go fishing. We found a local captain who has become a friend, and we make it a point to have a "boat date" at least once a month. When we go out with Captain Ramón, my husband will trawl fish and then we'll stop at a snorkeling spot for me.

Any time we've run into a hurdle, we've found a way to make it happen with help from our new friends. The people here are industrious and always find a way of getting something done. I've learned that when you reach out to someone here, you always first inquire how they're doing. In the States, I always led with what I needed or the questions I had. My life was about instant gratification and go, go, go. But here, time moves in "Mexican minutes."

I practice my Spanish daily and people here are more than happy to teach me new words. A friend turned me on to Duolingo, so every day I do a couple of lessons to supplement my learning. And Google Translate on our phones is always helpful.

We found health insurance and are very happy with our medical care. Most places don't take insurance, so we pay cash and then submit our receipts. When we see doctors, we have actual conversations; we get to know each other.

I respect the fact that although I have my residency card, I'm still a guest in this country. I try not to impose my "Americanness" on places and situations. I'm always surprised when I come across expats who don't even attempt to learn the language.

We live in a tourist area, so I frequently run into folks on vacation. Inevitably, the first questions I'm asked are if I'm bored with living such a slow pace of life, if I work, or how I deal with all the quiet. It led me to realize I've never been okay with being "bored." I wonder now if that's something a lot of Americans have in general: A need to always be doing something. To sit in silence, without distraction, can be very uncomfortable. Down here, with space and time, I've realized this, and I try to practice sitting in silence. It's a tough skill to learn after 50+ years of the opposite.

People ask me if I like where I live and I tell them I couldn't be happier. I love it here. I haven't worn closed-toe shoes since last November. Come to think of it, I don't think I've worn anything except shorts or bathing suits either! This isn't to say my life is all sunshine and unicorns. I still have the same types of problems, but with my sobriety and my journey in this new country, I'm trying to deal with them differently. For instance, I'm learning to keep my mouth shut instead of instantly reacting.

Small-town living isn't for everyone, but it's a lifestyle my husband and I have embraced, and it works for us. Will we ever move back to the States? I have absolutely no idea, and honestly, it's not something we ever talk about. We are where we're supposed to be right now, and loving every minute of it.

When people ask me what I miss most about the States, it's fountain Diet Coke, which I absolutely love. I can't get it here, but it's a trade-off I'm willing to make.

⌒

*Nancy Swan and husband Brec live in Loreto, Baja California Sur, with their two doggies Merlin and Ollie. Most days you can find her in or on the Sea of Cortez, GoPro in hand, and find Brec relaxing with a good book and his favorite drink, hibiscus iced tea. Follow along with their adventures at youtube.com/@BajaSwans.*

# 10. My Mexican McGyver

## Kristen Siefkin
## Puerto Vallarta, Jalisco

In the years leading up to June of 2021, my life could only have been described as a hot mess. My 16-year marriage had recently ended and even though it was for the best, I'd taken the divorce and his lightning-quick remarriage hard. Compounding matters, I had a relationship-terminating fight with my best friend of 25 years, which in many ways was more devastating than the dissolution of my marriage. On a professional level, I'd quit my lucrative job in public relations to start an interior design firm, and while my business was doing fine, it was still in its infancy and the learning curve was steep.

Things started looking up when I met and began dating someone, but soon after came the pandemic, and that relationship, like so many at the time, became a fatality. My eight-year alimony agreement turned into another COVID casualty when it was unceremoniously terminated after only 12 months.

Suddenly the city I'd called home for nearly three decades had become a minefield of memories. In the end, it felt like I was living in a life-sized game of Whack-A-Mole, with me swatting at recollections that would pop up randomly and relentlessly.

The final straw was the sudden death of a friend. We had met in our early 20s working in the restaurant industry, and together did all the debaucherous things one does in their youth. Over the years, we'd drifted apart as she raised a family, and I focused on my career. But later in life we reconnected, providing support during our divorces, and later, funny quips about our life's challenges and dating debacles.

The world seemed to be confronting me at every turn. I couldn't catch a break, and I was angry about it. So, as I do when I'm against a wall, I went looking for answers.

At a friend's recommendation, I set up a Zoom consultation with a life coach. In our very first session, she asked, "What gives you energy, Kristen?" I answered almost immediately: "Travel."

She probed further "What about travel does that for you?"

"I love feeling slightly uncomfortable. Like I'm standing on a precipice," I said. "I don't know anyone, I don't know where I'm going, I don't even know how to ask for what I want, and my only two options are to turn around and go back, or step off the cliff. Something about that excites me."

The conversation turned to what it would look like if I lived abroad for one month, then six, and finally 12. By the end of that hour-long session, I'd made my decision to move to Puerto Vallarta for a year. Two months later, I'd sold my house, my car, and 90 % of my belongings. Three months later, in the blazing heat and humidity of October, I was unpacking my suitcases in an open-air condo with my two little dogs panting beside me.

The first three months were the honeymoon phase. A lot of walks on the beach, going out to eat, making friends with snowbirds, and saying to myself, "I can't believe I get to live here." In my fourth month, I decided to dip my toe in the dating pool. I reinstated my Bumble account and updated my photos to include a few of me with my dogs at the beach. I carefully edited my profile, making sure to include assets and characteristics that were important to me in a man, such as a sense of humor, curiosity, spontaneity, a love of travel, and a liberal mindset.

Over those next several months, I went on approximately 10 dates with an equal mix of Americans, Canadians, Brits, and Mexican locals. I was careful to plan each date in a public place, usually for coffee or lunch. When on dates with Nationals, I was always cognizant of the stereotype that Mexican men are players or looking for *gringas* to be their "sugar momma," but neither rang true for me. None of my dates were a love match, but I had a fantastic time getting to know these men from various walks of life. A retired detective, an attorney, a tech consultant, a graphic designer, a real estate developer, and so on.

My therapist always cautioned me against what she called "future fantasizing" when dating, suggesting instead that I should be in the moment and avoid thinking ahead as to what could be. One of the ways I was able to keep level-headed was to pretend I was a journalist on an information-gathering mission. Later I would write about it for a humorous Facebook "column" I created called Dating Diaries.I kept all the dates anonymous and was careful not to reveal personal information about them, but the fact-finding strategy worked. For the first time in my adult life, I was able to truly date without expectation—and entertain my friends and family in the process.

On March 2, I went to lunch with Lu, a girlfriend from the Toronto area. She and I had met on the beach the first week I moved to Vallarta. She had a small dog as well, so we struck up a conversation about finding dog walkers, the best gyms in the area, and the challenges of finding people our age in the city (we were relatively young compared to the majority of Americans and Canadians living in Puerto Vallarta full-time). Eventually, our conversation turned to my online dating experiences.

"Wow! It sounds like you're having a lot of fun. Are you meeting these guys on Tinder?" she asked.

"Isn't that the one-night-stand app?" I replied.

"Not in Mexico! Everyone uses it. Everything else is lame here."

That evening, I opened a Tinder account. Most of the men I saw on Tinder were either Mexicans or foreigners visiting Vallarta for a short time. Within an hour, I'd stumbled upon a profile that interested me: Poncho, age 47. He had three photos and no bio. He was cute, but I had a rule: No bio was an instant disqualification. If a guy can't be bothered to write a few sentences about himself, he's either lazy or doesn't have anything interesting to say, I reasoned. I scrolled through his photos again. One of him flying a helicopter over a large city, one standing on a dune in the desert with jeans, no shirt, and a headscarf, and one in a well-fitted black suit. Who is this guy? I thought. Some kind of James Bond character? I was both intrigued and intimidated. I swiped right.

Over the next few days, he made multiple attempts to ask me out. Each time, I would have an excuse as to why I couldn't. They were all legitimate reasons, but as I learned later, he thought, "Why is she even on this site if she doesn't want to go on a date?"

On March 6, he made his final overture and to his surprise, I said yes. It was my 50th birthday.

I learned through our Tinder chat that Poncho worked just a few blocks away from where I lived at the time. He was the general manager at a high-end condo complex in the heart of Zona Romantica, Vallarta's gay district. We agreed to meet there shortly before sunset so he could show me the views from the rooftop pool.

I put on a dark blue tank dress and sandals and walked the block and a half from my house to his workplace.

"This probably won't amount to anything," I thought to myself, "but at least I'll get a good 'Dating Diary' story out of it."

I entered the cavernous, modern lobby with floor-to-ceiling marble and saw him sitting behind the desk. He stood to greet me, and I was startled by how much he towered over my 5'4" frame. The pandemic was still an ongoing concern, so we both wore face masks, making things even more awkward than they already were.

"Hola, I am Poncho."

"Hola, I'm Kristen." I pulled at my mask and fumbled self-consciously with my sunglasses as I tried to put them in their case.

He gestured toward the elevator and held the doors open for me. I pressed my back against the cold steel wall of the elevator and watched as his giant hand pressed the top button.

When the elevator doors opened again, we were greeted by a dozen taut-bodied gay men in Speedos and oversized designer sunglasses, lying on chaise lounges or wading in the gigantic pool. "Hiiii Ponchoooo!" they sang in unison. He stopped to say hello to a few of them before directing me to the bar where he pulled out a chair for me. He stood leaning casually against the marble bar top with his body facing me. We ordered drinks and made small talk, mostly about when he'd learned English (he spoke it perfectly) and interior design. He was articulate and inquisitive, but also extremely serious and hard to read.

Just after sunset, he suggested we get a bite to eat. We took the elevator back down to the garage and got in his car. When he turned the ignition on, "West End Girls" by The Pet Shop Boys came blasting out of the speakers. It was so loud that we both jumped in our seats. He reached down quickly to turn it off. We looked at each other and howled with laughter. It was just the ice-breaker we needed.

Over dinner at El Solar, a small beach bar—the kind where you put your feet in the sand while you eat—we got to know each other better. He grew up in Mexico City and Guadalajara, had lived in Torreon and San Miguel de Allende, but kept returning to Vallarta, most recently because his business in San Miguel was affected by Covid. His mother had died when he was four and his father was a prominent Mexican journalist, interviewing everyone from Che Guevarra to Salvador Dali and three Popes. Poncho's CV, though more diverse, was also impressive: he'd played soccer professionally, did furniture fabrication, and was a hot air balloon pilot. He'd also traveled the world, something that I'd noted was important to me in my Tinder profile. Like me, he'd been married once, was divorced, and had no children.

When it was time to go, Poncho asked for the bill and put his credit card down. "We are cash only," the waitress said apologetically. He looked at me. "I am really sorry—do you have any cash?"

"I'm on to you," I wagged my finger at him teasingly. "I just finished watching your series on Netflix," referring to the documentary "The Tinder Swindler," where a sleazy guy bilks dozens of women he'd met on the app out of hundreds of thousands of dollars. He laughed knowingly.

Over the next several months, Poncho and I went on many dates and he always insisted on paying, often refusing to let me even contribute or leave the *propina*, or tip. Most of our outings were to restaurants where he would order copious amounts of food: *ceviche*, tacos, tostadas, and soups. He would "prepare" each dish for us, adding lots of lime, chopped green chiles, cilantro, and a pinch of salt. He'd then carefully split it and give me half, or sometimes even feed me bites. At first, I found the latter uncomfortable, but he seemed to enjoy watching how much I loved Mexican food and that I could tolerate a significant amount of heat. "She eats everything!" he'd exclaim proudly to anyone who would listen.

One time when ordering he asked that they make our dish extra *picante*. The server looked at me dubiously. "Does your wife like it spicy?" He gestured up and down his body. "I think we both know the answer to that." He was ridiculously funny. His quick wit had me—and anyone within earshot—in stitches.

A few weeks before I'd met Ponch, the name I now called him, I'd put in an offer on a condo and it had been accepted. The place I'd been leasing was amazing and only three blocks from the beach, but I started to get the decorating itch, and as a renter, there was only so much I could do to make my place my own.

When my realtor took me to see Casa Cielo, my jaw dropped. It was a traditional hacienda-style condo with four small bedrooms, large arched windows, beautiful custom tiles, and a working travertine fountain. The biggest selling point for me, however, was that the previous owners had installed a huge skylight over what was once an open-air courtyard and made it a living room. I imagined laying on the sofa looking up at the stars. I took possession a few months later (the closing process here is much longer than it is in the States), and immediately encountered a series of issues: a leaking roof, no hot water, mold, relentless power outages, and even snakes. When I originally looked at the condo, it was February and the weather was perfect, but now in the heat of summer, standing in my living room under that glass sky felt like being in a convection oven.

All of the people I'd hired to help fix the problems seemed to either arrive late or not at all, and the quality of the work that was done was often subpar. I would spend my days vacillating between a state of fury and despair as I tried to communicate my needs to handymen, painters, and installers.I also encountered many frustrations trying to pay for things. Lack of credit card acceptance and daily ATM limits meant I had to get cash out nearly every morning to compensate my workers, because often ATMs would either be out of order or out of cash later in the day.

In the early days of ownership, I was certain I'd made a mistake and would often shut myself and my dogs in my bedroom, blast the a/c, and cry. Eventually I took up writing about my experiences again, looking to find ways to turn my frustrations into funny Facebook quips. Writing was the perfect distraction, providing the levity I desperately needed to keep me from plunging into a deep depression, packing my bags, and going home again. When I look back on it now, those first few months were probably painful because they challenged my notion of perfection, my need to control the outcome, and my desire for instant gratification. And while I am by no means Zen today, I am much better at managing my expectations than I was when I arrived. In addition, my experiences also allowed me to better communicate the emotional timeline of a move to another country to my interior design clients, and stress how important it is to keep perspective and a sense of humor throughout the process.

I'd only had two relationships of significance before meeting Ponch. In both, things had moved quickly; I'd mistook oversharing for intimacy, overlooked red flags, and moved in together within weeks. With Ponch, it was a slower burn. He worked a lot so we would see each other only two or three times a week, sometimes just for an hour during his lunch break or when I would tag along on a trip to Costco to stock up on supplies for the building he was managing. He also has a large circle of friends to whom he is fiercely allegiant. Monday night is *pozole* with Enrique, Wednesday is pizza with Pato, and so on. On some days, I'd have to temper my envy and remind myself that I'd chosen to leave my friends and our rituals behind in Portland.

A turning point came when he took me to Guadalajara for a birthday party to meet his "fancy" friends. The party was held on the 35th floor of a high-rise condominium complex with sweeping views. I noticed upon arrival that there were microphones but didn't think much of it. About two hours in, the host announced it was karaoke time. In the States, I was always up for belting out a tune or two in a dive bar but being the only non-Mexican in a sea of unfamiliar faces, I decided to watch and wait. Eventually, I gathered my courage and submitted a song request. A few minutes later, the intro to "Hit Me With Your Best Shot" by Pat Benatar began. I stood and began singing. About 20 seconds in, I notice 30 pairs of unimpressed eyes staring at me. Despite being mortified, I made it to the end and sat back down next to Ponch.

"Well, that was embarrassing," I mumbled.

"Yes, it was. But I'm proud of you and I thought you were great!" he replied.

That night back at our Airbnb, he told me he loved me.

After that weekend in Guadalajara, we began spending a lot more time together. Ponch and I shared a deep interest in interior design, so we would spend weekends and holidays going to furniture trade shows or checking out home goods stores together. He started helping me in my design business by making calls to lighting companies to verify pricing or confirm stock and scheduling appointments to tour factories so I could see the quality of their work in person. I'd never had a relationship with someone with whom I had this in common, and it was a whole new world. I didn't have to feel guilty about spending too much time in a showroom or asking him to interpret a product fact sheet about how a material would perform in the harsh conditions of Vallarta.

In January, Ponch's contract at the building he was managing was expiring. We decided that it was a good opportunity to see if we could join forces and take my interior design business to the next level. Not only could he be of service as a translator, but perhaps more importantly, he could assist in interpreting the cultural nuances of doing business in Mexico.

One of the first and most difficult lessons I had to learn is that delivering bad news must be avoided at all costs. When an answer begins with "*Si, pero no*," ("Yes, but no.") I know I'm in trouble. For example, if I check in with my furniture manufacturer on the status of an order and I hear those dreaded words, I know the order will not be ready as promised. No amount of begging or cajoling will speed up the process. In fact, subsequent messages will probably go unanswered until they're ready to deliver the news I want to hear.

Another truth I've had a hard time swallowing is that efficiency isn't a prized quality here the way it is in the States. When I lived in Portland, my installations would take one or two days maximum. I would line up painters, wallpaper hangers, art and window treatment installers, and furniture deliveries so that we could get everything done with minimal disruption to the homeowner.

Here, it can take weeks. Multiple trips to Sherwin-Williams, the local hardware store, and various other suppliers are the norm.

While Ponch helps me understand these nuances, he's also in violation of many of them. I've tried nearly every trick in the book to get him to improve communication and increase productivity—asking nicely, demanding firmly, and even screaming and crying. Unsurprisingly, my attempts to Americanize him are futile. "*Relajate*," he tells me on the regular.

Ponch is also a dreamer. It's one of the things we have in common, and we talk often about the next phase of our business and what it will look like. When he'll act on those plans is another story. I've had to learn to temper my excitement around ideas such as going to a trade show in Europe or opening a retail store, because when he brings it up, he may mean in five years—while I'm thinking five days.

On the other hand, I don't dare tell Ponch that something isn't possible. "That will never fit in the car," or "That artwork will never stay on the wall," is a challenge to his anything-is-possible, can-do character. I've nicknamed him the "Mexican McGyver" because the guy could probably start a motorcycle with a nail file, some toothpaste, and a handful of dirt.

Cultural issues aside, working together while maintaining a romantic relationship hasn't been especially easy. As a chronic worrier and a bona-fide people pleaser, long hours and sleepless nights are the norm. On the other hand, Ponch, like many men, can compartmentalize, setting work aside to have a nice dinner with friends or watch a movie. We've had to establish some ground rules whereby I can't discuss work before 9 a.m. or after 6 p.m. I have and probably will continue to transgress, but he's helping me find a better balance between personal and professional.

This spring, we bought a car that not only enables us to do our jobs more effectively but has allowed us to crisscross the country, buy furniture for clients, see Ponch's family, and visit places I would have been unlikely to see alone. The freedom and periodic change of scenery have been wonderful.

I'm often asked if I would make the same decision knowing what I know now. I like to say that 75% of the time I love the chaos and cacophony of my current life, while 25% longs for the familiarity and predictability of my days in the US. Now and again, I pine for the ability to shoot the breeze over pedicures with my best friend, to get cash back when buying groceries, or, as silly as it may sound, to just be able to wander the aisles of Target.

As my third anniversary in Mexico approaches, I look back at my decision to move here "temporarily" with a bit of amazement and a whole lot of amusement. I was naive to think this would be short-term, but even more so to believe it would be easy. Each day in Mexico may bring with it a series of surprises and challenges, but the mere idea of returning to the US and waking up every morning to my "normal" routine of dark skies and rain, commuter traffic, and the barrage of negativity in the news makes me depressed and anxious. It is the warmth of the people, the food, a sense of humor, and a whole lot of humility that get me through the tough days. Meeting and getting to know Ponch and his wide circle of friends has been the icing on the cake. As he reminds me fairly regularly, "We only have about 20 good years left, my love. Let's fill them with as much adventure as possible."

*Kristen Siefkin is an interior designer and founder of Interior Design Alchemy. Originally from Central California and later Portland, Oregon, she relocated to Puerto Vallarta, Mexico, in 2021, where she and her two small dogs live full-time in a restored hacienda-style condominium. She lives for travel, textiles, tortas ahogadas, and tomfoolery, in no particular order. Visit her website: interiordesignalchemy.com.*

# 11. Transformation

## Corrie McCluskey

## Santa Cruz Amilpas, Oaxaca

When I took my first trip to Oaxaca 15 years ago, I was seeking a transformative experience. It was not my first time to Mexico but was my first visit to Oaxaca. I wanted to immerse myself in the rich culture, practice my Spanish, and investigate the artisan studios and galleries that Oaxaca is known for. After 20 years of doing medium format black and white photography, I was shifting gears and learning to do sketch journaling and mixed media and wanted to meet and make connections with other like-minded creatives. Actually, it was more of a pilgrimage than a holiday. What I found in Oaxaca transformed my life.

My deep connection to Latin America began as soon as I was old enough to understand that I was born in Havana, Cuba, in January of 1959, right in the middle of the Revolution (but that's another story).

My parents' family legend—the story they told since we were little kids—was what fed and nurtured my love affair with Mexico. After saving for a year, my parents went on an amazing journey in 1953, driving from Connecticut to Mexico in an old woody station wagon for their belated honeymoon, and their stories and handwritten journals, photos of ruins, markets, dancers, and clay *ídolos,* were so enticing to my young adventurous soul. In high school, I naturally opted for Spanish as my foreign language, and when the Spanish teacher offered a week-long Mexico mini-course during spring break, I took on small jobs in order to save up enough to go. I went on this trip four years in a row, the highlight of all my school years, and each year we went to a different part of Mexico. The third year was to Yucatán, and the prospect of standing amongst Maya ruins sent me racing to the library and to the local community college to take some archaeology classes.

After graduating, I began my college career at UC Berkeley that fall as a Spanish major, but hated the focus on Castilian Spanish and literature—I wanted Latin America and nothing else. I came up with a plan: do my junior year as an exchange student and study anthropology at UNAM in Mexico City. Fate intervened when I met a fellow anthropology student (and future partner) in the Berkeley anthropology library. I didn't return to Mexico until 1986 (after the death of my partner) and didn't speak Spanish again for 20 years.

I felt the pull to regain my Spanish language chops and head south again, and between 2008-2023, I made one trip to Guatemala to study the K'iche' Maya language and 33 trips to Mexico, 27 of those to Oaxaca. My first trip back was to the Yucatán to photograph ruins, but then I discovered Oaxaca. By then I had transitioned to other art forms. Oaxaca was THE place for me; I knew it intuitively.

I met my now-partner and fellow artist Pedro 15 years ago in a coffeeshop in Oaxaca Centro, across from a plaza where he was selling his paintings. There was something magical about him and I started coming regularly to Oaxaca to hang out with him, to make and talk art, and to share new art mediums and materials with my art buddy. Our relationship turned romantic after a few years. We started doing art adventures together; jumping on a bus to Puebla for the weekend with a suitcase full of art supplies, going on ephemera treasure hunts in the antiquities bazaar, and making collages on the floor of our hotel room.

In 2018, we started teaching art workshops in Baja, Mexico, and then in 2022 we offered our first one in Oaxaca. We realized that we would eventually need our own art space rather than renting one or trying to give a class in a hotel patio. I was tired of going back and forth to California—long-distance relationships are very difficult in the long haul—and had always dreamed of finding a good piece of land to buy to build two art studios and a little *casita*. Pedro was somewhat doubtful that I'd ever make the leap, but

I firmly set my intention when I applied for temporary residency at the Mexican consulate in San Francisco. A few months later, in Oaxaca, I was thrilled to hold my new residency card in my hands.

I thought I needed to wait to seek residency until I was actually ready to move but had an epiphany: I qualified for residency and could use it to go back and forth until I could actually move full time. Why wait? It's a good thing I didn't, because I just squeaked by with the financial requirements in 2021, which were much lower than they are now, and increasing every year.

My intuition and every fiber of my being told me: If you have a dream, don't put it off. Begin. Figure out a way to start taking steps toward it as soon as you can and keep walking towards it. Educate yourself about what's required, visit the place and get to know it, solicit help from others who are a few steps ahead of you in the process and can give you current information and advice, and hire someone to help if necessary. But find a way to make your dream a reality.

When my mother died in 2023 after a long journey with dementia (and my father had died a few years earlier), I suddenly had the funds and the freedom to proceed with my dream. I seized the moment and made an instantaneous, solid decision to GO NOW, no matter what. I saw this quote by Doris Lessing and pasted it onto the cover of my journal: "Whatever you're meant to do, do it now. The conditions are always impossible." I didn't want to find myself on my deathbed someday, filled with deep, deep regret about not realizing my dream to live in Mexico and find out how far I could take my life as an artist.

There was a solid year of transition on every imaginable level. While helping my sister clear out my mother's home and sell it, I learned the importance of going through your closets and shelves to get rid of decades of accumulated "stuff" and not passing this awful task to your loved ones when you die. What to do with six sets of fancy antique dinner plates and serving silverware that you'll never use in your own modern life? Or a large collection of rooster figurines, canning jars, ancient yearbooks, linen closets full of twin sheets? The emotional energy required to deal with it all is considerable.

Immediately upon finishing with my mom's house, I started a major renovation of my own home (that was practically falling down around my ears) so that I could leave it for my daughter and granddaughters to take over. What was supposed to take six weeks dragged on for four months, and I had to get used to workmen never showing up when they said they would, everything I owned being scattered around in boxes, the rooms covered in dust, the exterior also in total disarray, the constant changes and impermanence surrounding me. It was a very liminal place to be in but actually helped me prepare for the sometimes-exasperating journey of building a home in Mexico.

I dove into the task of downsizing everything I owned: 30 years' worth of collected books, vinyl records, memorabilia, files and old bills, clothes and household items, and a two-car garage/art studio full of everything imaginable. It was as hard as I thought it would be, but I was relentless. I had to make a hundred decisions daily: what to keep, what to sell, what to give away, how to get it done. Going through drawers full of memories, each item demanded to be viewed, revisited, and considered. Selling my beloved cameras was hard, even though I hadn't been using them for a few years.

They say that when you get rid of the old, you make way for the new and allow flow into your life. This was my mantra as I sifted through dozens of full shelves and drawers, although I don't know if I was successful in getting rid of all that I should have. I ended up with 200 boxes that I couldn't part with, half of those being books! I had already downsized my book collection by half the year prior while my house was being renovated, but I simply couldn't imagine living without a home library. I kept the small taffy box filled with seashells collected on the shores of Cape Hatteras when I was 10 years old, and the bits and pieces of bottles, pottery, and ephemera collected from California and Nevada Gold Rush ghost towns, with plans to make a mosaic something-or-other out of them—an art project waiting to happen. I kept a collection of rocks that I picked up from all my travels in the world, and my windchimes. Kind of crazy perhaps, but odd things ground me and will take up residency in my new garden that's taking shape.

I chose a moving date of December 1, hired a moving company that specialized in Mexico and an assistant to help me. The mover gave me great advice: you actually don't have to get rid of everything you own; keep the things that give you comfort and joy (think: Marie Kondo). In my case, that was my favorite art books, good quality cookware and tools, some antiques and the furniture that Dad made me, years of journals, and the art supplies that were allowed to be imported. I bought a new couch, a couple of supremely comfortable vintage overstuffed armchairs (with hopes they'd actually fit in the *casita*), a solid quality bed and mattress with real linen sheets (a big splurge), and a gorgeous tall oak bureau to bring to Mexico; all of these things will last the rest of my life.

The process of doing a *menaje de casa*—the list of items going on the moving truck—was time consuming and nit-picky and had to be done exactly in order to pass through Customs. But the upside is that while my boxes sit in a storage unit here in Oaxaca as we wait for the house to be finished, I have a detailed list of what's in each one and can track down an item if I really need to find it. And when it actually comes time to unpack all these boxes, I may still chuck more things overboard in my quest to keep only what works.

I left behind my ESL teaching job at a community college, took a month to wrap up all the loose ends, bought my one-way plane ticket for the beginning of the new year, and off I went. I recognized right away when I arrived and started to get settled that living here is absolutely different from visiting. A huge internal shift happens; you're no longer the tourist visiting the *Pueblo Mágico* and wandering around downtown looking for the latest diversion, but a person searching for their new daily routine, a way to function in a different culture and where to fit in, leaving behind your language and favorite comfort foods and ways of doing things.

If you're wise, you'll consciously make an ongoing effort to assimilate upon arrival: Get out of your comfort zone and be willing to interact with everyone around you, in their language as best you can. I was hit with unexpected and strange waves of existential fear (mostly at night) for several weeks, silently howling, "What have I done?! How will I do this, can I make a go of my business here? What if, what if, what if…" and was thankful for a couple of close friends that I could call to get reassurance that I wasn't falling apart or crazy for doing this. Eventually it subsided to a manageable dull roar in my head that I can choose to ignore as I go about my day.

Buying land in Mexico is a journey with a hundred twists and turns; you learn the process as you go, and nothing is as we're used to in the US. You have to be willing to be persistent and vigilant, have a great deal of patience, learn a lot of new legal terms in Spanish (or hire someone to translate and help you), and not expect the process to be familiar. Be sure to buy private land that's fully documented—never buy *ejido* (communal) land or you open yourself up to possible heartbreak and loss.

And expect that the unexpected will happen. Building a new home is no less convoluted; timelines are only theoretical; contractors do what they please. I'm fortunate that I had a Oaxacan partner who could help: getting electricity hooked up, filling a roof-top *tinaco* with water, calling the gas company to come refill the tanks, paying the homeowner's taxes at the *municipio*. The land we chose is in Pedro's small hometown, with his parent's home (with a working well, worth gold here) a couple of streets away and his siblings nearby, so I literally landed in the bosom of an established and respected family, with all that entails.

I'm known as "*la guera*" (the white lady) in my *colonia*, and I'm finding ways to fit in. I've participated in the annual *calenda* (parade) in May that winds through the streets of my *pueblo*, complete with giant street puppets and dancers, blaring brass bands, and exploding fireworks. I'm as polite as possible when interacting with locals, and always share a "*buenos días / buenas tardes*" and "*que le vaya bien*" because manners and politeness matter here.

My sense of time and obligations don't always match my Mexican partner's, and he chuckles and reminds me often that things are different here; *ahorita* can mean now, in a couple of hours, or whenever he feels like it, and things should be done "*con calma*." Practicing patience and flexibility while we live in a 600-sq-ft studio together with four energetic juvenile cats, waiting for our house to be built, has become a rather Zen path I have to walk and I'm getting better at it.

In between working online to grow our business and finding time to be in the art studio, I helped sow our own *milpa* (cornfield) by hand and watched my partner start and tend a large garden of vegetables and fruit trees (sometimes helping when I could be useful). One of the most enjoyable tasks has been to choose the plants and trees for the landscaping around our studios; we have mostly native species that are culturally important to Oaxaca. Pedro knows all their names and has stories about eating this or planting that from throughout his life. I love watching the men plant the trees, digging the holes with just a long iron bar and small shovel. They know what they're doing. I love the ritual of deciding on the right location, everyone standing around the hole as it's dug, the tree is set, and the earth is patted down around it, as if blessing the process. There's such an attachment to the seasons, the planting cycles, and the land, rain and sun here in the countryside.

I'm learning basic animal husbandry with the eight chickens, three goats, and Luna the baby burro that we now have: how to tie her halter correctly, how to herd chickens, how you must not feed animals fresh-cut alfalfa that's still warm from the fields, how to put them to bed in their stalls at night, what to do when a chicken has a cold. It's hard to believe we're only 15 minutes from the bustling capitol city and live out amongst pastures where they still use yoked oxen to plow the fields. There are grazing sheep, packs of stray dogs roaming around the nearby river and through the fields, and dirt roads that are nearly impassible with mud in the rainy season. The beauty of the tall hills on either side of us is stunning, and the pace of life is slower and more sane, and feels ancestral.

I love the rustling sound of the corn stalks at night and the hundreds of birds singing at daybreak. On weekdays, the workmen listen to *cumbia* and *corridos* as they do the construction nearly entirely by hand, and you can hear them joking and riffing on each other all day. There's no OSHA here, and one prays for their safety sometimes when they're up on the roof or lowering a cistern into the ground. Customs and traditions are taken seriously in these *pueblos,* and you learn to walk gently through all manner of situations because you really don't know the backstory and how you now fit into it. I was already used to the incredible noise level (and our roosters are adding to it), the trash issues, and services and infrastructure not being the same as back home; none of that came as a big surprise, and you learn to deal with different ways of doing things and taking it all in stride.

I have no regrets about leaving my former life behind, although some days I miss the ease of doing things in the hyper-efficient digital California lifestyle, the regular meet-ups at a coffeeshop with old friends, a visit with my daughter and grandkids, enjoying the lunch special at my favorite neighborhood Thai place where I was a regular, or the ease of buying some specialty item or art material that you simply can't find here. I'll have to wait for the next visit to restock what I need and see those I miss.

Here I learn something new every single day—how to do something, a new word, where to look for "x" and what kind of store you'll find it in. I'm not going back because "back there" is no longer my home. I'm mostly resilient and adaptable; although once in a while days are tough, you get through it and when the sun comes up the next day you can't believe your luck at being here.

Nothing about this first year is especially easy because it's still fairly new and we live a rural life, but it's a worthwhile and meaningful life, and one that I chose and have worked toward for years. My current task is to make new friends and add to my routine so that I never feel socially isolated; a mix of Oaxaqueños and a couple expat friends would be ideal.

I have to pinch myself sometimes to realize that I actually made it all happen—getting residency, finding expat health insurance, finding the right piece of land to buy, the downsizing, the packing and inventorying, the move—and that I'm finally HERE. I'm finding out who I am in this new place, and I'm working to create the kind of life I want here while the place shapes and changes me at the same time. When I post on social media, I get messages from friends that marvel at me living my dream. I want to ask them, are you doing the same? If not, why not? Life is very short, and the goal is to have lived it well. There are no do-overs. Being brave doesn't mean you aren't afraid, it just means you do your due diligence, then walk into the unknown and do it anyway. And now that I'm here and my art studio has been built, I must create and nurture a weekly routine that includes the deep art practice I've dreamed of having in my life. I always had some other priority that had to come before art making. The time is now to prioritize this. I can't wait to see what shows up on my paper.

What helps most in adjusting to life here is choosing to be happy and reveling in small but meaningful things: sharing a roast chicken dinner with the cousins who just helped you build the goat shed, celebrating a family member's birthday with a live band and dancing till dawn, Sunday afternoon family lunch under the shade tree out in the field, the morning visits with food vendors who sell *churros* and *atole, tamales,* or fresh fruit picked from their backyard for a few pesos, marveling at how the place explodes with green and life after the rainy season starts.

Having happiness as a mindset is something I'm cultivating; finding a way to be content with what I have and being willing to grow. People enjoy life here and there are always the sounds of music, fireworks, or a party in the air. My partner and I can make an adventure out of anything— a trip to the store to pick out a washing machine, going to the Sunday market to buy corn seeds or drink some *tejate,* taking a bus trip to Puebla to visit the antiquities bazaar, or driving to the mountains for the weekend and stopping at the plant nurseries on the way. Other joys: making a *quesadilla* with fresh tortillas, *quesillo* (Oaxacan white cheese), homegrown squash blossoms and chile peppers. Savoring a cup of tea made from our own lemongrass. Learning the Zapotec and Nahuatl names of the plants and trees in our field, and the songs of all the birds that live in this valley. On Saturday mornings I meet a friend at a yoga class downtown and then enjoy a great chat with her over brunch. All of this together makes a great life.

Moving to Oaxaca was a vivid dream for me for more than a decade. I've found my forever home for the last third of my life and it's the right decision for me. I never let the voice of "no" persuade me to abandon my dream. I'm supposed to be here, and I listened when Oaxaca called to me. Although I would have done it even if I'd been single, having a partner certainly has made it easier and quicker to integrate. I'm an immigrant, and I can proudly say I'm a *Oaxaqueña adoptada.*

꙳

*Corrie McCluskey is an artist and teacher who lives in Santa Cruz Amilpas, Oaxaca, Mexico, a small pueblo 15 minutes from Oaxaca city. For decades she resided in the San Francisco Bay Area. She taught ESL and Spanish language literacy at a community college for 10 years and is now teaching English to her neighbors. Corrie also worked in black & white medium format photography for nearly 20 years and her images were published internationally.*

*Today, Corrie is a visual artist working in mixed media, collage, encaustic monotypes, cold wax and oils, ink, graphite, and natural pigments found in Oaxaca: cochinilla, cempasuchil, añil. She and her partner Pedro own Galería Talismán Oaxaca, an art space with innovative "industrial rustic" art studios built in the middle of milpas (cornfields). It's a place for viewing art, individualized art classes, private art retreats and art + culture workshops. They love to share their insiders' perspective on the art, culture, and traditions of Oaxaca with travelers who crave an art adventure and a real experience of cultural immersion, who need to reignite their creativity and make art from the soul. Visit her websites at corriemccluskey.com and talismanoaxaca.com.*

# 12. Creating & Living a Damn Good Life

## Heather Shoning

## Puerta Vallarta, Jalisco

I'd been vacationing in Puerto Vallarta for at least 15 years with my (then) husband and our two daughters when I decided—on a whim—to move there. I'd long since gotten over the heartbreak of my failed marriage, but when the ink was finally wet on the paperwork, I found myself feeling restless and wondering, "what now?" That's when Hanna, my younger daughter—21 at the time and on a hiatus from junior college thanks to the pandemic—said to me, "I'm bored, Mom. We should move to Mexico."

Hmmm. I could almost feel the wheels turning in my brain.

Could I move to Mexico? I'm a freelance writer and editor, so I'm not tied to an office. My kids are grown and (mostly) self-sufficient. I already lived far from my family of origin, so what's a little farther?

As excited as I was feeling about this prospect, I felt like I needed a sign. So I flipped a coin. For real. I traced the outline of a quarter onto a sticky note, cut the circles out, and stuck them to my 25-cent piece. On one side, I wrote "Mexico" and on the other, "Not Mexico." I flipped it. I'm sure you can guess how it landed. I flipped it a few more times just to be sure. Ultimately, I decided that's it's just a decision and those are a dime a dozen. If it turns out that I don't love the decision, I can always make a new one.

Why Puerto Vallarta?

I'd visited other locations in Mexico but always felt called back to Vallarta, as the locals call it. As a young wife and mother, I was not a well-traveled person—I'm still not by many standards—so Puerto Vallarta is where I cut my travel chops. In the early years, my husband and I would stick to the resort, the malecón, and well-established (read: gringo) restaurants. I still only ate rice and beans, as the meat tasted gamey to me.

I'll never forget the time we decided to exit our comfort zone. Wandering through the side streets of the Romantic Zone, we stumbled upon a couple of women in one of those rickety, fold-up taco stands, chopping meat *thud-thud-thud*, a crowd three-deep standing around eating and waiting for tacos. We decided to go for it, and the *carnitas* tacos, dripping grease on the colorful plastic-bag-covered plastic plates, were divine. It changed my life, and I'm not being hyperbolic. At the time, it seemed like such a quaint experience, but as I branched out into the depths of the city and away from the safety net of the tourist areas, I quickly learned that this was just everyday life.

With more and more visits and exploring, I've come to know the real Puerto Vallarta with its flaws and blemishes, but also its genuinely sweet people, colorful cultural traditions, and unabashed natural beauty.

Many people making this leap would look for a place to rent. But I went all in, as I am wont to do with most things. I didn't spend a lot of time thinking it through, as I am also wont to do. Many times over the past four years, I've wondered if maybe a little time pondering before doing would have benefitted me. Maybe, but it probably wouldn't have changed the outcome, and I'm OK with that.

So, with my tiny budget and a referral for a real estate agent, I got online to start my search for a home in Puerto Vallarta. I emailed about a house that was out of my budget, thinking maybe they'd be interested in dealing. The response was, "That's cute. Let us know if you can increase your budget." Moving on.

The second house that caught my eye online was the one I eventually purchased. It was—to put it mildly—a fixer-upper. Let me preface this by saying I have remodeled many homes throughout my life, and I have a keen eye for "potential." I happen to be one of those people who sees and is inspired by potential, be it in people, job opportunities or, in this case, a fixer-upper house perched on a hillside where the city breaches the jungle. It has stunning views of Banderas Bay, which is really what I bought because the house itself … let's just say, I found it lacking. But not in potential.

Let me also preface this by saying that I had sold the home I "got" in the divorce because I didn't want all the work associated with it. I'd moved into an apartment that was shiny and new. It had a gym, pool, dog park, and coworking spaces. It was neat, tidy, and easy. My new home … not so much.

This all happened during the pandemic shutdown, so I made an offer on the house, but didn't go see it until two months later. My real estate agent was a sweet woman. She passed away unexpectedly about a year later, and I attended her funeral—she'd been living in PV for more than 20 years—and it was a bit like a smalltown gathering. I saw so many people there that I knew from "around town."

But I digress. When she took me to see the house, she insisted I look at a shiny new condo in a neighboring *colonia* (neighborhood). I said, "Fine, if you insist, but I know I'm going to buy this house." I looked at the condo, which looked significantly like my apartment in Colorado at the time. I didn't want to move to Mexico to live with expats in a building that looked like any condo in Anytown, USA. I wanted Mexico—bright colors, Saltillo tiles, arches, traditional metal-framed doors and windows, and Mexican neighbors. Now, almost four years later, it's still not finished, but it's shaping up to be the authentic Mexican-style home I envisioned from the moment my coin landed Mexico-side-up.

I told almost no one what I was doing until it was almost time to leave the country, mostly because a small fear gripped me that somehow something would go wrong, and this coin-toss-turned-dream would somehow become the proverbial rug. But my fears were for naught.

When I did tell people, I faced two breeds of negativity. One born from a certain concern for my well-being and safety, and another born of jealousy—not everyone has the *pelotas* (slang for balls) to do what I was doing. And, hey, to each her own. Then, four months after the fateful coin toss, Hanna and I packed up our belongings, loaded the most important ones, along with our dogs, into her older Isuzu Rodeo, and set off on our three-day drive south from Colorado.

Honestly, the trip did have me a bit nervous. I'd read too many awful things on social media, and I let it get into my head. As it turned out, it was thankfully—potholes aside—uneventful. We did get pulled over for a shakedown once, but thanks to said social media, I knew it was coming and exactly where it would happen. We politely declined to pay, repeatedly, until they got bored and let us go.

I rented an Airbnb for a week that I chose because the photos from its rooftop showed that I could see my house on the hillside. But Hanna and I only went to the rooftop once to look. We busied ourselves with buying beds and bedding, a refrigerator, lots of storage containers-cum-dressers. Let me be clear, we spent the first solid year in a glorified state of camping. For nine months, I had no hot water heater. I also had no *tinaco* (water storage tank), which means that when the city water shut off, so did mine. And it happens all the time—once, in the wake of a storm, I had no water for nine days.

A top priority was getting internet so I could work. The first company never showed up. Antonio, my neighbor at the bottom of the hill, told me about another one, and helped me communicate with the installer when he came. I was up and running in no time, and since then (knock wood) my internet has been surprisingly reliable. Much better than the water service.

One of the biggest challenges we faced was getting everything we had to buy *into* the house. In many areas of town, especially the hilly areas, the "street" is actually a pedestrian staircase. My house is on one of those, so from the closest street, it's 90 stairs to my front door. It was not all that fun with Costco trip after Costco trip. My calves, however, look amazing these days.

My casa continues to be a work in process—I can hear the contractors pounding as I write this. But each new project and update only serves to solidify what is already true: This is my home. It's not neat, tidy, or easy, but—damn!—this life is good.

I'd been in Puerto Vallarta for an extended stay in 2018 and adopted a dog, my sweet Juniper. When I was leaving, I had a dog crate I couldn't take with me, so I posted it in a Facebook group—there are a zillion dog rescuers here. Through that process, I connected with a woman who lives here full-time and happens to be a real estate agent. When I moved back, she reached out and asked if I was now living in Vallarta. (I didn't use her as my real estate agent because I didn't know she did that at the time.) She's since wildly grown her business and frequently hosts mixers, which she invited me to. Now, I belong to a large group of expats who I frequently see for events such as a wine fest or that I run into when I'm out and about. That led to my developing a small, tight-knit group of ladies whom I adore and spend a lot of time with. They are here six months or on-and-off, and I love to have their company whenever I can.

Living here, I've learned a lot about this place. Of course, I have some favorite eateries that I've been going to for years, including La Piazzetta, an Italian restaurant in the Romantic Zone; Margarita Grill, a campy, touristy place with great live music and even better strawberry basil margaritas; and Joe Jack's Fish Shack, which has a fried chicken dinner twice a week during low season.

But today, I'm much more likely to frequent inland places, and by that, I mean the non-tourist spots you discover by lots and lots of walking. One such spot is Pizza Papa Don, a place near El Estadio (a sports park) that sells $7 peso slices of pizza most nights of the week for hungry sports players and fans. Another is a taco stand that has a name, but I don't know it. To me, it's the *suadero* taco stand across from Ley (a grocery store in *el centro*). "*Suadero*" is a cut of beef. I won't go into the details, but I will say it's delicious when it's cooked right, and this taco stand is tops. Another favorite hidden gem is a Sonoran hot dog stand in my *colonia*. Again, it has a name, but I don't know it. There's not really a need to know because it doesn't show up on a map, so I just have to take people there for them to try it. The owner thinks I'm *loca* because I don't get all the peppers and *panela* cheese and other toppings. I like just the hot dog wrapped in *tocino* (bacon) on a steamed bun.

My daily life is comprised of things other than food. I work from home, so it's very much a normal existence, in that respect. For a while, it was a big pet peeve to me that my colleagues all imagined my life to be like what they experience when they go on a tropical vacation. It couldn't be farther from that. I take my clothes to the *lavandería* in my *colonia* because I don't have a washer and dryer in my house (although when this current remodel is finished, that will change).

One of my favorite things is my evening walk. I take the bus to the other side of the mountain and hop off at the river. Then I walk the river path to the malecón. Sometimes I watch the sunset, depending on the time. Sometimes I make it a long loop, walking all the way back to my house. When I'm feeling lazy, I make it a shorter trek, stopping by my favorite liquor store for a bottle of wine, then I hop on the bus back home. A few nights a week my walk ends at the gym, which I love—sometimes just for the simple fact that it has air conditioning.

My Spanish is awful, which is really embarrassing. Thankfully, people in my neighborhood forgive easily. But I did recently find lessons that seem to be working for me—when I make the time to commit and show up. I've realized that I spend an inordinate amount of time speaking Spanish in my head, practicing what I'm going to say, checking Google Translate to be sure I've got it right, only to freeze and have English come out of my mouth. I try to be forgiving and patient with myself, but I've been here long enough that I should be fluent!

I'm most looking forward to having the construction done on my house so I'll have a new sitting place where I can while away hours staring at the ocean. As a creative, and especially a writer, daydreaming and thinking is very much a part of my process for working. I've just about got it mastered. I love watching the cruise ships arrive in the morning and then sail off into the sunset in the evening. I love seeing the outline of the lighted pirate ship that entertains visitors two or three times a day and shoots off fireworks for its nighttime show.

But mostly, my time spent staring at the sea is when I think about how lucky I am that my daughter was bored, and that I flipped a coin that landed right-side up. This has been quite the adventure, and I stand a bit taller having undertaken it on my own. People used to tell me how brave I was for doing this, but I always wrote it off as being impulsive—maybe even stupid. But not anymore. I scroll through my Instagram feed as a gentle reminder of all I've been through, and even through the many videos of me crying through my construction woes, I can see the strength, will, and determination I've gained. Who knows, maybe I'll flip another coin one day, make another decision, and embark on another journey. For now, I'm happy, knowing whatever I decide, I can do.

My daughter recently returned to the United States, but I'm not alone. I have my dog and a second, who I rescued from the streets a year ago. I have my neighbors and business owners of the *lavandería, tienda,* and coffee shop that I frequent in my *colonia.* It's nearly impossible for me to go downtown without running into expat friends I've made since moving here, and I often have a little smirk on my face because I feel like the luckiest girl in the world to be living this amazing life.

〜

*Heather Shoning is a freelance editor and writer currently residing in Puerto Vallarta, Mexico. Originally from Iowa, Heather's work is grounded in Midwestern sensibility. She is currently working remotely as editor of both a Colorado luxury lifestyle publication and a national home and design magazine. Heather also writes lifestyle, design, and travel articles for several other US magazines. In her spare time, Heather continues to write, finding joy in the creative process of wordsmithing. She is looking for a publisher for her first novel, a romance, and has two women's fiction novels in various stages of production. Follow her at: @casavistajourney.*

# 13. Peace at Last

Denise Perry

Tlaquepaque, Jalisco

July 22, 2019.

As the plane flew over the Sierra Madre mountains, I felt tears welling up in my eyes—not out of sadness, but rather from the sheer beauty of what I was seeing. It felt like a welcome home, though it was all unfamiliar to me. The sultry humid air hit me like a wave as the plane landed in Puerto Vallarta, a severe contrast to the cold climate I'd just left in upper northern Minnesota. I don't remember exactly what I was wearing but no matter what I would have worn, it would have clung to my suddenly very sweaty body. Once we landed, my naturally curly hair became a wild mess, something I knew would happen and now didn't care at all what it looked like. It felt like freedom to let my hair go wild.

I had two checked bags and one carry-on, the extent of my life's possessions. I had sold or given away almost everything except for a limited amount of summery clothes and electronic devices. As I moved through the customs inspection line in the overcrowded airport, I kept my eye on the system indicating whether or not you would be pulled aside for a thorough baggage search. If you got the red light, this meant an intense search of your belongings, in Spanish of course. If you got the green light, no further check was required. It reminded me of a child's game except the stakes of this game were high. Thankfully, I breezed through with no further inspection warranted.

I had rented an apartment sight unseen while I was still in the United States, something which in hindsight I would not recommend but which was necessary for me at the time. I'd left behind almost everything in my life in exchange for this move to Puerto Vallarta, Mexico, where I knew no one. I didn't even speak Spanish. I felt overwhelmed, like a five-year-old who can't read signs or even know which bathroom to use. Despite what could have been an extremely stressful predicament, all I remember feeling was peace. It strangely felt like home. It never felt scary.

I suppose it's natural to wonder how someone reaches the point where they abandon everything familiar to them in exchange for a world where everything is unknown. Here is my story.

I retired in 2015 from a 30-year career in criminal justice. Unfortunately, my pension was insufficient, so I had to continue working full-time in another capacity. I was tired, stressed, and not taking good care of myself. Then fate intervened, delivering an unexpected and severe turn-of-events that ultimately saved my life.

Due to all of my obligations, I'd postponed having an important cancer screening. In 2017, I finally had the procedure. They discovered a large polyp and told me it was dangerously close to becoming cancerous. Had I delayed any longer, I might not be writing this essay. I had an epiphany: I had to start living for me or I would surely lose my life. Self-care, I decided, was not selfish, it was necessary. The constant stress was literally killing me. I knew I had to get to a place where I could have time to think and plan the rest of my life. I still fantasized about living outside the US but didn't feel like I had time to plan that big of a move. At the same time, I felt that I must move as soon as possible; I had to get out of this rat race I was in, no matter how painful it was to leave everything I knew behind.

In 2018, I moved from Ohio to northern Minnesota, where I had friends. For the next year, I pondered the direction of my life. Here, with extremely cold weather a majority of the year, I had time to focus on myself and think clearly. Then, the Universe offered an opportunity: a friend and her husband invited me to Puerto Vallarta for a week's vacation in February, 2019.

I'd always been interested in the Mexican culture. I remember being particularly moved by the song, "*Eres Tú*" in the early 1970s. I would sing it in Spanish (or mimic what I thought the words were) and dream of living in another country. Even before I fully understood what living in another country involved, I fantasized about being elsewhere. The place was vague. I just knew I envisioned more for my life.

As I grew older and began to take vacations to such places as Montreal, Toronto, Chicago, San Diego, and New York City, I was simply enchanted with wanting to live elsewhere. The more foreign the location, the greater appeal it had for me. I loved walking or driving by the houses or apartments and imagining what it would be like to live there. What would my life be like? I nearly always imagined myself being a successful single lady living in a beautiful historical house or a modern high-rise in the city. I dreamed of a life as a bohemian living in Greenwich Village in New York City and working in the fashion district.

I still have "*Eres Tú*" on my favorite playlist and to this day, it brings happy tears to my eyes. It's particularly poignant to me as I listen to it in my Mexico home and am transported back in time to the little girl who dreamed of living in another country. I wish I could tell that little girl to hold on, have faith, and lose her fear, because her wishes will come true one day and she'll have peace in her heart and in her life.

Unfortunately, before the fear would leave and the peace could be found, there would be much pain. As a small child, I'd become fearful of almost every situation. I was afraid of failing in school, of not getting perfect grades, of being in embarrassing situations, of not being popular enough, smart enough, or pretty enough. I became fearful of taking chances in doing anything new since I felt that I would likely fail as I wasn't smart enough or good enough.

These feelings of inferiority lingered into my adulthood until one day, a friend who was an experienced skydiver invited me to join him in a skydiving adventure. I would be jumping tandem with a skilled instructor while my friend would be jumping solo. As the plane was climbing to our jump altitude, I remember thinking it odd that I felt no fear. I'd made the decision to jump and, at that point, there was no turning back. There was no other way down but by jumping.

I remember everyone telling me I was crazy. They were certain I was going to die, break bones, that the security harness would come undone and leave me dangling by a thread, or a myriad of other horrific things. They would drone on about how badly this would end. But once I decided to go, the only thing I felt was excitement. So I donned the jumpsuit and the safety goggles, and my instructor hooked himself to me and set up all the apparatus.

My friend jumped first. I remember watching him jump out the door of the plane and then quickly disappear into the horizon. It was my turn next. I sat in the little doorway of the tiny plane with my instructor behind me, attached to my back by a harness. My legs dangled high above the Earth I could see far below. When he gave the signal, all I had to do was sort of tumble out, face down.

I'll never forget the rush of the cold air on my face. The force was so powerful it felt like the skin on my face would be ripped off. But more than anything, I loved the sheer insanity of the free fall and the feeling of freedom.

There were no broken bones, no harness mishaps. None of the ghastly things predicted by my friends had happened. I felt incredibly flushed with adrenaline. My first words were, "Let's go again!" All day long I felt incredibly confident, like I could do anything. I was superwoman for a day. I can see how people get easily hooked on skydiving; adrenaline is a very addictive hormone. One very unexpected result of my skydiving experience was that I began to notice that my fears were gone. Once I'd jumped out of that plane, nothing else was scary.

I started to take trips by myself and do other things that I'd previously not done because I'd been held back by my fears. It was so incredibly liberating. I don't believe I would have ever had the courage to move to Mexico, especially by myself, if I hadn't gone skydiving.

So, rather naturally, I jumped at the chance to visit Puerto Vallarta when my friends extended the invitation. I was immediately enamored with the Mexican charm and began talking to the locals about moving there. My friends back home couldn't believe it. "You can't move to Mexico!" they said. They inundated me with all the horrific things that could happen to me if I followed my heart.

I wasn't deterred by any of their concerns. I trusted my intuition and previous training, and, just like with skydiving, I forged ahead with my plan. I was sad that my friends were not more supportive. It occurred to me that they were very fearful and lacked any experience in living anywhere other than where they'd been born and raised. I also sensed prejudiced undertones because it was Mexico where I was intending to move. I suspect they may have reacted differently if I'd been talking about moving to Europe.

Five months later, after exhaustive research, I did just that. I applied to the Mexican consulate in the United States and obtained approval for permanent residency. I sold or gave away the remainder of my belongings. I also got a long-term health insurance policy which would cover me in Mexico.

My first apartment was located on the beach, which sounds luxurious but was far from it. The refrigerator was propped up on bricks, there were no screens in the windows, and the furnishings were basic and old. The apartment was located above a convenience store and I was routinely awakened around 2 a.m. to the sound and smell of a diesel truck making a delivery to the store. But, being new to Mexico, I found all of this charming. And the price of the apartment fit my budget nicely. I walked the beach every morning before the heat became too unbearable. The apartment building was quiet and boasted a beautiful rooftop terrace with a small view of the ocean. Despite some inconveniences and challenges, I still reflect upon my first apartment fondly and have wonderful memories of my time there.

When I moved to Minnesota, I learned to make friends easily and found the change of scenery refreshing. This definitely eased the transition to Mexico. Amazingly, I've had little problem adjusting culturally. I do have the occasional frustration while waiting for a repair person to come to the house as they always seem to be late and sometimes don't show up at all. I've also dedicated a lot of time working on my Spanish, which helps significantly in acclimating.

The Covid-19 pandemic struck eight months after I moved to Puerto Vallarta, an unanticipated event that kept me in place for another year and a half. I had made many lasting friendships, participated in a writer's group that met online, and had some amazing experiences, but overall, I was finding that Puerto Vallarta lacked cultural depth for me. Also, it's a very transitional town, and in fact, it was expected with new friendships that the person might not be in town long-term.

In Puerto Vallarta, most things are geared toward pleasing the tourists. There are plenty of bars, touristy restaurants serving traditional bar food and other tourist attractions. Naturally, a lot of these closed during the pandemic and a lot of the snowbirds (people who live in Puerto Vallarta half the year) returned to their home countries. The pandemic prevented me from exploring other places in Mexico or even within Puerto Vallarta. Mexico did not have access to the Covid-19 vaccinations until mid-2021, so for the most part I was staying in my apartment and not socializing much, especially until I was vaccinated.

I rented a house for six months that exceeded my budget but had a private pool. During the worst of the pandemic, I swam several times a day for exercise. To me, living in Puerto Vallarta was like living on the sun. It was so hot that it was impossible for me to enjoy a walk at any time of the day or during any season. It was too hot to go to the beach. I realized that I do not tolerate heat well nor am I fond of the beach for anything more than a vacation.

Occasionally, I would meet my best friend in a park and we would catch up while maintaining social distancing. It was a very lonely time. Soon I found myself longing for the symphony, performing arts, a mix of cultures, art, music, history, architecture, and a cooler climate. I wanted to walk and exercise without the threat of heat exhaustion. Despite my initial enchantment with Puerto Vallarta, I felt unfulfilled and restless, yearning for a deeper connection with Mexican culture. I felt like I was simply adrift with no identifiable plan.

I took advantage of the Covid lockdown to research other locations in Mexico and worked briefly with a life coach to clearly focus on my goals. Torn between Mexico City and Guadalajara (the two biggest cities in Mexico), I chose the latter believing that Mexico City with 22 million people would be overwhelming to me. In November 2021, I moved to Guadalajara without ever having visited.

One skill I've learned that has been an important part of my expat success is networking. Friends joke that I'm the "master concierge." I've learned that through networking, I can find the people who are essential to my life. For example, immigration facilitators/ lawyers, insurance agents, movers, etc. No matter where I live in Mexico, these are important people to have in my life.

When I first arrived in Guadalajara, I was struck by the significant language barrier. Though Spanish was spoken in Puerto Vallarta, I could get by without learning much Spanish since it was a tourist town and most people spoke English. The opposite is true in Guadalajara since there aren't many expats. The overall expat population is very small in comparison to the total population of Guadalajara, at 5.5 million people. Being all alone and not knowing Spanish was definitely daunting.

I've since taken online Spanish classes, attended language exchanges and of course I get lessons just going about my daily life. I've found that the best way to learn is by surrounding myself with locals. A few of my friends speak no English, so I'm forced to learn and practice Spanish. It certainly makes things easier and less stressful when I can converse on at least a basic level. My friend and I still laugh about the time in Puerto Vallarta when I ordered a margarita with red limes! I don't focus too much on speaking Spanish perfectly and know my verb tenses are often wrong, but for right now it's important for me to learn the words and be able to convey simple thoughts.

I'm trying very hard and can laugh at myself. It's all very humbling, for sure. I've never been shamed for not speaking Spanish fluently, and in fact, most times others chime in and tell me the correct pronunciation or words. They're very patient and eager to help me adjust.

Another difficulty in moving to Guadalajara was the housing situation. It's an extremely competitive rental market for locals and is difficult for foreigners to qualify. Many landlords still insist that renters have an "*aval*" or "*fiador*," a legally binding document from someone who owns property in Guadalajara and is willing to co-sign for the renter if they default. Without this guarantor, the renter is subjected to alternative legal contracts in an effort to protect the landlord. Additionally, many landlords require an investigation, similar to a background check, which examines the renter's credit and any court involvement in Mexico, their employment history, personal references, etc. Without a guarantor, the renter must also pay more money in advance. It's difficult to even get a landlord or realtor to work with you or return a phone call.

I was experiencing great difficulty in finding a long-term apartment and after two or more months in a small temporary dwelling, I was becoming disheartened with my move to Guadalajara. I was questioning whether I'd made the right choice despite still feeling that I'd found the home I'd dreamed of long ago. Just when I was seriously contemplating leaving and heading to a new destination, a random person on a Facebook group suggested I consult a particular lawyer. Thinking I had nothing to lose, I contacted the lawyer and scheduled an appointment. He was very helpful and was able to direct me to a long-term housing prospect. The process was arduous and painful, but I eventually moved to a high-rise condo where I lived happily for nearly three years. Sometimes, it's not about the journey—it truly is the people you meet along the way.

Guadalajara was the perfect choice for me. The climate is one of the best in the world, all year round. The tree-lined streets reminded me of back home. I volunteered at a charity thrift shop for more than a year where I improved my Spanish, made more friends and uncovered my passion for fashion while fulfilling my love of thrifting. I discovered an interest in styling the mannequins and I co-produced a fashion show using the thrift shop clothing. All this was a far cry from my previous career in criminal justice and it was fun to explore something so foreign to what I'd done before.

For nearly three years, I loved living in the big city. I loved the busyness of the city and the ease in obtaining modern goods and services. Guadalajara is recognized as having the top medical community in Mexico, so as I age, I know I can receive the best medical care available. The high-end shopping malls offer everything imaginable in keeping with the current fashion trends. The restaurants are some of the finest in Mexico. It seems that the culinary options are endless.

Despite my love for Guadalajara, I began longing for a deeper dive into Mexican culture and I wanted to learn more Spanish. I felt that, in some ways, the city whitewashes some of the Mexican charm in an effort to be modern. The rent for my condo increased every year and also sometimes increased when the value of the US dollar fell in comparison to the Mexican peso. It began stretching my budget beyond its means. Rental prices in Guadalajara have risen drastically, and that, combined with the additional money necessary to keep or obtain a lease, began to wear thin. But every time I considered leaving Guadalajara, I felt very sad and tearful. My conclusion was that I was in the right city, but I needed to find the right place.

Then, a few months ago, a friend invited me to visit her in nearby Tlaquepaque, a small historic town recognized by the government as a *"Pueblo Mágico,"* or "magical town." This status is given to certain towns either for their exquisite beauty, historical importance, or natural wonders. I immediately fell in love with the tiny town and felt the depth of the culture there was just what I was craving. She connected me with another friend whose apartment would soon be available, as she was returning to the US. This seemed to be the perfect arrangement, as Tlaquepaque is just outside of Guadalajara. I could have the deeper dive into culture I was craving while still being close enough to satisfy my "big city" needs.

My new apartment is not the beautiful, modern, high-rise I enjoyed in Guadalajara. The two dwellings are incomparable. As beautiful as my condo was for all things modern and big-city-like, my new apartment bursts with Mexican charm, with its arched doorways, stained glass window, and spaciousness. I feel a greater sense of community and a stronger support system than I had in Guadalajara. While I had friends in the big city, most of them didn't live near me, and I still felt very much isolated and alone. In Tlaquepaque, I feel like I have a blanket of support wrapped around me.

I haven't driven since I moved to Mexico, instead relying mostly on walking or using platforms like Uber. These were readily available in Guadalajara, so I moved around with relative ease. Tlaquepaque is more focused on walking to accomplish errands. There are no major grocery stores, so I walk to the market to buy most of my food. Nearly all of my needs for a gym, groceries, pharmacy, etc. are easily within walking distance. Guadalajara is about

45 minutes away, just close enough to attend to my medical needs, visit my hairdresser, and pick up items I can't find in Tlaquepaque. Right now, it feels perfect for me.

I haven't visited the United States since I left in 2019. Initially, I planned to, but for a few years the Covid-19 pandemic prevented me from traveling. My parents have passed away and, aside from cousins and friends, there simply hasn't been a compelling reason to visit. Plus, the trip is quite cost prohibitive. I've invited them to visit, but media portrayals of Mexico keep them away. So, I settle for the occasional phone calls, text messages or Facebook interactions. The perception of my life in Mexico among my friends is mixed. Some think it's awesome and inspiring, while others still seem baffled by my decision.

I also no longer identify with many of the values I previously held. I'm much more patient, and far more simple and less materialistic. For example, I don't have a dryer, so I hang all my bedding and clothes to line dry. I see the United States through a much different lens nowadays.

It's said that you never know how truly capable you are until you move abroad by yourself. I've found this to be true and I'm proud of my bravery and resilience. I've done a great job in keeping my life as stress-free as possible and staying as healthy as I can. I embrace each move I make and welcome changes in my lifestyle and location. I look forward to learning new things and the amazing people I meet wherever my path leads me.

Only time will tell what my future holds, but I will always be proud of my courage to move abroad and challenge myself to embrace the unexpected.

*After living the majority of her life in Ohio and spending a year in Minnesota, Denise Perry made the leap to emigrate to Mexico. She lived in Puerto Vallarta and Guadalajara before moving to Tlaquepaque, a small town founded in 1530. She's now living her best life in a spacious apartment with historical charms along with her two rescue cats, Fernando and Marcos.*

*Denise enjoys walking every morning, meeting new neighbors, and lifting weights at the gym. Retired after a successful 30- year career in criminal justice, Denise spends her time reading, writing in her blog, "She's Gone Nomad," exploring Tlaquepaque's many historical and cultural sights, shopping, attending cultural events, and socializing with the many good friends she's made since moving to the greater Guadalajara area in 2021. She especially enjoys the wonderful climate that allows her to enjoy a myriad of outdoor activities, be more physically active, and eat healthier.*

# 14. Gringo House

### Eric Streit

### Mazatlán, Sinaloa

Caught up in the excitement of a two-week vacation on Mexico's Pacific Coast, I inexplicably found myself making a spontaneous purchase: A hillside house overlooking the Pacific Ocean and the historic old town of Mazatlán.

To refer to my purchase as an actual "house" would be a gross exaggeration.

What the realtor described as *"pre-revolución hacienda"* was, in reality, a 120-year-old pile of rocks with no roof, no electricity, no water ... not even a road to gain access to the ruin which I enthusiastically purchased with $20,000 in cash.

What would motivate me to drop $20,000 dollars cash on a ruinous money pit in a Third World country where I don't even speak the language?

Considering that all I got for the money was a hand-written receipt in a language I couldn't comprehend, did I even know beyond the shadow of any doubt that I actually held the legal title to the place?

Not really.

Was there anything to guarantee that Pancho Villa's great-great grandson would not ride in tomorrow and take it away from me?

The answer was a simple and resounding, "Nope."

But I could see beyond the horrible state of disrepair. I knew that the ferocious roosters, feral cats, and wild iguanas running rampant throughout the property were merely temporary fixtures.

It was my genuine belief that with tremendous effort, the miles of red tape and bureaucracy that are a huge part of any dealings with legal issues in Mexico could be understood and overcome.

Deep in the heart of a falling-down hillside folly, I saw the amazing potential of what this unique property might become. With hard work, laser focus, and total commitment to my vision, this place could be far more than a mid-19th century ruin. My expectation was that over the next six grueling months, a tropical Paradise would emerge from what was now my pile of rubble. It may have been just an old pile of rocks in Nov. 2006, but when I stood on the site of my future front lawn, there was a city-to-ocean view that would cost millions if it was located 1,500 miles north.

Mesmerized by the spell of enchanting cobblestone streets, sun-drenched plazas, and breathtaking Pacific sunsets, enthralled by the sights and sounds of daily fiestas that filled the air, I threw caution to the wind and embarked upon a new adventure in Mazatlán, Mexico.

I knew that the American Dream was alive and well, and I intended to find it … in Mexico.

At the time, I had a job working two weeks on and two weeks off in Portland, Oregon. Every two weeks, I would fly to Mazatlán, where I kept an apartment at the Hotel Belmar in Olas Altas, the beachfront neighborhood of Centro Historico.

The atmosphere of the Belmar was unlike anything I've experienced before or since. It's a behemoth of a building that covers an entire city block and has tens of thousands of square feet, much of it not in use due to its extreme state of disrepair and decay. I spent countless hours strolling the hallways and corridors at all hours of the day and night.

The Belmar is a unique place with a funky vibe, amazing prices, and a lot of history. To say it's even a two-star hotel would be a stretch. The Belmar is not for everybody. But the combination of an excellent location, friendly staff, and mystic atmosphere made it a great choice for my temporary home in Mazatlán as I learned the lay of the land and figured out how to build a house. From the front desk to the water's edge is less than 100 steps. My first stop on most mornings was through the lobby and into the waves of Olas Altas beach.

The Belmar is located along the malecón, and there were a variety of places where one could get a meal for under $4, which was unbelievably inexpensive even 20 years ago. Puerto Viejo, Copa de Leche, and the Shrimp Bucket were historic restaurants nearby that had been Mazatlán institutions for decades. During the early 2000s, service at these places moved at such a slow pace that it felt like you'd stepped into a time machine and arrived in 1950s Mexico, which was like the 1930s United States. Sadly, all but one of these original spots have been replaced by more modern coffee shops and restaurants; only La Fonda de Chalio remains, a portal to another time, having changed little since opening its doors in 1948.

During its heyday in the 1940s and 1950s, Hotel Belmar hosted John Wayne, Tyrone Power, Yul Bryner, and Errol Flynn, among other show business luminaries. In 1944, the grand ballroom was the site of the unfortunate assassination of Sinaloa's governor. When walking the halls, one can literally feel the history of this once-luxurious hotel calling from the walls.

My rooftop apartment was reputedly the preferred suite of Errol Flynn when he was in residence. Unlike the rest of the hotel, it featured a large bedroom, well-appointed living room, and a kitchenette that would've been quite suitable in the 1940s (although not so much in 2007). I always kept the windows open as I drifted off to sleep and have never had such a clear sound of the ocean. For the $120 a month I was paying, it was hard to believe it was real.

I no longer live at the Belmar but I walk by almost daily. I've spent many evenings having dinner along the malecón with my wife and son, and although most of my old neighbors have long since cast off their mortal coils, I fondly recall my time there and tell people that it was like living in a Wes Anderson movie for two years. Hotel Belmar is not for everybody, but if you do ever have the opportunity to stay there and absorb the energy that fills the place, it will always be a part of your life.

While living at the Belmar, my time was divided fairly equally between figuring out how to build a house and getting to know other members of the expat community. There were no cell phones to speak of, and when somebody new showed up, within a few days they would meet the very small, core group of foreigners who called Centro Historico home. What was immediately apparent to me about Americans who move to different countries is that they are supremely optimistic, adventurous, and weird, not necessarily in that order.

There were (and are) a fair amount of raconteurs of dubious distinction. Unfortunately, a lot of expats who claim to be builders, contractors, carpenters, and architects share far more in common with P.T. Barnum than actual skilled tradesmen. I was taken in by quite a few of them as they skillfully separated me from my hard-earned money, but eventually learned to ask a lot of questions before hiring anybody for any project of consequence.

To that end, I spent a year searching for an architect who would work with me to create a design for the house that I had in mind, which was a combination of art deco, rustic farmhouse, and just plain weird. When I finally found the right guy, it took about nine months and $65,000 to build the main house, which has two bedrooms and three baths, with living space of about 2,500 square feet. We also built a swimming pool on the hillside that cost an additional $6,500.

I won't go into detail about the challenges of building a house in a foreign country in a language I didn't understand. There's not enough ink to share the many highs and lows of Mazatlán construction. To do so would require an entire book, rather than a single chapter, but I will share one story that gives some insight.

My house is located on a hill above a dead-end street. Road frontage would certainly make my house more valuable. A road might also make it safer, as access would mean police patrols could more easily include us in their routes.

On the negative side, a road would bring traffic. One of the best things about my house is the absence of traffic. A road to the top of the hill would bring an endless parade of cars coming to enjoy the magnificent view.

As one who was eschewing the need for an automobile and trying to simplify my life, I would have preferred that no road be built at all. Conversely, my neighbor O'Neil saw extending the road as an absolute necessity.

O'Neil was the proprietor of the Old Mazatlán Inn, a beautifully appointed hotel with some of the best views of the city and ocean. The construction of a road would gain O'Neil valuable and necessary additional parking. He'd asked me and my architect, Oscar, to join him and a city planning inspector to discuss the potential construction of a road between our two properties.

I was not openly campaigning against the road but would not have been disappointed if the road extension proved to be impractical or impossible from a construction standpoint. Truthfully, I was quietly hoping for that conclusion.

Strangely enough, on the city's master plans, my street, Calle Compania, was shown as already connected to the road at the top of the hill that overlooked the ocean. The plans were drawn up more than 50 years ago, but nobody had gotten around to actually building the road yet.

Before I move on with this story, one must understand the psychology of a Mexican bureaucrat. He is a unique breed of individual who has a strong belief system firmly tied to plans, rubber stamps, and enormous stacks of paperwork.

The inspector's plans showed a finished road. Though we were standing on a spot where no road existed, the inspector insisted that the road was there. There had to be a road, even though there wasn't. The plans were stamped four times. Each stamp was a different color. There was paperwork, in triplicate, to back up the multi-colored, elaborately stamped plans. The road simply had to be there. The trinity of plans, stamps and paperwork were irrefutable and every bit as divine as the holy trinity of Catholic fame. There must be a road. It was that simple.

Oscar cautiously attempted to convince the inspector that somehow, the road—although it appeared on the plans—did not currently exist. Oscar's seeming lack of faith in the obvious truth of an invisible road caused our Mexican bureaucrat considerable tension. How could a man of Oscar's stature, a well-educated and highly skilled architect, question the irrefutable, undeniable truth of plans? This was inconceivable, and the inspector was not taking the insubordination well.

Before it became a full-scale argument, Oscar artfully conceded that a road may have possibly been there at one time, but surely we could all agree that it was not there now. We were, after all, standing on a plant-covered hillside with lots of trees, scrub brush, cactus, and chickens. There was no pavement beneath our feet, so how could this possibly be a road?

The inspector could not agree. Not without an explanation. What could have happened to a road that must have been here at some point?

A long, awkward silence ensued. Finally, Oscar cautiously suggested, "*Tal vez La Revolución?*" ("Perhaps the Revolution?") Thank God for the outlaw Pancho Villa. Any time there's a stalemate with government officials and a need to save face, it's always convenient to dig up the bones of Pancho Villa and the glorious Revolution.

Mexico enjoys a long history of amazing storytellers, and everybody loves to solve a complicated puzzle. We were all suddenly and miraculously imbued with a deep knowledge of the Mexican Revolution. We all agreed that the road had clearly been bombed out. After pinning the formerly missing, but now bombed-out road on Pancho Villa, it was not too far a jump to expand on the explanation and allow the mystery of the missing road to unfold naturally.

After a few minutes of heated debate, deep thought, and scientific contemplation, we realized that, not only had the road been bombed, but this was most certainly the very spot of the world's second aerial bombing, which took place in Mazatlán during the Mexican Revolution in 1914.

We were standing on hallowed ground and all quickly agreed that Pancho Villa's bandits dropped a bomb from a biplane 94 years ago, and that was why there was no road today, even though the city's plans showed the road was there. Problem solved. *Viva la Revolución!*

I did not dare mention that the plans that showed the road were drawn up 50 years ago while the bombing was 94 years ago. We simply agreed it was Pancho Villa's revolution that caused the misunderstanding, and we could now move forward with confidence—and have a really cool story to boot.

Eighteen years later, the road has still not been built, but someday I hope to commemorate the world's second aerial bombing. Perhaps it can become a tourist attraction. I might put in a souvenir stand and sell snacks, and even commission of statue of Pancho Villa himself to stand vigil over something that may or may not exist.

That is just one small example of the complexities of building one's dream home in Mexico.

During the time I was building a house in Mazatlán, I was also building a circle of friends and a sense of community. Though the population of Mazatlán then was about half a million, the gringo population was quite small, and in those days it took on a very small-town atmosphere with all the positive and negative qualities that accompany living one's life under the microscope of prying eyes.

Simultaneously, I had also fallen in love with Jenna, the woman who became my wife. We had known one another since 2001, having met at the Friars Club in Beverly Hills. Between her enrolling in a Chinese medical school and me traipsing around the world producing television, running for Congress, and building a house in Mexico, it took quite a while for us to finally get together, but we finally did.

Her first trip to Mazatlán opened up an entire new chapter in the evolution of what is now our house. As a bachelor, there were many things I'd neglected and failed to take into consideration. Jenna brought a magnificent design aesthetic and sense of style that truly turned the house into a home. Matching cutlery, comfortable furniture, quality sheets, and a higher level of quality in every aspect imaginable brought our house in Mazatlán up to a new level I hadn't thought possible or even imagined.

Our son, Sidney Lazarus, took his first steps in the living room. We enjoyed whiling away our visits riding around town in *pulmonías*, Mazatlán's unique open-air taxis, floating in our pool, or sitting on the deck enjoying the majestic view that had been just a dream a few short years ago.

But our short visits were also stressful. Managing a house from a different country is not easy. There are bills to pay. Repairs to be done. Property managers to be managed. Expenses to be dealt with. As much as we loved being at our house in Mazatlán, it was very challenging on many levels. But it was worth it.

We were far too young to retire, so between projects, Jenna, Sidney and I would fly down from Los Angeles to deal with issues and problems that cropped up, trying to soak in as much of the city as possible while dreaming of how we might someday make Mazatlán our full-time home.

That day arrived in 2020, via a global pandemic.

Covid-19 struck the entertainment industry hard. The television industry may never recover from those two years of inactivity. When one cannot work, that doesn't mean there aren't bills to pay—and Los Angeles is a very expensive city. Like everybody, Jenna and I were deeply concerned for our future. There were several false starts and times we almost returned to work, but the "almosts" quickly became "not yets."

Although we lived a short walk from a beautiful park, even when it reopened, the playground equipment was deemed off-limits. We had a seven-year-old little boy who was cooped up in a two-bedroom condo, which was not good for his development or our daily life. We decided to head to Mazatlán for six weeks, where we had breathing room. Sidney would have a swimming pool, a swing set, a yard to play in, and space to roam and be.

As the six weeks began to wind down, we dreaded returning because Los Angeles still had not opened up. It was then that I got a call offering me a job as a producer on a series. The only downside, they said, was that I'd have to do all of the prep work from home, as offices were still off-limits. Suddenly, we were earning US dollars while staying in Mexico. Articles began to be published with headlines like, "Americans Will be Working From Home for a Long Time" and "Remote Work is the Future of America." We began making plans to move to Mazatlán full time.

We returned to LA to spend a few months boxing up our possessions, deciding what to keep and what to get rid of. In August of 2020, we drove two U-Hauls to Tijuana and transferred the contents to a Mexican moving company, who delivered our household goods to Mazatlán.

Once we moved in, the enormity of our decision began to set in. The difference between living in Mexico part-time and full-time is vast.

The most adaptable was Sidney. He enrolled in third grade. We hired an after-school tutor three days a week, and within six months he'd learned the language well enough to get very good grades and make many good friends. Few things give me greater pleasure than to hear him and his buddies chattering away in rapid-fire Spanish when they're running around the house playing chase, hide-and-seek, or video games. I can't understand most of what they're saying, but their sheer joy is punctuated with frequent laughter, and I sometimes believe that's more gratifying than if they were speaking English. Being focused on the happiness in the tone of their speech is a separate and different experience than knowing what they're actually saying. It also encourages me to study Spanish more so I can understand more of what they're talking about before they reach their teens. Jenna speaks very good Spanish, but I remain at what one might charitably call "caveman level," but at this point have perhaps improved enough to say I'm at "intelligent caveman level."

Jenna has cultivated a very good clientele for her Chinese medical practice and has set up her clinic and treatment room in what was formerly our guest studio. It's not uncommon for her to see four to six patients a day. Word of mouth is critical in Mazatlán, and she has earned a stellar reputation as a caring and professional practitioner who helps many people live their best lives.

I continue to work in television as a producer and director. Although the television industry is still very slow compared to what was happening before the pandemic, my location work is usually six to eight weeks at a time; and I typically have eight to 12 weeks between jobs.

We enjoy living in Mazatlán tremendously. We have a beautiful house and a good quality of life for a very small fraction of the cost of living in the United States. But I'd be lying if I said everything was perfect. Los Angeles is a city of 11 million with such a vast array of cultural activities available that it's impossible to take them all in. Mazatlán is growing, and there are a lot more activities now than there were when I first arrived in 2007, but Jenna and I both miss living in a place where there's world-class entertainment every single day and night of the week.

There's a song that sums it up very well: "How Ya Gonna Keep 'em Down on the Farm (After They've Seen Paree)?" This song rose to popularity in 1918. The lyrics speak to a concern that soldiers wouldn't want to return to the slow pace of life in their old home-towns after experiencing the life in European cities and high culture of Paris during World War I. The song was made popular by Eddie Cantor, a world-famous vaudevillian of the era. Our son went to kindergarten, first, and second grade with his great grandson.

While the restaurant scene has exploded in Mazatlán during the last decade and there are some very good chefs and many op-tions, it will be decades before our city's cuisine achieves "world-class status." In Los Angeles, one can find Korean, Tibetan, Peru-vian, French, Haitian, Romanian, Hungarian, Ethiopian, and just about any other food, made authentically, from every corner of the globe.

This is not to speak poorly of Mazatlán; the hundreds of new condominiums currently under construction indicate a rapidly growing cosmopolitan future for the city I call home. When I first came to town in 2006, the population was not quite 500,000. To-day, it's 610,000.

In many ways, Mazatlán is safer than when I first came. Al-though there are daily headlines in the United States about the dangers of the cartels, unless one is involved in that industry, it's highly unlikely one will fall victim to it. Cartels are typically very specific and targeted in their shootings, while random mass shoot-ings happen on an almost-daily basis in the USA in schools, malls, churches, and movie theaters.

There are many things to love about living in Mazatlán. But there are also many things we miss about home. We've carved out a niche for ourselves here that I'm very proud of.

Every time I step out on the deck and take in the majestic city-to-ocean view that was just a dream in 2006 when I first came to town, there's an indescribable sense of peace. I feel more at home here than in any place I've ever lived but am also mindful of the fact that it's a very big world.

Jenna, Sidney, and I frequently talk about the possibility of moving to Italy; both of them have Italian passports through Jenna's heritage. Rome is a city we all enjoy, and it certainly has an amazing history and an electric present.

But wherever we may find ourselves in the short term, Mazatlán is now my permanent home, and—unlike the boys who didn't want to return to the farm after seeing the lights of Paris—Mazatlán is the place I shall always return to.

⌒

*Eric Streit is a veteran producer of unscripted, reality, and documentary television. His credits include some of TV's biggest hits, including "Naked and Afraid," "Little People, Big World," and "Gator Boys."*

*In addition to his television career, Eric's many adventures include touring the US and Canada as a stand-up comedian, portraying "Balthazar the Monkey Boy" in a carnival sideshow attraction, a stint in the US Navy, and touring Eastern Europe with a bluegrass band. He has traveled to 60 countries to ford rivers, explore jungles, climb mountains, and experience as many adventures as possible. Eric is a two-term president of the Adventurer's Club, and a member of the Friars Club and the Kentucky Colonels Association.*

*Since 2020, Eric has lived in Mazatlán, Mexico, with his wife and their 12-year-old son, Sidney Lazarus. He continues to work producing television programs world-wide.*

# 15. Beach Dog in Mexico

## Melanie Blair

## Lo de Marcos, Nayarit

Mexico has been a part of my life since I was a youth. My adventurous parents and brother loved to fish so every Easter and Christmas vacation we'd get in our motorhome and tow our boat to Mexico. We spent the first few years in the mid '60s going to San Blas, and then our destination became beautiful Teacapán, Sinaloa—the northern side of the large mangroves from San Blas. My parents even purchased beachfront land in Teacapán and built the California Trailer Park. There's now a school on that property for the local kids.

My early years in Mexico were magical. Every Christmas Eve our family went to midnight mass in Teacapán with the locals. I'm kind of a warped Catholic and although I'd been to many midnight masses this was always my favorite. Of course it was in Spanish, and I couldn't understand the words any more than I could understand Latin, but it was always about the energy. Everything felt so much more connected and down to earth in that little church on the plaza full of locals of all ages.

When you're young you don't realize how unique something like this is, or any other experience that a different culture offers you. When I see young gringos today experiencing Mexico with their parents, I just want to run up to them and let them know how very lucky they are to experience a culture outside of the United States. Any culture—just give them the exposure outside of the US, especially in this day and age.

When my brother and I got older and my parents quit going to Mexico, we decided to drive down in my van. Mind you, this was 1974: I was 18 and he was 21. Our two friends that joined us were also 21. We towed a boat and left it with friends in Teacapán so we could drive all the way to Acapulco, where we had never been. That was an epic and dangerous adventure all in one. We had a little run-in with the Federales which could have put us in a Mexican jail since we were actually guilty, but lucky for us our guardian angels were with us that afternoon. My brother had a pistol and some marijuana hidden in the van that the Federales didn't find. Not a big deal up north, but definitely illegal in Mexico. In this day and age, you would never risk bringing a gun into Mexico.

After that experience I swore that I wouldn't drive to Mexico again. I was in my 20s and decided to be a "normal tourist" and fly into breathtaking Puerto Vallarta Bay, hugged on all sides by the Sierra Madres. It was a place my brother and I had discovered a few years earlier. I flew down numerous times with girlfriends, and we would check into a hotel, and then catch the first party boat to Yelapa. We couldn't wait to get on the water and out of traffic.

After two failed marriages, my son Randy and I moved to Calistoga in the Napa Valley in 1992, where I 'd been working as a project manager building mansions. It was a fun and fabulous chapter in both our lives. In 2001, I returned from a short vacation in Puerto Vallarta with a friend. We stayed in Mismaloya and I fell in love with a little dog on the beach. When I found out he didn't have an owner I decided to bring him home with me.

Once back in the US, I needed to get him groomed, but there was a 2-3 week wait for an appointment. A lightbulb went off in my head: You need a change! Right then and there, I decided to get into the dog grooming business. There was obviously a need. After research and consulting with our wonderful, small-town vet, I bought a brand-new mobile dog grooming trailer. I was fortunate to be able to volunteer at a high-end grooming salon with a few groomers and successfully learned how to groom purebred dogs. I loved going from mansions to wineries, grooming dogs all day in my beautiful new trailer. It was hard work, but it paid well and was very rewarding. Lots of my tips were bottles of fine wine I could never have afforded to buy, even though the income was great! At this time in my life, I was a single mom and had other priorities.

You work all your life accumulating things to be comfortable, and then suddenly something changes, and you decide to downsize. For me this happened in 2000, when I backpacked for five weeks around Europe with my son after he graduated high school. I realized I didn't really need anything except what was in my backpack; I could be comfortable with less. I went back home and looked at everything with a different attitude. I had so many things that I didn't need. My son was close to finishing school but wasn't sure where he wanted to live. I'd sold my house in Calistoga and my grooming business and moved into my motorhome. I didn't know which direction I was going. After a big yard sale, the things I ended up keeping went into storage.

I was turning 50 in March 2006 and, of course, I wanted to celebrate it in Puerto Vallarta, one of my favorite destinations. My son and I often traveled to different countries around the world, especially around Christmas. I liked to get him away from the commercialism of Christmas that you find everywhere in the States, which seems to get worse every year.

My son was attending the University of Wyoming on a football scholarship, and I flew him to PV to celebrate my birthday with me. I'd lost my strong, charismatic brother in 2004 from a sudden heart attack at age 51, and then both my parents passed away in 2005. I needed a dose of Mexico to help heal my broken heart and celebrate a special occasion.

One day I rented a jeep and my son and I headed up the coast to San Blas, a place I hadn't visited since my youth. As I drove on the exact same road that I'd driven with my brother 31 years earlier on our trip to Acapulco, I wondered if I would recognize anything in San Blas after so much time. Back then I knew nothing about the amazing beachside pueblos north of Puerto Vallarta like La Cruz, Sayulita, San Pancho, and Lo de Marcos.

It was a long day of driving, and I didn't recognize anything in San Blas. Not surprising since I was about six years old the last time I visited, and everything had changed, but it was a fun day, nonetheless. We passed a few trailer parks and it made me think about driving my small motorhome down in the fall. What a marvelous idea, I thought; I need to look into that. After recently losing my parents and brother, the idea of driving my motorhome to Mexico to spend a few months healing my heart in a place where I'd had so many wonderful adventures with the three of them became my new plan.

I started doing some due diligence on trailer parks on the Nayarit coast north of Puerto Vallarta. La Peñita Trailer Park was one of the few parks at that time that had Wi-Fi, so I made reservations for November 1, 2006, the day they opened for the season. The wonderful woman who runs the park told me about a caravan that drives down at the end of October every year. As a single woman driving an older, classic motorhome, towing a cargo trailer, it was a no-brainer. Yes! I'd love to join the caravan! She also told me about a lady who was putting together the first local spay and neuter clinic, in case I wanted to get involved. Absolutely I wanted to get involved! I'd sold my grooming business but saved some clippers and a blow dryer, intending to groom matted Mexican mutts. A perfect connection!

I met up with the caravan and we spent four comfortable days driving to La Peñita. I made some very special, life-long friends on that trip. We settled into La Peñita Trailer Park, which is terraced on a big hillside overlooking the ocean. There are many levels and the park can accommodate 200 big rigs. In November there were only 30-50 of us in the park, so it was ideal for what I needed—lots of space. Then on December 1, lots of Canadians arrived, and suddenly there were 200 rigs in the park. I quickly felt claustrophobic.

The cargo trailer I'd towed behind my motorhome held my Harley Davidson Sportster and everything else I'd brought along with me. In search of a smaller place to stay, I jumped on my Harley and headed south. I turned into the little pueblo of Lo de Marcos, which had a beach sign on the highway. (Of course I'd love to stay on the beach front!) Let's go check things out, I thought. As I slowly rode down the main street into town, I couldn't help but notice the magical energy of this little *pueblo*. I ended up finding a little trailer park on the beach and was lucky enough to get their last available spot for the season. I felt like I'd struck gold, like I'd arrived in Paradise!

When I spent my first month at the La Peñita Trailer Park it seemed like almost everyone had a dog. Most of them needed grooming, and people knew I had equipment, so I started grooming all my new friend's dogs for free. All the dogs loved me! I worked outside in the sun on a little concrete table with a water hose while all my new friends were down enjoying the beach. My back was screaming, "Charge, woman, you need to charge!" And then they started asking if I could watch their dogs for "a few days" while they went off exploring places like Guadalajara and Tequila.

That's when I decided that since I had to continue working my ass off anyway, why not work my ass off in Paradise? Plus, Bush had just been elected to a second term, and the reality was I couldn't afford to live in the United States anymore. No way I could afford medical coverage. I had to either go back to the expensive, yet gorgeous, Napa Valley to start all over again, or figure it out here in Mexico.

It was back to basic supply and demand. I already had lots of clients here. It was also very important to me that I wasn't starting a business that would compete with any Mexican businesses. Eventually, when my business grew, I employed Mexicans, so I was helping the community in that respect.

I had some savings put aside, and knew I had to purchase property so I could start building my new business. I found the perfect lot in Lo de Marcos, five short blocks from the beach. Property was more expensive than I expected, and I didn't have enough, but I did have a nice monthly income for the next 18 months from the sale of my grooming business. The lot was $60,000 dollars and I only had $30,000 to put down. I asked the owner if I could make the balance in payments. He said no. I was crushed. This was the perfect lot. He ended up coming back two days later and said, "I'll finance you if you give me your Harley Davidson and an extra $1,500 dollars." I quickly agreed and suddenly the lot was mine!

Most of us have a vision of how our life will be as we age. I had no plans whatsoever of moving to Mexico and starting a dog and cat boarding and dog grooming business at age 50. It never crossed my mind, but this is where the south winds blew me, and it felt so right. And it was! Eighteen years later, I still know it was the best decision I've ever made for myself, especially with all the challenges the United States has had, particularly in the past decade. I feel so much safer in Mexico. It's a culture shock to me when I go north of the border, especially seeing homeless people everywhere. We have homeless dogs down here, not people.

I'd been deep in debt for years getting my son through university, and was overweight, depressed, and always stressed. I'd lost my parents and brother and was always struggling to keep my head above water. Now it was time to put my energy into something I knew was achievable. It was the perfect prescription for the challenges I was facing in my life, and the perfect time.

My new lot had a big solid brick wall all the way around, and it was full of weeds up to my chest. First, I hired help to clear the lot, then I had to get water and electricity connected and then figure out a toilet. I hired a backhoe to dig a trench to get city water to my lot. I paid the electric company about $2,000 dollars to put in a power pole nearby so I could get electric; there was none around me. Then the backhoe returned to dig a hole for my septic tank. Things were challenging, to say the least. Thankfully I had lots of camping experience, so I was able to get by until I finally got water, electric … and a toilet. Once that was all done, I had a big metal gate installed and moved my motorhome in. I was home for the first time in a long time, and it felt good, even though I was physically exhausted every day. There was no time to be depressed or to worry about life.

I didn't have much extra money, but I had to continue to slowly build. I already had clients, so one of the first things I built was a big, walk-in, tiled tub for bathing dogs, and a concrete table for grooming. I was still paying a hefty monthly fee for my storage unit up north where one of things being stored was my Jeep Cherokee, which I needed now that my Harley was gone. That had to be addressed as soon as possible.

Another new life-long friend, Dan, asked if I would drive his one-ton, stick-shift pickup to the States while he drove his motorhome. He knew about my storage issue and said I could tow my cargo trailer with the truck. Thank you, amigo! I followed Dan to Arizona, driving his truck and towing my cargo trailer. It pulled like a breeze. I got my Jeep out of storage, booked a hotel for two nights, and then spent all my time going through my big storage unit, which was mostly filled with things I didn't need for my now full-time life in Mexico. I had to downsize big time. I didn't need my oak dresser and nightstands in Mexico; they'd just be destroyed by termites. I didn't need all those books or jackets or blankets … the list went on and on.

It was really hard having to rush through those two downsizing days, but I didn't have the luxury of staying longer and doing it slower. I needed to get back to my animals and new income. As I look back on some of my downsizing decisions, I wish I'd kept more small, memorable things, like my mother's vintage sequin top. As it was, I filled my Jeep and cargo trailer up to the point where you couldn't fit a tennis ball in either of them! (I love packing; it's like a Tetris game.) I ended up hauling down my mother's washing machine, which was almost brand new. Eighteen years later and that washing machine is still going strong! Lots of my things, like furniture, went to Goodwill; there was no time to have a yard sale. I just had to give it all up and move on to the new chapter of my life.

The trip back home to Lo de Marcos went smoothly, and it felt great to have all my belongings together for the first time in almost two years.

After getting the salon built up enough for business, I started building kennels for the dogs, and then a palapa for shade. News spread by word-of-mouth and my business got bigger and busier.

I was always closed on Sundays so I could regain some of my sanity, catch my breath, and not have to put on a bra. I was doing all the grooming, taking care of all the dogs staying with me, keeping everything clean, and handling all reservations and appointments. I loved every minute of it! I was making good money by Mexican standards, so I was very grateful for that, but I was also working my butt off to have a great business with a great reputation.

Women entrepreneurs tend to be very passionate about the reputation of the business they've built from the ground up with their own blood, sweat, and tears. When I was caring for 20-25 dogs a day, and also grooming a few a day, I sometimes wondered if I was hard-working or just plain crazy. But that was usually during the nights when my fur guests wouldn't quit barking. I definitely needed my sleep, and I didn't always get it. I look back at those times and can't believe I survived. I'm 68 now so I look at things differently.

There was something very magical about the camaraderie we experienced in Lo de Marcos in those early years. It really raised my faith in humanity. I'd been used plenty in my earlier years in life, yet here I was in a strange, new, tiny *pueblo* on the west coast of Mexico, and every day I'd meet other expats offering all kinds of help. This didn't exist in the States, or at least wasn't my experience. Everyone is too busy to have any genuine connection with their neighbors, or to take the time to simply enjoy life. Your calendar is always busy with something, but often it's not about enjoying life to the fullest.

It's different down here. I've never felt as safe as I do living in Lo de Marcos, Mexico. Everyone knows everyone and when shady characters pass through, everyone is aware. I've been here 18 years and have never been broken into once. (I'm sure the dogs help!) Dogs always help keep an eye on things in Mexico.

As years went by and Lo de Marcos became more and more popular, us "originals" would walk around town or go to events and say, "Who ARE all these people?" But they're just the new people lucky enough to discover this beautiful place. And every season I meet new friends; we have a lot in common already by being south of the border. I've also made lots of wonderful new animal-lover friends through the many spay-and-neuter clinics we've held in different *pueblos,* and some business clients have become close friends, too.

One of the things I love about expats and snowbirds in general is that they love to party (maybe because most are retired) and they love to donate, so we have lots of entertaining fundraisers. Part of the magic of LdM are all the talented musicians that live here seasonally. Through the years, they've put together a calendar of regular shows and special musical events for our viewing and hearing pleasure. Some of the most magical and priceless times are when expats are playing music on the beach; it seems that all retired musicians bring their instruments of choice while on vacation.

Another LdM original, snowbird Claire, my fun, life-long friend of 16 years, decided one day that she was going to open a coffee shop because no one had fresh coffee in the morning. I asked her if she'd ever had a restaurant before and she said she'd "figure it out." She opened Clarita's on the main street, a stone's throw from the plaza, and people were lined up down the street from the very first day. The restaurant was only open Friday, Saturday, and Sunday for breakfast. She hired all Mexicans and after her first season, leased Clarita's out to her head waitress and chef. Claire absolutely loved going from table to table visiting with everyone and making sure they had everything they needed. Her new title was *"mariposa social"* (social butterfly). Lo de Marcos has always loved her warm energy and we've been lucky to have her here.

I love the ocean and the water, but in all truth, I don't like hanging out on a hot, sandy beach. I prefer sitting in the shade with good food and a drink *looking* at the beach. And our beach is absolutely picturesque! My favorite place to do this in LdM was Rejilio's, now Olivia's; it's at the end of the main street, right on the beach. The ambience is like no other. Then about five years ago Tomatina's restaurant came along at the southern end of the beach. It's a dream come true for our little *pueblo*, with high-quality food, amazing grilled meats, specialized pizzas, and live music in the evenings.

There are good grocery stores in town with everything I need, and 15 minutes north is the bigger town of La Peñita, with everything Lo de Marcos doesn't have, like a bank, housewares stores, computer repair services, insurance agents, etc.

My lifetime passion is travel. It started from an adventurous young age. A year ago, I booked an African safari, and then a few months later I discovered I needed a hip replacement. I couldn't afford both these expenses at once but had already made a substantial down payment on the safari. One of my Lo de Marcos friends offered to help me with the surgery costs, so I didn't have to cancel my trip and lose the safari downpayment. I just feel so blessed to have found these kinds of people, and to have them in my life, here in little Lo de Marcos, of all places. My 18 years of memories here are priceless.

As I recuperated for a few weeks with my new hip, surrounded by my Mexican family in Mazatlán, I made the decision to sell my property and travel for as long as I physically can, with my home base always in and around Lo de Marcos. All the blood, sweat, and tears that I put in forthe past 18 years in Mexico is going to pay off. Bucket list travels ahead!

〜

*Melanie Blair was born to adventurous parents and raised in the San Francisco Bay Area. Most of her childhood consisted of the beautiful and isolated family camp on the Eel River outside of Willits, trips to Mexico for almost every Christmas and Easter school vacation, and numerous motorhome trips to Minnesota for family visits. Her own adventurous spirit continued to grow as she got older and traveled whenever possible while raising her son as a single parent. Melanie worked for the family excavation business for many years, doing everything from running the office to driving trucks and operating heavy equipment.*

*She spent more than 20 years in Calistoga, Napa Valley, raising her son. It was an exciting chapter where she worked as a Project Manager or Estimating Manager building multi-million-dollar mansions. It was also a beautiful place to live, raise a son, and enjoy fine wine.*

*In 2006, after her son finished university, Melanie drove her own motorhome to Mexico with her original rescue dog, Conan and her two cats and never looked back. She settled in the beautiful coastal pueblo of Lo de Marcos and built a successful dog and cat boarding and dog grooming business. She also enjoyed working with various spay and neuter clinics and rescuing a multitude of dogs and cats. After 18 years she has decided to retire, sell her Mexican property, and travel the world as long as she can.*

# 16. Leap Into Life!

## Karen Blue

## Ajijic, Jalisco

When I announced my decision to retire at age 51 and move from the Bay Area in California to Mexico, both my grown children and my best friend rebelled. I'd been a single mother since my kids were toddlers.

"But Mom, what if you don't like it?" My son asked. I hugged him and said, "Sport, it's not the last decision I get to make."

I had been working 60- to 80-hour weeks in Silicon Valley consulting with high-tech Fortune 500 companies and spending too much time in airports and on airplanes. I needed to get some balance in my life—physically, emotionally and mentally. My financial advisor shook his head as he confirmed that early retirement was not financially possible for me in California.

My best friend implored me, "Blue, you can afford to stay if you downsize your lifestyle."

"And do what?" I asked. "Play bingo at the senior center? All my friends will still be working."

Of course, everyone wanted to know, "Why Mexico?" It's actually a good story.

Dreams had often helped me make major decisions. While on a week of rest and relaxation, I had a dream in which the word "enclave" played a predominant role. I looked it up: "A distinct group of people that lives or operates together within a foreign community." Like Chinatown in San Francisco—but what could this dream or this word possibly mean for me? Certainly not Chinatown!

I returned home to find a complimentary issue of "International Living" magazine in my mail with this headline: "Lake Chapala:

An Enclave of American Retirees." Goose bumps covered my arms. That article promoted their first "Retire in Mexico" conference to be held two weeks hence in Guadalajara. I signed up. This was, for all intents and purposes, before the Internet, before cell phones, before GPS and before social media. There was no other way to gather the information I'd need to make such a life-changing decision.

There were about 130 people at the conference and at 51, I was the youngest. They brought in lawyers, accountants, bankers, medics, realtors, and other professionals to introduce us to life in Mexico. My note-book bulged and my brain regurgitated the information we received.

I knew no one in the Lake Chapala area, had a Spanish vocabulary of about six words, and would be giving up about 15 years of income by retiring that soon. Could I afford to live in Mexico until my Social Security kicked in? Excel became my ally while I made my best guesses on the growth of the investments I currently had and compared that to the anticipated cost of living in Mexico.

My friends and family were divided into two groups. One group begged me to stay. "It's dangerous in Mexico." "You won't be safe." "You'll be lonely." The other group envied me my upcoming adventure. After all, over the years I'd moved with my kids to Idaho, Washington, and Germany while working for Hewlett-Packard. We were all accustomed to change. Having had seven careers and at least 15 different jobs gave me the courage and even a sense of excitement and anticipation to learn a new culture and figure out what I was going to do when I grew up.

Having difficulty making such a momentous decision with all this push you/pull me going on, I left it up to the Universe. I listed my home in a down market. If it sold, I'd go; if it didn't, I'd stay. It sold within two weeks with an unconditional offer. I sold or gave away most of my possessions. Then I set myself two goals. Number one: Never have another goal. Number two: Never let pantyhose touch my legs again. The second one I kept.

No more goals? I wanted to be open to all new experiences and had learned in my career that focusing intently on the next goal or promotion often blindsided me to other opportunities. I had no idea what I'd do in Mexico to fill my need for purpose or to meet like-minded people. But I suspected that the Universe did since it sent me here because of my "enclave" dream and the quick sale of my home. I've learned to call this synchronicity, and having talked to thousands of expats over the years, I've realized that it's a thread which weaves many of our unique decisions and experiences together.

Although I had no intention of buying a house, on my third day in Ajijic I bought the worst house in the best neighborhood. It was unlivable. It had been deserted for about six years and the ants and termites had taken over. I paid $48,000 dollars for it. Why? Well, it was what I thought I could afford, and I knew that if I didn't have a project, I'd spend my time home sitting behind a computer. It needed new plumbing, new electricity, a new kitchen and bathroom, new tile floors, and not one stitch of furniture in it. My realtor said he would manage the construction until I returned for a 10% fee. What was I thinking? What did I do?

So my first project (and goal) was that house renovation. That's another story. However, I did happily live there for my first 12 years in Ajijic. Then I wanted a view and moved to where I live now, on the west end of Ajijic in a neighborhood called Arroyo Alto, with a beautiful lake and mountain view.

During much of the time it took to make my house livable, I lived with a Mexican family in Guadalajara. I took Spanish immersion classes five hours a day, five days a week, assuming I'd be proficient at the end. Who was I kidding? Now, 30 years later, I've probably taken thousands of hours of classes, in person and on-line. Still, although I have a sufficient vocabulary and can understand most Spanish if spoken slowly enough, I struggle to speak it. The reason is that because I'm living in Ajijic, I'm not frequently forced to use it. Use it or lose it!

## What next?

One day I saw a notice posted on the Lake Chapala Society bulletin board for a fiction and poetry class, taught by a professor on sabbatical from the University of California San Diego. LCS is the local community center in Ajijic with more than 3,000 members, the largest English library outside of English-speaking countries, and an organization whose mission is to help both expats and the local Mexican population. I thought, "Why not?" Never having written anything other than marketing and business proposals, I wanted to see how I could do writing a novel.

I attended a writers' group that still meets today. I dared to read a synopsis of the novel I thought was within me. "Write what you know," the teacher had encouraged us, so I drew upon many of my own experiences. Reading my first work before all those talented writers, I felt like I'd just opened my kimono and was standing in front of them naked. One older woman suggested I consider including other women's stories in my book as well.

Hmm, I thought. That's a good idea and it would be easier to market a non-fiction book than a fiction one. I asked how many women who had moved here on their own would be willing to be interviewed, and several raised their hands. During the next year, I interviewed 39 women and wrote my first book, "Midlife Mavericks: Women Reinventing their Lives in Mexico." I included 16 of their stories and intertwined some of my own experiences betwixt and between theirs.

As the internet blossomed, I took online writing classes and belonged to international critique groups which helped my writing tremendously. The websites hadn't yet learned how to charge for anything online, so it was a wealth of free education.

Upon completing the book, I spent a year learning how to find an editor and publisher, investigating the new print-on-demand technology and educating myself on self-publishing. My book was published in 2000 and has sold more than 2,000 copies in print and e-book formats.

## What next?

I yearned for another project. I met Judy King. Over coffee she and I decided we'd like to publish an online magazine. Since neither of us wanted to sell advertising, we'd have to create a high-quality magazine that subscribers would be willing to pay for. We called it "Living at Lake Chapala" and included about 12 well-researched articles each month about moving to and living at Lakeside. I resigned after the first two or three years, and she kept it going for

145

a few years longer. Using non-fiction articles from our magazine, Judy and I also developed material for our weekly newcomer seminars. This was a great way to meet new people and help them decide if becoming an expat in the Lake Chapala area was the right decision for them.

One of the things we often joked about with the single women in our seminars was, "Don't come down here looking for a man. If they're not married or gay, they're gone by Sunday." Another popular expression was that single, older men coming to Mexico were either looking for "a nurse or a purse." For some reason, there are many more women who venture here on their own than there are men. I'd need a psychological or sociological background to figure that one out.

## What next?

I remember telling one of my best friends, "What I would like is a long-distance relationship." I wasn't interested in a long-term, 24/7 relationship. I'd lived alone since my kids left the nest and I still wanted my independence. But I forgot to be specific about what I put out there. And, of course, the Universe was listening.

As fate would have it, I met Joe. He'd joined a caravan of RVs driving from the US to Panama and back. One of the RVers was a gal I'd gone to high school with some 40 years before, and we hadn't been in touch since. A friend of hers knew she'd be driving through Mexico and just happened to have my book which she lent to Mary. More synchronicity. Mary recognized my photo and emailed me to see if I'd like the caravan to stop in Ajijic for a few days.

Joe was the only single member of the caravan. We connected instantly. The caravan spent two weeks here and I lost my right to say, "I'm a born-again virgin!" Tall, good looking, and kind, with a great sense of humor, Joe wanted to RV in Europe and I thought it would be great fun. That became my next project. I spent scores of hours on the internet researching RVing in Europe, places to visit, where to rent an RV, learning about the differences in electricity, plumbing, and other helpful information. Joe lived in Florida. He still does. Neither of us wanted to ever marry again. He'd tried it four times. Once had been enough for me.

We spent four months in Europe in 2005 and went back for another three months in 2006. After that we travelled together in his 21-foot RV through many of the US national parks and up into Canada and Alaska. Another year we explored Mexico.

Although we didn't travel together the whole year, when we did it was definitely 24/7 and included shopping, cooking, laundry, and cleaning, in addition to the wonderful experiences these places afforded us. In between trips, we went on a couple of cruises, and I decided that was my preferred way to travel. Someone else did the shopping, cooking, and cleaning. I've since been on many cruises. My favorites are repositioning across the Atlantic. One cruise took me around the world.

By 2009, I'd had my fill of RVing in his small rig. We're still online friends and I'm thankful we created and shared so many good memories together.

## What next?

I needed another project and thought I might write a second book. I had met some really interesting singles, couples, gays, and straights who were doing exciting things in their retirement. This was the same time that the baby boomers began retiring and voila! "Baby Boomers: Reinvent Your Retirement in Mexico."

The folks I interviewed had invented lives they were passionate about and were excited to talk about. One man started an aquaculture facility growing lettuce. Another couple collected used children's shoes, cleaned them up, and passed them out to poor Mexican children who had none. A neighbor woman found sponsors to pay college tuitions for smart but poor Mexican children. Her husband became active as an actor in the Little Theater. I had permission to ask personal questions about income, expenses, health, and personal feelings. Writing that book allowed me to meet fascinating new folks and make new friends.

## What next?

What do they say? Getting old isn't for sissies. About three years ago, I found I could only stand or walk for 15 minutes before sciatic pain forced me to sit down. The neurosurgeon recommended back surgery where they would put pins in my spine. He only offered about a 50% recovery rate. I said, "No. Thank you very much." And then along came COVID. After three years of sitting in solitude with no partner, no roommate, and no pets, my back problems became worse. Depression threatened to envelop me. Eventually I could only stand or walk for two minutes at a time.

As Covid quarantine ended, I met with another specialist. He suggested a different back surgery. By that time, I felt that I had no choice. I was lucky—it was successful. The following year I had two hip replacements. Then, in the first four months of 2024, I was in and out of four hospitals and two nursing homes half a dozen times. The hospitals and care in Guadalajara are exceptional if you have good insurance or sufficient savings. Although the doctors told my kids they almost lost me three times, I prevailed and have been bestowed the nickname of "Miracle Girl."

Even if I could afford assisted care in the US, I would choose assisted care in Mexico. Not only is it much more affordable, but the Mexican culture has a great respect for the elderly and infirm. They treat us like family.

That brings up the subject of medical insurance. It's a sticky wicket question. I chose to get private Mexican insurance when I arrived. It was very reasonable. I was 51. I declined Medicare when it was offered because it didn't cover me in Mexico. This year I turned 80 and my health insurance cost me $14,000 dollars. That's about half of my social security. It's no longer reasonable. Today, if you have Medicare with an Advantage plan, it covers emergency situations here in certain hospitals.

If I had to do it over, I would have self-insured, putting away the equivalent amount of money I paid to an insurance company in a separate account. Although prices here have risen dramatically over the past 30 years, a visit to a specialist is still only about $50 dollars. Property taxes are about $200 dollars per year. Electricity and gas are much cheaper here than in areas which are either very cold or very hot and need air conditioning or central heating; we don't need either. Except for this year: it was the hottest March, April, May, and June since I've lived here. I finally bought a small air conditioning unit for my bedroom.

However—and this is a very important point—expats who come with no insurance and insufficient funds to deal with unexpected illnesses have a very difficult time. There are many insurance and medical options available in Mexico, especially in the Lakeside area, and researching them thoroughly should be a high priority.

I have a friend who does personal JOY workshops. On Jan. 4, 2024, I received an email from her asking me what two things I would work on in 2024 to increase my level of joy. I immediately replied, "health and friends." On Jan. 6, I found myself in the hospital emergency room at the beginning of my six-month medical ordeals. I said to her, "Perhaps I should have been more specific and asked for *good* health! During those six months, however, friends and acquaintances came out of the woodwork to offer help in any way they could. This warmed the cockles of my heart and reaffirmed my decision to have chosen Ajijic as my "heart home" for the last 30 years.

## What next?

As Scarlett O'Hara says in "Gone with the Wind," "After all, tomorrow is another day." Now that I'm more mobile and can be more social, I'm not sure how to answer that question. I try to live in the moment, appreciating each additional day life offers me. I'm in what the Mexicans call *tercera edad*. That translates into "third life." It includes anyone over 60. It sounds so much better than "old folks."

I enjoy spending time with friends, playing scrabble, bridge, euchre, and board games. I read a lot, write some, listen to TED podcasts, and take Zoom classes. I belong to an e-book club and the writers' group. We have so many choices here for eating out at various international restaurants and having meals and food delivered. We have talented writers, poets, actors, musicians, singers, and dancers who provide almost unlimited entertainment now that Covid is mostly behind us. Folks play pickleball, tennis, and golf, and get involved with a wide variety of religious and worthwhile volunteer organizations. There literally is something for everyone—from growing orchids to playing poker. Strangers and friends greet each other on the streets, and each day here is "another beautiful day in Paradise."

## What have I learned?

The Mexican culture has taught me much about values. I've come to think that US values are upside down. Here, family is first, religion and/or friends are second, and way down at the bottom are position and possessions. Handshakes are promises. Laws change frequently and we learn to go with the flow.

I feel safe, happy, and blessed that I've been able to live my third age in Ajijic with the great weather, fascinating people, beauty, and a cost of living that allows me to have a house cleaner and gardener. I can't remember the last time I've cleaned a toilet!

Is Mexico for everyone? Absolutely not. Generally, the kind of people who are happy here are well-travelled, enjoy change and new challenges, are interested in different cultures, can live in the moment, and have high self-esteem. They're outgoing and do not have Type A personalities. Folks who were unhappy before they came stand a good chance of remaining unhappy here. Wherever we go, there we are!

The other day I watched a TED presentation on "The Four Phases of Retirement" by Dr. Riley Moynes. I looked back at my 30 years here and had to agree. The first phase he related to a vacation. My working friends had asked me, "But what do you do all day?" "Whatever I want," I replied. I took writing lessons and Spanish lessons. I renovated a house.

The second phase was to develop purpose, passion, and new relationships. Getting involved with projects such as writing articles for local newspapers and publishing an online magazine and two books did that for me.

The third phase he talked about concentrated on contribution and trial and error. For me, that involved serving on three different boards of directors and teaching English at one of the local orphanages. I also volunteer at the Lake Chapala Society information desk as needed and volunteered at their bazaar for a year. I've financially supported a few young Mexican girls through school. I enjoy helping friends with my limited computer savvy and editing experience.

His fourth phase talked about reinventing and revising your life. Funny, I thought, that he used the word "reinventing" since

I'd used that in the titles of both my books. That's what this whole journey has been about for me. My corporate journey goal prior to retirement was to reach and possibly break through the glass ceiling. Perhaps I just scratched its surface, but …

This journey through retirement has provided me with much more purpose and fulfillment than the corporate journey had, by making a difference in people's lives rather than making a difference in shareholders' pockets. I know this through the many emails I've received from readers of my books and articles, telling me what a difference the stories we expats shared had made in their own lives.

Have things changed since I got here 30 years ago? You betcha. There was only one traffic light at Lakeside then; there are 15 now. The traffic has become difficult to deal with. The weather has become hotter due to climate change. The kinds of people who choose to move to Mexico has changed. Younger folks are coming, some with their children, others because they can work remotely, many because of economic or political reasons. Some folks coming recently seem to feel they're entitled. They want Mexico to be like it was back home. Some even expect the Mexicans to speak English. That's just rude.

On the plus side, we have many more options for eating, shopping, entertainment, and taking classes. We have Zoom, Google Meet, social media, and Skype for staying in touch with family and friends back home. It's also been a boon for me to realize that, in general, the type of people who choose an expat life are much more interesting and interested than those who choose to live their entire lives in the same place. And because of the culture and the weather, it's much easier to make new friends here than any other place I've lived. We become each other's family—by choice, not by DNA.

To sum it up for me, I came because I could retire early and put some balance back into my life. If I had to choose one reason I've stayed, it's because of the communities—both the expat and the Mexican.

"Enclave" (the same word in English and in Spanish) has a special new meaning for me now. And I still pay attention to my dreams.

〜

*Now 81, "Blue" was raised in the San Francisco Bay area of California. At age 20, she worked in public relations for a semester on the University of Seven Seas which provided a curriculum for students as the ship sailed around the world. She returned from that once-in-a-lifetime experience with gypsy blood in her veins.*

*Blue became a single mother when her two children were six and 18 months. She received a B.S. degree in Business Administration from St. Mary's and worked for Hewlett-Packard for 16 years, changing careers five times before leaving to start her own consulting business. At age 51 she retired, deciding that she needed more balance in her life—physical, mental, and social. She moved to Ajijic, Mexico in 1996.*

*Learning to write via online classes and having interviewed scores of expats, she is now the author of hundreds of articles and publisher of two books: "Midlife Mavericks: Women Reinventing Their Lives in Mexico" and "Baby Boomers: Reinvent your Retirement in Mexico." She believes that the Lake Chapala area is perhaps the best place in the world for a single woman to live. Her website is mexicoblue.com.*

# 17. Hidden in Plain Sight

Wayne Brewster

Morelia, Michoacán

Through years of exhausting and inconsequential personal research, I've discovered that nine out of 10 Americans would fail a geography exam if asked to point out Morelia, Michoacán, Mexico, on a map. Hold on a second! Forget them trying to find it on a map; they've never even heard of it! "Where's that?" "Does it have a beach?" I've wanted to scream and deny them guacamole and chip privileges. That'd teach them!

Now, don't spill your tequila shooter over my angst. I'm indeed calling out my fellow US citizens for their obliviousness about their southern neighbor. I'm saying that Mexico only enters most Americans' conscious thoughts when a Corona beer ad appears on their television screens. To most of my fellow compatriots, Mexico is a distant beach where you fly to an all-inclusive resort, drink copious amounts of margaritas, and eat tacos daily. The ubiquitous sunburn is a bonus.

Allow me to flesh out this thought. Perhaps Americans focus so much on "The Wall" separating our two countries that it blocks their vision of what lies on the other side. For example, when I lived in Arizona, a border state, and I watched the weather on our local television channels, the radar only showed what was happening on our side of the border. No weather existed south of that wall. Therefore, in theory, people believe nothing exists south of the border besides some cactus, adobe huts, and breweries. And then they remember those beach resorts with endless piña coladas. That's all Mexico has to offer. Wrong!

If I haven't lost you yet with my sarcastic humor, let me provide you with some details.

Hello. My name is Wayne Brewster, and I live in Morelia, Mexico. I moved to Morelia in June 2009, and I love it! (Gosh, I sound like a newcomer to a Mexico Anonymous meeting. Maybe it is time to admit my addiction and get some help.)

Why Morelia? I guess you'll have to keep reading to discover my reasoning. The short answer is that the US recession forced me to advance my retirement timetable of moving to Mexico. It seemed a more reasonable option than starving to death in the States. I could rent out my home in Phoenix, Arizona and live on Social Security in a more economically feasible place.

Family and friends questioned my sanity. "Are you crazy?" Perhaps. But I've done my research. Is it safe? Is Phoenix safe? Or any other US city? I got tired of defending my decision, so I got creative. My standard sarcastic response became, "I'm surprised by your questions since you're so Mexico-aware after visiting Cancun for a week last year."

I'll never forget my eldest brother, who assured me I was making the biggest life mistake ever and would soon regret it. Fortunately, I didn't take to heart his warped, biased American news-influenced comment. I was a member of the same ill-informed masses before I started exploring Central Mexico in the early-21st century. My discoveries erased my prejudice towards our southern neighbor. Mexico is so much more than the invented Cinco de Mayo image hyped annually in the US. Although very popular with the citizenry, it promotes the warped image of Mexico as a never-ending beer-soaked fiesta and not as a modern land of immense history and culture that predates the United States.

Allow me to digress and give you my backstory. During the mid-90s, my then-partner suggested that we visit Rocky Point, Sonora, for a few days. Correctly named Puerto Peñasco, this small fishing village on the Sea of Cortez had long been a destination for Arizonians wanting a little beach time and fresh shrimp. Its location was a quick three-and-a-half-hour drive from Phoenix and Tucson.

I had heard horror stories of camping on the beach. All that sand invading my body cavities was a significant deterrent. However, my partner convinced me that there were new, modern beachfront condos we could rent that would suit my unique needs of cleanliness and comfort. I reluctantly agreed. At that time, my only exposure to Mexico had been day trips to Nogales, Juarez, Tijuana, and a Spring Break week in San Carlos, Sonora, where I slept on the beach and got dysentery.

As a result of these visits, Mexico was not high on my list of desired destinations. Additionally, I had spent a great deal of time working and vacationing in Europe, where my standards of dining and culture were elevated and enjoyed. But, one must sometimes agree to spousal wishes to keep peace and happiness in a relationship. To tell the truth, I was dreading the trip and didn't have high expectations.

Drum roll. Naturally, I fell in love with this Mexican experience after the first day. Picture turquoise blue water lapping at a golden sand beach a few steps from our condo, which had air conditioning, running water, and indoor plumbing. In the evening, we sat on the terrace, watched fishing boats cruising back to port, sipped adult beverages, and saw the sun set over the distant Baja peninsula. Of course, we dined at kitschy restaurants with decent food and strolling mariachis. What's not to like?

At the time, I spoke no Spanish but knew the difference between a taco and an enchilada. Of course, my language skills had the rudimentary verbiage of "*gracias, por favor, y cerveza.*" I could point to items on a menu and get served my correct meal. What more do you need to enjoy a Mexican visit?

After the initial trip, there were semi-annual excursions to this seafront town. I organized extensive group visits with my friends to experience this special place. Then, tired of being the leader and chief organizer, I started making frequent solo visits. (Yes, I was single once again! Please, there is no need for your tears!)

Slowly I met some locals who shared my similar persuasion, and developed friendships. Thus began my introduction to the real Mexico and Mexicans. As happened, I created close relationships with Mexicans who spoke no English, so I learned Spanish *poco a poco*. Believe me, when you have a Mexican boyfriend who speaks no English, you learn Spanish quickly!

Ten years after that first Rocky Point exposure, I decided living in Mexico would be my goal after retirement. Since a 1966 visit to Australia, I'd always fantasized about living in another country.

Life happened, and that dream never materialized. Marriage and family kept me tied to Arizona. I had considered Italy for all the obvious reasons. But logically, Mexico was the better option for economic reasons and quick access to my Phoenix-based family.

But where to live? I eliminated Rocky Point because of its small size and stifling summer heat. Then where? For pre-internet searches, I had to rely on maps, guide-book s, videos, and word-of-mouth. Research was essential, and I developed a list of potential cities to visit. My first trip took me to Mexico City, Toluca, Cuernavaca, and Taxco.

During one of my frequent Rocky Point visits, I met a young man and began a romantic relationship. He was from a small village near Toluca, in the state of Mexico, and was going to accompany me on my week-long tour of these cities. The first 36 hours went well until he passed out drunk in his small village on the second night and left me alone to find my way back to my Toluca-based hotel via my rental car.

Great! What now? It was harrowing due to the late hour, around midnight, and I had no idea how to return to Toluca. I was able to exit the village and find a road. Imagine how scared I was as it was pitch black without street lights or signage. Nothing but an empty country road. Which way do I go? I stopped and asked numerous strangers for directions with my limited Spanish. One kind individual said, "You go down this road past the Benito Juarez statue, then veer to your right till you see a series of trees. Hidden among those trees, you will see a road that will take you back to the main Toluca highway."

Naturally, I never found the hidden road, and I wandered here and there till I finally saw a sign pointing me to Metepec, where I (and my then-sober boyfriend) had visited earlier that day. I knew then I could find my way to the hotel. After three torturous hours, I made it to the hotel. You may laugh, but please remember we didn't have GPS or cell phones then, and Mexican highways had little or no directional signage. This unnerving exercise taught me the kindness of Mexicans when you need help.

The next day, I awoke and decided to forge ahead with my itinerary sans my paramour. I traveled to Taxco and spent two days there. Beautifully situated on steep hills, I parked the car at my hotel and used taxis to navigate the winding, scary streets. It's permanent *siesta* time once you buy some silver, see the magnificent church, and take beautiful photographs. There's nothing to do. Taxco is an eight on the yawn scale.

Cuernavaca, billed as the perpetual spring city, was blah and disappointing. As a key weekend destination for Mexico City residents, I had expected to be blown away by its beauty. Perpetual spring, my posterior! It's hot and ugly. Cue the hate mail.

In 2007, I planned a two-week vacation exploring Morelia, Patzcuaro, and Valle de Bravo. Several people had told me that Morelia had a "soul." Intrigued, I bought a guide-book and booked my ticket to Guadalajara, where I rented a car to travel the three hours to my destinations. What could go wrong?

Getting the rental car was confusing and surprising, as I had only the slightest understanding of the contract I signed. The insurance cost two times more than the car rental, but I'd have been responsible for every single peso of replacement value without it. I love taking risks, but going without insurance would have been terminally stupid.

"Is there a map available of Guadalajara?" I asked the rental agent.

"No," he responded.

"Could you please give me directions to the toll road to Morelia?"

"Of course!"

I listened intently to his instructions in Spanish and felt like I'd entered an alternate universe. I wasn't jet-lagged, but it seemed like complete language immersion without a life preserver. I listened and nodded my head like I understood every syllable. Sure. Okay. After a positive affirmation of "I can do this," I hopped into my manual transmission Nissan Tsuru, then jerked and shuddered my way out of the parking lot. All the while, I thought of John Candy's car in the movie, "Uncle Buck." All I lacked was the backfiring belch of smoke.

After negotiating a roundabout while dodging kamikaze-driven buses and taxis, I finally headed in the right direction. I immediately took the first exit, which pointed to Morelia and Lake Chapala. Of course, this was the free road to Morelia and the wrong exit.

A slow and panicky realization hit that it would take almost eight hours to drive to Morelia if I stayed on this road.

Naturally, I stopped numerous times and, in my halting Spanish, asked for directions to the toll highway. The elusive answers varied with each stop and did nothing to solve my problem. My frustration was mounting, and the hundreds of *topes*, those ubiquitous Mexican speedbumps, on this two-lane road only added to my angst.

In the town of Ocotlán, I received some good news. A kind lady told me to find a particular street and continue north until I saw the highway. I would find an entrance there. I let out an audible sigh of relief and thanked her for her help.

I located what I thought was the street and continued north out of Ocotlán. Hurrah. I spied the toll road ahead. Suddenly, I passed over it without seeing any entrances. I stopped and carefully turned around on this narrow road with no shoulders. I drove slowly over the toll road, looking for any sign of an entrance.

On both sides of the road were *milpas* (cornfields.) Wait, what was that? I spied a primitive dirt road on the side of one of the fields, and it appeared to go to the shoulder of the expressway. I decided to take it as it was my only option. It was rough, and I felt every rock and pothole in my little car as I bumped along this pathway. Within a few seconds, engulfed in a dust cloud, I left the highly illegal access road and safely entered the toll road. I didn't care if I had just broken my first Mexican law. The relief I felt was akin to being released from prison for my crime of being a stupid *gringo*.

The continued trip to Morelia was uneventful but beautiful. In central Mexico, everything is green and lush in September due to the summer rains. I remember remarking on all the wildflowers along the roadway.

I stayed at a motel on the highway the first night, not wanting to get lost looking for a hotel downtown. Later that evening, I got a taxi and asked the driver to take me to a nightclub. As we made our way to Morelia's center, I was stunned by the city's architecture and beauty. The buildings constructed from pink cantera stone were in colonial Baroque style, and I felt like I was in Spain or Italy. My head spun in every direction, trying to take in as much as possible.

The city glowed from the many flood-lit historic buildings that filled the narrow cobblestone streets, which were lighted by sizeable wrought-iron lanterns. The scene was so charming and magical that I felt I'd made the right decision to visit here. I also felt ignorant, not knowing this beautiful colonial treasure existed only a three-hour flight from my Phoenix home. (There are many direct flights from Morelia to the US, but there isn't one to Phoenix as of this writing.)

Later that night, as I drifted to sleep, I remembered how life-altering this first day had been. Morelia instantly captivated me with her beautiful architecture, European ambiance, and friendly people. Had I discovered my perfect place to retire? Perhaps.

After numerous days of exploring the city and subsequent visits, I knew Morelia was where I wanted to live. Now let me tell you why. Let me switch my expat ballcap for my Chamber of Commerce chapeau.

Morelia is the capital city of Michoacan state and a UNESCO World Heritage Site. Founded in 1541, its historic center has impressive 17th- and 18th-century architecture that mimics its European roots. Because of the 6,400-foot elevation, the city sports a mild year-round climate with two distinct dry and wet seasons. I like to say that the weather resembles northern California, but where the rainy season occurs in the summer and brings delightfully cool weather.

Morelia is a modern city with the necessary resources of Costco, Sam's Club, Home Depot, Walmart, and other big box stores to support a million residents. If you shun those global companies, you can embrace thousands of local entrepreneurs instead. The local cuisine was also named a UNESCO Intangible Cultural Heritage of Humanity item. The cuisine survives and flourishes using indigenous ingredients to celebrate its New World roots. Beyond Mexican cuisine, Morelia supports innumerable restaurants and cafés featuring diverse foods and beverages. Italian, French, Korean, Japanese, Argentinian, and even McDonald's compete for your dining dollars. (I have to speak the truth: in my 15 years of living here, the restaurant scene has exploded with outstanding venues. Our city has become a foodie destination.)

The most frequently asked question, other than about safety, is about health care. Having had personal experiences with two major surgeries and countless old-man medical needs, I can assure you that we have world-class doctors and facilities here. Three private hospitals (Star Medica, Angeles, and Victoria) are internationally certified, and the care is exceptional and almost resort-like. Many of the doctors and dentists have international certifications and speak English fluently. Medical care is subjective and highly based on individual needs and expectations. I suggest you approach it with an open mind and decide for yourself. Cash outlays for office visits, procedures, and medicine are a fraction of the cost charged in the US.

The expat community is surprisingly small but growing. For the apparent reason stated initially, Morelia has been below the expat radar. The beach communities (Puerto Vallarta, Mazatlán, and Cancun), Ajijic/Lake Chapala, and San Miguel de Allende have the most extensive expat populations. Many individuals love living in those places for hundreds of reasons.

However, I believe the interior colonial cities and towns tend to be more authentic. For example, Morelia, Patzcuaro, Guanajuato, and Queretaro are culturally more Mexican-oriented than the tourist or expat orientation of the locations mentioned above. I'm being kind and politically correct in this discussion. I didn't move to Mexico to live in a Disneyland version of the country. Too harsh? I think not. I've gained more from the Morelia experience than I could have living with a gaggle of *gringos* pretending to be living the "Mexican Dream."

Geez Louise. I had better finish on a high note, or I'll have to go into a witness protection program. The "Expat Posse" is forming as we speak.

Michoacán is called the Soul of Mexico, and for good reason. It's friggin' beautiful. Imagine pine, fir, and oak forests to take your breath away. Imagine alpine lakes and streams. Imagine mountains that scrape the sky. Imagine Monarch butterfly preserves where millions of those delicate creatures return to winter. Imagine beautiful Pacific beaches with sun-kissed sand and turquoise water. Imagine villages unchanged through the centuries. Imagine a culture so rich you stand in awe. Imagine a vibrant music and arts scene to rival any US city. Imagine a world-class film festival with global stars and movie industry honchos mingling with locals for 10 days every year. Imagine the epicenter of the beautifully unique Day of the Dead festivities and ceremonies. Imagine endless fiestas and festivals celebrating local handcrafts and foods. Imagine a life living in the center of all the above with one foot in the past and one in the future.

So you have to ask why am I living in Morelia, Michoacan? Really?

⤳

*Sadly, I've never won an Oscar, or for that matter, a Pulitzer Prize, for my prose. My writing chops have been honed through self-humiliation of trial and error, and editors with the patience of saints. It all started innocently after I arrived in Mexico in 2009 with encouragement from my social media followers. For some reason, they liked my witty observations on life in Mexico and other subjects. Their encouragement boosted my fragile ego and made me believe I could write a novel. Always an over-achiever, it took me eight years to write three books: two historical fiction works and one book of short stories. I'm working on another short story collection that reflects my twisted personality and fluctuates between sarcastic humor and nostalgic stories of my youth. Hopefully, Hollywood will finally recognize my genius, and I will be offered a substantial payment for the movie rights.*

*I forgot to mention that I have unrealistic expectations for my efforts. I still live in Morelia, Michoacán, where I work in real estate, have a tour business, and founded a community social organization. Come visit our beautiful city and see the secret jewel of Mexico! It will captivate you.*

# 18. The Unfolding of a Grand Adventure

## Karen Kinney
## Mexico City, DF

It's Saturday, and I'm strolling through the lush park just a few blocks from where we live in Mexico City, enjoying all the sights and sounds of the weekend: kids running and families strolling, groups of people swaying their bodies in rhythm to salsa or *bachata*, a vendor calling out and trailing a huge cluster of animal-shaped balloons behind him, a musician playing classical guitar on the sidewalk, an elderly man selling *churros*, an impromptu soccer game. Everywhere I look, there's a sense of life buzzing and over-flowing.

This large park is a hub of community, as so many public places are in Mexico. And this abundance of community is one of the things I love most about my adopted country. I pinch myself to take in the fullness of my surroundings and the reality of having established an international life outside of the US.

Eight years prior, I'd made a vision board in my art studio in Los Angeles and taped it to my wall. It was a fairly simple vision board—a short list of expansive desires scrawled on a sheet of printer paper. One of the visions I'd written down was living and working in another country. And before this idea made it onto the paper taped to my wall, it was a recurring thought for years. This morning, I'm enjoying reflecting on just how this vision came about and celebrating its manifestation.

My husband and I have had a long-held wish to try living in another country. We have always enjoyed other cultures and carry within us a desire to travel and explore. Our friend group is quite diverse, and we have always felt at home with people from other parts of the world. And, despite the fact that our lives had taken a fairly conventional path (marriage, jobs, a mortgage), we also hungered for newness and adventure.

We'd been living by the ocean in Los Angeles for 12 years—I was a professional artist doing gallery shows and public art projects and my husband worked remotely for a health care company. Through my connections in the creative community, I'd often heard of San Miguel de Allende, a small pueblo in the hills of Central Mexico. Similar to LA, it was also full of artists and writers. And so in 2016, we decided to travel there and spend a month exploring. As luck would have it, during our stay I met a woman in search of artists to help beautify a public alleyway. I ended up making a plan with her to return to San Miguel the following year and paint a mural.

By the end of 2017, the mural was finished and we had two extended visits to Mexico under our belt. We were now more open to entertaining the idea of a longer stay. I'd just completed a public art project for the airport in LA and had also published my first book, *The Reluctant Artist: Navigating and Sustaining a Creative Path*. I was also at a new juncture in my career. I was beginning to switch gears creatively and move from art towards writing, with the goal of establishing myself as an author.

With this change in sight, and the fact that I would now only need a computer to work (and could let go of my large studio space with all of my unwieldy art supplies), we were finally both in a position to look more seriously at leaving California.

The initial plan was to move to San Miguel for eight months, experience what life was like, and then return to Los Angeles. So, the first thing we had to do was find a renter for our condo—ideally someone who was OK moving in for less than a year. To encourage that kind of flexibility, we asked for a slightly below-market-value rent.

After finding our renter, we sold all of our furniture and packed the rest of our belongings into boxes. Combined with a few other odds and ends, we moved the boxes into an eight cubic foot storage unit and locked the door. I admit I felt a bit of pride that we'd been able to whittle down our possessions from the past 18 years to fit into such a compact space. Less is more, as they say. And simplicity definitely aids adventure! I figured we'd be back in eight months to retrieve it all.

Well, no one is more surprised than we are that the initially planned eight months has now turned into six and a half years— and counting. Mexico has been more than I ever could have imagined or expected, and my life has been enriched in ways far too numerous to count. Some days I still can't believe that we actually live here and have crafted such interesting, cross-cultural lives. It is a daily reminder to me of the power of visioning, and that we have the ability to create what we want to see and experience in the world.

We began our journey in Mexico in 2018 in San Miguel de Allende, and spent five wonderful years there. It could not have been a better entry point into the country. San Miguel is accessible to those who don't speak very much (or any) Spanish, has the most wonderful and easiest sense of community I've ever experienced (for example, routinely being invited over to someone's home for dinner a few days after meeting them). It also has beautiful and varied cultural celebrations that honor both Mexican and indigenous traditions, and is quaint and picturesque.

During my time in San Miguel, I vowed to "become a writer." Even though I'd written a book prior to moving there, I still wanted to grow into and embody the calling of writer more fully. I found a supportive writers' group to join, and, in addition to completing and publishing my second book, I began speaking and teaching, including at the San Miguel Writers' Conference & Literary Festival held there each year. We also bought a house, something we'd never been able to afford in California, where we'd spent most of our adult lives.

San Miguel gently introduced us to Mexico and to all of the practicalities of daily living (both the good and the frustrating), and to the challenge of figuring things out in another language. But after five full years there, we began to feel that it was time to return to a city again. Both my husband and I are urban people at heart, and while we found many joys in pueblo life, we missed the energy and expansive feeling of a big metropolis.

In the summer of 2023, we moved from San Miguel to Condesa, a neighborhood in Mexico City that's chock full of parks, sidewalk cafes, and tree-lined avenues. In many ways, the Art Deco architecture and leafy green trees feel reminiscent of Europe. It also reminds me of some of the Chicago neighborhoods I lived in during my young adult years.

Mexico City was not new to us; we'd been visiting the city for several weeks each year, ever since arriving in Mexico in 2018. And, as charming as San Miguel is, we felt too young to enter retirement mode and wanted to be around a younger population that's still working. We are both in self-driven fields, and the energy of being around people who are working in all kinds of industries fuels our own goals and projects. Also, my creative ambitions align more with an outward and international focus, and Mexico City supports this kind of energy well.

We also resonate much more with the creative vibe in Mexico City. Although San Miguel is full of artists and writers, my preferences have always skewed more urban in taste—whether that be visuals I find inspiring, or a more eclectic and diverse array of people and projects. As the seventh largest city in the world, Mexico City offers all of this and more.

During my time in San Miguel, my art practice really went underground as I focused on becoming a writer. But since relocating to Mexico City, my art-making has blossomed again and I've been in two different art exhibits (including one that traveled to Italy), with plans for a third next year. I've also had my first international teaching experience at a university in England. International work opportunities are part of the direction I'm heading, and access to the airport here is much easier and faster than in San Miguel (20 minutes vs. an hour and a half). This makes travel for both work and pleasure quite convenient.

For me, one of the big unknowns in moving to Mexico City was how much social interaction I'd find in comparison to San Miguel. San Miguel, after all, is an epicenter of community. So I've been very pleased to experience a social infrastructure that's just as full and just as rich. When you move to another country, foreigners tend to seek one another out, no matter where they live. And I'm continually meeting people from all over the world—Cuba, Sweden, South Africa, Cyprus, Taiwan, etc. I've enjoyed starting a writing group, and through that have met several published authors and writers, all of whom inspire me to take the next steps in my work. My husband and I have even started taking *bachata* dance classes in the large park that's just blocks from our apartment.

I've grown and expanded in countless respects since moving to Mexico. Both the joys and the frustrations of living in another country have ultimately enriched my life and helped me evolve in valuable ways. For example, I've been challenged to view task completion and time very differently. (If you're interested in efficiency, Mexico is not the country to move to!) But I've found that adapting to a slower pace and navigating things not "working" in the same way they do in the US to be an antidote to the never-ending American pressures of speed, perfection, and climbing a ladder.

Mexican culture is more conducive to taking a winding road instead of a linear one. And not only do you learn to become OK with this (that is, if you decide to stay), you also start to see the immense value in another way of experiencing time. Life becomes something to be enjoyed instead of rushed through. And the false sense of urgency we experience so often in the US no longer has such an over-inflated influence on decision-making.

I've also learned about contentment on an entirely new level. Mexican culture, as a whole, models this well. There isn't the same restless hunger for "more" and "newer" that I routinely sense in the US. Over and over again, I've experienced life becoming *enough* in all of the ways it's presented to us.

Coupled with this is having fewer choices. Sometimes I miss being able to easily find certain items I'd buy in the States. Or, being forced to purchase a much more expensive alternative. (Yes, some items are much pricier here than their US equivalent!) But over-availability of material things is unrelated to life satisfaction. At the end of the day, what actually matters is our connection to others, finding meaning and inner fulfillment, and celebrating life. And Mexico offers all of these in abundance.

Another upside of a culture that regularly models contentment is that you begin to learn what truly warrants irritation or frustration and what does not. And what I've learned is that, at the end of the day, most of the things we want to be irritated about are simply not worth the energy.

When we first moved to Mexico, I used the internet to search out most things (as I'd done in the States). I was surprised to find that the information on websites would often be incorrect. For example, I'd go in search of a store I'd found online, only to find out it didn't exist. Or that it was closed when it should have been open (or vice versa). Many businesses didn't have websites at all. The internet became less useful, and I learned that word of mouth was the best way to source most information.

Utilities were sporadically inconsistent. The electricity would sometimes go out for a few hours with no notice, and it would always be when I was in the middle of a Zoom call or some other work-related task needing the internet. Sometimes the water from the city would be shut off due to a repair, and again, with no notice given. We'd have to find out what was happening from our neighbors, as the kind of communication you get from utility companies or from the city where you live in the States simply doesn't happen here.

As Americans, coming from a country where infrastructure can generally be counted on to work with greater consistency and communication, there are days when inconveniences like these can get under your skin. But I've found that shifting expectations and holding things more loosely helps tremendously. The day goes on, you find another way, and you learn to accept "what is" with far more ease and grace. As a result, you end up cultivating a much greater sense of peace with life, despite things not always functioning at the level you're used to.

One of the things I love most about Mexico is the wealth of community I've found here. But a close second is the unparalleled kindness I've received. Perhaps this feels like a significant cultural contrast to me because, for the most part, I've only lived in large cities in the US, where being more aggressive and self-sufficient is the norm. But in this country, I've received so much unexpected kindness from strangers that my heart has been permanently altered.

One of my earliest and most memorable experiences was on a very hot summer day shortly after our arrival. I was sweltering at home, and so to escape the heat, I decided to venture out to a café for a cold drink. As I settled into a chair, the man at the next table accidentally bumped into mine. He apologized profusely and then returned to conversing with his wife and child. A few moments later, he turned and struck up a conversation in English, asking inquisitively where I was from. As I chatted with him and his wife, I learned they were from Guadalajara and on vacation for a few days. In a few weeks they were headed to Ontario, California to visit extended family.

When I told him I was from Los Angeles, he joked that LA was pretty much like Mexico, to which I laughed and agreed. The conversation continued for a while as we discussed their family in the States and details about my time in Mexico. They asked how I was enjoying their country and sincerely welcomed me as a foreigner multiple times, repeatedly remarking that they hoped I enjoyed my stay. He ended by saying, "You are truly welcome here." His last line left me taken aback, as I was unexpectedly moved by this display of sincere kindness. And I couldn't help but think, with chagrin, how Spanish-speaking foreigners with very little English are so rarely welcomed in the same manner in many parts of the US.

I would say one of the greatest lessons of moving abroad has been learning to trust more fully in the unfolding of life. Both before and after moving, I've been on a continued growth curve of staying open to dreams and possibilities, and, as best I can, detaching from specific outcomes. Holding things loosely is key. (I've gotten much better at this, but still have room for improvement!)

Sometimes it can be easy to place too tight a grip on the details of how we want our dreams to play out, and we can be tempted to force an exact outcome. Yes, we can plan and have goals and bring structure to how we move towards those goals—these things definitely help! But at the end of the day, no one knows the future or the details of how life will transpire.

Our plan to stay long-term in Mexico was certainly nowhere in sight when we first moved. And most of the other foreigners I've met here didn't have a grand, over-arching plan when they came either. They were motivated to take the leap for a variety of different reasons, but many never expected to stay as long as they have.

The challenge, then, becomes both embracing a sense of possibility over and over again, and then releasing it, and trusting that life will eventually work itself out the way it's meant to. Because, despite our best efforts, it's impossible to imagine the radical fullness of any particular vision. We can have our aspirations, but often the Universe will have an even grander plan in mind, one we can't possibly see with clarity ahead of time.

If moving to another country excites you, I'd encourage you to take small steps of faith and see what happens! Most decisions can always be undone, so there isn't any harm in trying what's calling to you. Having some anxiety is a normal response to the unknowns, the what ifs, or the "worst case scenarios" that surface in our minds. But the truth is that we always have the choice to shift our thought patterns, our mindset, and how we ultimately decide to show up in the world. We can move forward rooted in our own power.

Above all, keep allowing yourself the freedom to dream! (Remember my vision board?) By dreaming, we start to cultivate the seeds of those places inside of us that are yet unlived. Going after what we long for with open hands gives voice to our desires, and helps us picture what being fully alive looks and feels like. It turns what could be an otherwise stagnant life into one where dreams and hopes are seen, nurtured, and honored.

In essence, we can begin to partner with the Universe and say, "Let's go on this grand adventure together!" The outcome is unknown. But when we stay open to what could be and release the limits of our thinking, beautiful surprises await us.

↜

*Karen Kinney is an award-winning author, internationally exhibited artist, and teacher. For more than 20 years, she has practiced and studied contemplative spirituality, the basis from which her creativity is birthed. She uses a multitude of mediums as vessels for inspiration, connection, and beauty.*

*Her most recent book, "Doorways to Transformation: Everyday Wisdom for the Creative Soul," is a companion for personal and spiritual growth and includes meditations to bolster your creative spirit and your larger life. Her first book, "The Reluctant Artist: Navigating and Sustaining a Creative Path," is a guide to fully owning and nurturing your creative work.*

*As a speaker, Karen has taught around the world, including at Cambridge University, the University of Hong Kong, and the San Miguel Writers' Conference & Literary Festival. She helps people find greater levels of creative freedom and speaks about inner transformation, the sacred feminine, and the innate connection between spirituality and creativity.*

*She has also pursued a multifaceted art career, and her work resides in numerous private collections, including those of Stanford University, actor Bob Odenkirk, and NPR's Guy Raz. She has designed installation work for the Los Angeles International Airport and painted murals in LA and Mexico.*

*Karen's current passion and work centers on the divine feminine. She authors a quarterly newsletter that explores spirituality and transformation from a feminist perspective and is writing a new book that explores this topic in depth. She is based in Mexico City. Contact her at karenkinney.com/*

# 19. Say Yes & Show Up

Janet Blaser

San Antonio Tlayacapan, Jalisco

My story at this point is more about living-in-Mexico, as opposed to moving-to-Mexico. After 19 years, my life here has become, well, the norm. When I visit the States, I feel awkward. Each time I go I realize how different I am from most of the people I'm around. Adding to that mild culture shock is that I'm always confronted by a barrage of new "things:" new words and jargon, new kinds of cars, new technology, new ways of doing things, and of course, new prices for even the most basic of items. It can be overwhelming, and I'll admit I do feel the total of my 68 years during those moments.

To recap: I moved to Mexico in 2006, following a lifelong dream of living in a tropical climate and wanting a simpler lifestyle. I felt increasingly unable to afford California and it felt like I was just treading water, working to pay the bills and never getting ahead. I chose Mazatlán, a mid-size city on the west coast, which I'd fallen in love with while on vacation. I was 50, and although I resigned from my full-time job, I kept one part-time editing job online. I had an idea, a plan, to start my own business: a monthly English magazine to serve the burgeoning foreign community I'd seen there. I had some savings I thought would get me through until I got the business up and running.

This loose, not-quite-formed financial plan somehow ended up being pretty successful. Part of it was luck: I was in the right place at the right time with the right skill-set and a niche product there was a need for. And I was young enough (in my early 50s) to have the energy to do everything that was needed to start and run the magazine. One could say I was plucky; I had the attitude to get it done, too, barreling ahead into a million unknowns, confident that I could and would figure everything out and make it work. And somehow, I did.

Over time, I learned Spanish—not fluently, but enough to communicate well, speak publicly (sort of LOL), and feel comfortable doing so in most situations. With the business, I had to learn—and fast. I built a warm, supportive community of both locals and expats that made my everyday life brighter and more fun. I started an organic farmers' market, the city's first and still the only, where farmers sold their produce directly to consumers. Living right on the Pacific Ocean, I learned to surf—another longtime dream—and spent countless happy hours in the water. I traveled around México visiting iconic places like Oaxaca, San Miguel de Allende, Sayulita, Guanajuato, and Puerto Vallarta. And I started that magazine, M!, publishing it for 10 years before selling it when I began taking my Social Security.

Somewhere in the midst of all that, I wrote a book about living in Mexico, *Why We Left: An Anthology of American Women Expats*. It became an Amazon bestseller; my freelance career blossomed. Life was good.

Then came Covid, bringing with it the isolation, fears, and changes that people all over the world were experiencing. Worried about the capability of the local hospitals and any possible need for care as a foreigner during a pandemic, I thought I'd ride it out in the US with one of my grown kids, a vacation of sorts. I closed up my apartment, paid my rent and bills a few months in advance, and loaded my cats and a couple of suitcases into my car. Little did I know it would be a year to the day before I would return to my beloved Mazatlán.

It was a harrowing time to be in the United States, and for me 2021 was a dichotomy of wonderful family time juxtaposed with the harsh reality of what the US had become since I'd left almost 20 years earlier. "Open carry" and guns in public terrified me; the political anger and harsh divisions felt abrasive, unnecessary and just plain scary. I struggled to deal with the grey, cold, rainy weather and short, dark days in the Pacific Northwest, where I was. I'd grown accustomed to blue, sunny skies and warm weather all year round, and this was depressing and a shock to my system.

That year confirmed for me that America was not my home anymore. I packed my car once again, and my cats and I made the long, long drive from Portland, Oregon back to Mazatlán.

Good friends offered me their vacation home to stay in while I looked for a place to rent. As I drove around to my old haunts, I was shocked. Somehow Mazatlán had been able to capitalize on the pandemic, promoting the laid-back beachfront town all over Mexico as a great place to let kids do their online classes and ride it out. People came; the city boomed.

The town I'd left had grown, and was now bursting at the seams with development, tourists, and all the issues that come with too much growth, way too fast. The iconic malecón fronting the ocean was now lined with 20- and 30-story condos and hotels—or construction sites heralding more to come. Instead of palm trees, Mazatlán's beautiful sunsets now had a backdrop of giant cranes and bumper-to-bumper traffic. It was not where I wanted to live anymore. I was increasingly unhappy and dissatisfied and knew I had to leave Mazatlán before all of my wonderful memories became negative ones. But where to go?

I know that many people stay in the same place, the same town, their whole lives. Or they move once, maybe for work, then settle and stay. I'd always thought that's who I was, but as the years have gone by, I see that that's not quite true. I do settle—deeply and quickly—wherever I am, for sure; friends always remark on how fast my rentals become my "home." But when undeniable change is staring me in the face, whether it's coming from inside of me or from something external, I'm just as quick to go with the new flow. As fast as my home felt "right," it can feel "not right," and then I know it's time to move. It may take me a little while to get off the fence, so to speak, but what's always true is that change is inevitable, and it's better to accept it than fight it.

I guess I'm lucky also in that I'm not very attached to "stuff." My experience has been that wherever you are, there's always more stuff to be had! Plus each place I've lived has its own vibe, its own energy, that requires different furnishings, décor, etc. There are some things I do keep, either out of sentiment or aesthetics, but for the most part, everything gets sold.

And so I found myself at one of those junctures again.

The Lake Chapala area—about six hours south and inland—suddenly popped into my head as an option. I started mentally checking off things that mattered to me. I knew I would miss the ocean; that was the hardest thing. But a quieter, more peaceful lifestyle in a smaller town without the 24/7 party vibe of Mazatlán felt like what I needed.

I had a few friends there already, folks I'd met in Mazatlán years before who'd moved there because of the milder climate and small-town lifestyle. Intrigued, I arranged a visit, opting for the bus instead of driving. I'd booked an Airbnb, but a few days before my departure I saw a last-minute pet sitting post, for two cats, on HousesitMexico.com, in exactly the area where my friends lived— for the dates I was planning to go! The home was in San Antonio Tlayacapan, a small pueblo of about 7,000 people that's halfway between the bigger, more popular and well-known towns of Chapala and Ajijic, right on the lake. "Bigger" is relative, though: Chapala's population is around 57,000, and Ajijic about 22,000. (Much smaller than Mazatlán, a bustling city of 650,000.)

One of my friends took me under her wing and showed me around the area, and together we found a perfect place for me to rent. I'd told myself that if I was supposed to move, the Universe needed to give me an unmistakable sign—and it did. The cute little yellow house we found was on a quiet dead-end street, with a gated yard and parking, two bedrooms, a nice kitchen, enclosed patio, and rooftop deck. It was just a few blocks from her, in a rural area, and was below my budget, at only $9,000 pesos a month, including water (about $450 dollars, depending on the exchange rate). I met with the landlord, gave a deposit, and signed a one-year lease that would begin in three weeks.

On the bus back to Mazatlán, I decided I'd sell my furniture and appliances and start anew. As fate would have it, my best friend wanted to move into my apartment—and buy everything! It was a win-win for everyone and made the move much easier. I saw all of this as another sign from the Universe that this was the right thing for me to be doing.

I have a mental list of things I need for wherever I live, whether in Mexico or elsewhere. Top of the list is convenient, modern medical care; a modern, international airport nearby, and reliable services, meaning dependable Wi-Fi, water supply, electricity, banks, mechanics, an immigration office, and shipping options, like FedEx and Amazon deliveries. Seem silly? It's not. I've lived in places where these things were not guaranteed, and believe me, not having dependable running water gets old fast.

This next thing some of you may think is trivial, but it's not a trade-off I want to make anymore.

I love to cook and bake, and having a wide variety of food options, both fresh and packaged ingredients, is important to me. Don't get me wrong: I love Mexican food, but sometimes I want to make authentic lasagna or an Indian meal. I want to be able to find the ingredients I want and spend an afternoon cooking something new and different. The year-round temperate climate of the Lakeside area means more things grow much easier than in the heat and humidity along the coast. Stores and markets have blueberries, strawberries, and raspberries year-round at unbelievable prices, and asparagus, artichokes, salad greens, and tomatoes, too. A more affluent expat community and proximity to Guadalajara's big stores and import companies means access to "gourmet" products like burrata, phyllo dough, aged Cheddar cheese, organic spices, and "Beyond Burgers." I can't tell you how exciting it is to be able to easily get products like these!

For so many years, on my trips to the States, I would plan carefully what foods I could bring back, carefully rationing suitcase space, dollars, and desires. (Pumpkin puree or couscous? Basmati rice or steel-cut oats?)

You'll note that "safety" is not on my list. That's because it's a given, and not something I've ever had to worry about in the places I've lived or visited in Mexico.

As I write this, I've been here about six months. The little yellow *casita* is home now, and I love sitting in the garden at the start and end of each day, listening to the birds as the day begins or ends. It's peaceful, which is what I wanted and needed, and has given me time for my writing work (including this book), and to focus on my family, and examine my priorities for the next 10 or 15 years of my life.

The world is so different now than when I first moved to Mexico. America is a mess, getting more worrisome by the day. Since the election, I'm receiving countless messages from readers and followers asking, "How can I do what you did?" Since my first book was published and I've developed more of a media presence, that's not unusual for me. But what is notable is the attitude behind these messages now: People are scared. They're "running away from" more than "going to." Many sound desperate. Frantic. Expat Facebook pages in a myriad of countries—Portugal, Italy, Spain, Canada, Costa Rica, Panama, the UK, Ireland, and of course Mexico—are filled with requests for advice, suggestions, and help. Moving to Mexico is no longer just about sunny weather, a lower cost of living, and a less-stressful lifestyle. Of course, those things still matter, but it seems that foremost now in many people's minds is something altogether different.

Mexico feels like freedom to them—and they're correct. Here, no one really cares what you do; there's a "live-and-let-live" attitude. (Within reason, of course.) You're free to live your own life, peacefully. Nobody wants problems. There are no shootings at the Walmart or elementary school; people don't own guns. Let that sink in for a minute: People don't own guns. And they don't want to own guns, despite what the US media says. Millions and millions and millions of people live peacefully, happily, and violence-free. Mexico is not a chaotic, lawless, scary nation; of course there's crime, just like anywhere else in the world. Yes, there's the cartel, but really, think about it: They're busy running their multi-billion-dollar international business and you and I are not even blips on their screen. Is it perfect? No. But is anywhere perfect? Again, no.

It's hard to be writing this now when so much is happening that has changed the attitude and reasons for leaving America and moving to Mexico. (Or Canada, Portugal, or any other country, for that matter.) It's a very different climate than when I made this decision almost 20 years ago.

I know Mexico isn't perfect, and for many reasons it's probably not my "forever" home. More and more I'm missing my family and grandkids, missing the milestones in their lives, the chance to know them better and for them to get to know me more, too.

My grandkids only know me as a visitor, and have never seen my home, how I live and what I do in my day-to-day life. Sadly, I'm like a traveler passing through, and although I'm not saying we don't have a relationship—we do—a big part of me yearns for it to be more. I think seriously about becoming a snowbird but can't see how that could work financially. (Yet!)

I also don't want to die here away from my family. I'd like to grow old(er) and make that final transition surrounded by my loved ones. Of course, you never know, but you get my point.

The life I've built for myself in Mexico works for now, and really, it's hard to imagine living in the States considering the direction it's headed. I went to Italy recently, my first trip to Europe, and my heart came alive in ways it hasn't since I first set foot in Mexico. I wonder often if that's my next place; but there are obstacles, financially and visa-wise, that I can't see my way through. (Yet!)

If my life in Mexico has taught me anything, it's that everything is possible. Dreams do come true. Some of it is luck, some of it is hard work, and some of it is simply that life is full of change. You never know what's around the next corner, through the next door, or about to appear on the horizon. All you can do is try to somehow be aware and ready to take that next step when it's presented, to say yes and show up.

⌒

*Janet Blaser is an author, writer, and consultant who has lived in Mexico since 2006. A former journalist in California, her work now focuses on expat living. Janet has been a writer and storyteller her entire life, and has been fortunate to write about great food, amazing places, fascinating people, and unique events. She is a regular contributor to CNBC's "Make It," International Living magazine, and various other publications.*

*Her first book, "Why We Left: An Anthology of American Women Expats" is an Amazon bestseller. She's currently working on a series of "Going Expat Guides" about Mexico, Italy, Portugal, and Costa Rica. Janet also offers individualized Expat Consultations via Zoom to encourage and assist folks wanting to move to Mexico.*

*A writer by nature, Janet also likes to surf, garden, read, cook, and, at times, rabble-rouse. She counts among her many blessings three wonderful adult children as well as a trio of delightful grandchildren. Stay connected and learn more about expat life in Mexico by following @TheJanetBlaser on Facebook and Instagram or visiting JanetBlaser. com.*

# 20. Following the Breadcrumbs

## Ann Woodward

## Puebla, state of Puebla

New York City, 2011.

On a chilly, gray Sunday afternoon, I sat alone in a Mexican restaurant in Noho. Over a margarita and some tacos, I scribbled down in a note-book a list of places where I was itching to travel immediately:

India
Petra
Thailand
Angkor Wat
Bali
Vietnam
Beirut
Laos

I also jotted down how long I thought I'd need in each location. Clearly, this trip would be measurable in months instead of days or weeks. My soul was yearning for something much larger than a vacation.

Foreign places piqued my interest at a young age. My mother taught social studies, and the bookcase in our den was lined with issues of "National Geographic" and various cultural reference books. I spent countless hours flipping through the pages and staring at the photos with wonderment. I travelled outside the US for

179

the first time when I was 15. It was a whirlwind tour of western Europe, five countries in 10 days. I basically slept through Germany due to jet lag. That trip taught me that I never wanted to travel that way ever again, and it also opened my eyes to what lay beyond my hometown in rural south Georgia.

I interned in New York City between my junior and senior year of college and then moved there after graduation. NYC is a world unto itself. Navigating the city, deciphering my colleagues' Yiddish phrases and partaking in the nightlife kept me occupied.

In May 2000, I spent a week in Barcelona with my friend Tina. It was my first grown-up vacation outside the US. We savored the *menu del dia*, drank copious amounts of sangria, and danced until the sun came up. I remember sitting at an outdoor café at one point during the trip, looking around and thinking, "I love this place. I could live here. Should I move to Spain?" I worked for a large global advertising agency. I'd watched colleagues transfer for assignments in Australia and Poland and wondered whether I could do the same.

Several weeks later, my father died unexpectedly of a heart attack at age 52, four days after my 26th birthday. Sometimes life-altering events such as a sudden death or a serious illness propel you into choosing a different path. In my case, moving abroad no longer seemed appropriate, so I suppressed those thoughts. Instead, I spent more time in Georgia, worrying about my mother and muddling through my own grief.

After that immediate crisis passed, I performed a dutiful dance for several years, working incredibly long hours and using my vacation days to visit far-flung destinations. Eventually, though, I reached a breaking point. Not only was I exhausted and burned out, but business trips to Capetown and Istanbul and vacations in Brazil, Egypt, and Sri Lanka didn't satiate me. At all. They only fueled my desire to see more of the world. Some people are obsessed with eating chocolate or shoe shopping. I was obsessed with travel.

Stacks of travel magazines and Lonely Planet guide-books littered my apartment. I started following several travel bloggers, studying their advice on how to prepare and pack for long-term travel. I met with people in NYC who'd taken career breaks to travel the world; I just needed to gather the courage to set out on mine.

Then, in summer 2011, I was laid off, a few months after I'd penned my travel wish list in the Mexican restaurant. Once the initial wave of shock, nausea, and embarrassment passed, I realized I had the perfect opportunity to enact my plan to travel.

That same week, my friend Brian—someone I'd known since we were teenagers—called me to announce he was moving to NYC and looking for apartment leads. He wound up subletting my apartment. He arrived with only two suitcases of clothes and wanted my place furnished as it was, alleviating the logistical burden of having to sell or store my possessions.

I also exchanged a bag of miscellaneous foreign currency I had in my apartment from prior trips, and the dollar amount was exactly what was needed to pay for two visas and adding additional pages to my passport. The Universe was conspiring to help me leave, in both big and small ways.

My two biggest fears about the impending trip were losing all of my belongings somehow and whether or not I'd be able to "hold it" on long bus rides with no bathroom breaks. I also fretted about what others thought of me and whether I was making a fatal career mistake in not getting another job right away.

Looking back, the most difficult, nerve-wracking sequence of this adventure was walking out of my apartment with my backpack, taking a taxi to JFK airport and boarding the flight to my first destination, Jordan. Leaving NYC was the scariest part. Once I was in motion, things fell into place.

I didn't know if I'd enjoy long-term travel; it's not the same as vacationing. Perhaps unsurprisingly, I took to nomadic life right away. Much of my time was dedicated to typical touristic pursuits of sightseeing, trying local foods, and simply appreciating being in new environments. However, I also volunteered for a women's empowerment organization in Rajasthan and stayed with a family in Madrid for some months to tutor the kids in English. (I got my chance to live in Spain after all!)

When I returned to the US after being away for 13 months, I decided to set out again, this time focusing on Latin America. Although I'd checked off everything from my wish list and more, one year of full-time travel had shown me how much there was to see in the world. I didn't have work commitments, so why not continue to travel?

My inner voice also whispered, "do it now." My father's death at a relatively young age taught me that tomorrow is not promised. After a year of scaling Cambodian temples in searing heat and humidity and clambering onto the top bunk of overnight trains in India, I also understood how physical the act of travelling can be. I knew it was unlikely I'd have the same mobility and stamina at retirement age.

I started with countries I'd never visited in South America and made my way north through Central America. During this time, I completed two rounds of intensive Spanish classes, with at least four hours a day of one-on-one instruction. Headaches after class were a common occurrence, but I persevered. Spanish is a useful language skill, but another motivator was that I didn't want to be a traveler from the US who could only speak English.

In Jan. 2014, I crossed the border from Guatemala into Mexico. I'd travelled to Mexico several times for quick beach vacations and always enjoyed them, though aside from a couple of nights in Mexico City back in 2007, I'd never been anywhere in Mexico other than the coast. I thought I knew Mexico because I'd spent some tequila-fueled days in a few beach areas. As it turned out, I didn't know much about the country at all.

Because I was travelling overland, I realized just how big a country Mexico is. I'd never given that much consideration before. San Cristobal and Oaxaca appear close to one another on a map. Today a bus trip between the two places takes between 12 and 13 hours. I recall the bus ride taking even longer back then; I think the road conditions have improved during the past 10 years.

For the next several weeks, I backpacked through the interior of Mexico, stopping in San Cristobal de las Casas, Oaxaca de Juárez, Puebla, Mexico City, San Miguel de Allende, Guanajuato, and Guadalajara.

I was struck by the vibrancy of, well, everything: Bands and dancing in the *zocalos*. Colorful homes and architectural details. Traditional pottery and textiles. Gorgeous churches.

The food was incredible. I scarfed down *moles* and *tlayudas* in Oaxaca, more *moles* and *tacos árabes* in Puebla, and delicious *tortas* and a life-changing shrimp tostada from Mexico City street stands. The level of spice, in terms of heat as well as the complexity of the seasoning, was immediately apparent as soon as I entered Mexico. Aside from my time in San Miguel, I encountered almost no one from the US. My educated guess is that the food in touristic beach areas has been adapted to better meet the preferences of foreign palates, whereas the rest of the country is geared toward Mexicans.

This journey through Mexico was a pivotal point on my life path. The trip completely changed my perception of Mexico and my relationship with it as well. How could the energy—and the food—of each place be so different? I left curious and quite literally hungry for more.

My time in Mexico ended in an unexpected way: I learned that my aunt had received a liver transplant at Emory University Hospital in Atlanta. She'd been on a waiting list, but the sudden availability of an organ match and immediate surgery was a huge surprise. I flew to Georgia to help my family.

While in Atlanta, I met with an endometriosis specialist because my periods had become unbearable. I'd seriously considered going to a hospital emergency room in Mexico during one terrifying and excruciatingly painful episode. I had a partial hysterectomy a few months later. I didn't realize how sick I'd been until I felt better post-surgery.

The months in Georgia gave me time to reflect. I'd been travelling untethered for more than two and a half years. I had no desire to return to live in the US. I still wanted to travel but needed to move at a much slower pace. And so, with that intention, I headed out once more.

Choosing to base yourself in a location, even for a short while, is a dramatic mental and behavioral shift. Conducting your life somewhere for weeks or months fosters a different experience than just passing through for a few days to see the sights. For example, renting an apartment in a residential neighborhood and buying groceries creates a different relationship with a place than when you're staying in centrally located hotels and eating every meal in restaurants.

Cultural immersion can be an aspect of slower travel. I realized the part of travel I enjoyed most was behaving like an amateur anthropologist—understanding the realities of the place I was visiting, learning about and experiencing its unique aspects, and observing the differences from my own culture.

As a way to stay in places longer, I applied my skills to participate in various work exchanges, including managing a surf school in Morocco, marketing a bed & breakfast in Italy, and serving as the hostess for a vineyard restaurant in Chile. These opportunities definitely helped me learn more about the cultures of these countries. I spent nearly two years in an Amazigh (Berber) village in coastal Morocco, undoubtedly an immersion.

I returned to Mexico in 2018 for another extended stay, this time renting a room in a Mexico City apartment shared with two Mexican doctors and a terrier named Coco. I deliberately selected a living arrangement outside of the areas popular with foreigners and tourists. Choosing to live with Mexicans who couldn't speak English and to surround myself with Spanish in as many situations as possible made for a type of cultural immersion that deepened my relationship with and understanding of Mexico.

By this time, I was quite functional in Spanish. I used Spanish more often than English: writing WhatsApp messages in Spanish, making phone calls in Spanish, even dating in Spanish. Of course, my Spanish was not perfect and I made mistakes, but I was relieved to be understood most of the time.

One thing I learned during this visit is that Mexicans eat their main meal of the day around

3 p.m. This custom may not be apparent in tourist areas, but the restaurant across the street from my apartment wouldn't begin accepting lunch orders until 2 p.m. With such a large meal so late in the day, many people skip dinner altogether or only have something light like tacos or a dessert.

Mexico City is dynamic, with countless cultural offerings. It's also more sprawling and car-centric than NYC. While I was grateful for the time to explore neighborhoods more fully and experience attractions I'd missed on previous visits, I realized I'd rather visit Mexico City for a few days at a time than live there.

During this stay, I also visited Copper Canyon, Querétaro, San Luis Potosí, Zipolite and Bacalar.

Once again, I was impressed by Mexico's varied landscapes and how different one destination was from the next. The more I conversed with Mexicans, the more I learned about other small towns and areas that sounded interesting. My list of places to explore in Mexico continued to grow.

I spent most of the next 18 months traveling in Eastern Europe, Central Asia, and Turkey. Mexico was top of mind for places where I could spend the winter.

I arrived in Mexico for a third extended stay in January 2020, with a couple months planned and no onward ticket. When Covid became a disruptor, I chose to remain in Mexico. Most people assume I was trapped in Mexico when international travel came to a halt. However, that's not accurate, and it was not a difficult decision for me to stay in Mexico.

In September 2020, I applied for and received permanent residency in Mexico. The question "should I seek residency in Mexico?" had been on my mind before I arrived, and I interpreted the ongoing global pandemic as an affirmative sign. The more time I spent outside the US, the more I recognized a deep disconnect between the actuality of everyday life in my birth country and what I wanted for myself. Knowing I could legally live in a country other than the US was an immense relief, and it felt expansive to have a tangible option to create a life elsewhere.

I continued to explore different parts of Mexico. In the spring of 2021, I booked an apartment in a town near Puebla city for several weeks to learn more about that area but also to have a place to hide during the busy Easter vacation period. I was pleasantly surprised by the town's walkability, volcano views, history and culture, level of services, and overall vibe. By this time, I had rented apartments in nine different parts of Mexico for a month or longer and visited dozens of other places. Every location has its charms, though none had called to me to stay longer. But this town seemed different and definitely resonated more, and it became my home base in Mexico.

Nowhere is perfect, including this town. The weather here is magnificent overall, but for me, the colder months are uncomfortable with no interior heating. So I decided to spend winters at the beach. I love being by the sea, but I discovered through various stays during the pandemic that Mexico's coastal areas are too hot and humid for me to live there year-round.

I'm able to maintain this duality of shifting between the highlands and the coast because I rent fully furnished apartments on a monthly basis, and I travel with just one suitcase and a small backpack. I don't consider that to be a sacrifice. This lifestyle may not suit everyone, but I mention it so others can be aware that the option exists. I value the flexibility and freedom that comes with not having leases or many possessions.

Puebla, where I've chosen to live, does not have a high concentration of foreign residents, especially compared to places like San Miguel de Allende, Ajijic, or Mexico's beach areas. English speakers do exist but finding them requires concerted effort. I believe it's beneficial for US citizens in foreign countries to have contact with both the local residents and other foreigners. However, I prefer the learning opportunities that arise from being in a predominantly Spanish-speaking environment.

Culture shock is real, though I haven't experienced it in Mexico. The sum total of my life experiences has made it comfortable for me to live in Mexico. Living in NYC prepared me for big cities like Mexico City or Guadalajara. My childhood in the rural Deep South prepared me for Mexico's pueblos and remote areas. The growing pains of learning Spanish earlier in my journey paved the way for better, smoother communication here. The times when I was in a constant state of bewilderment in other countries around the world gave me a greater appreciation for the relative ease of my day-to-day existence in Mexico. Although plenty of things are handled differently in Mexico than the US, I'm willing—and able—to adapt and adjust.

Why has a traveler like me remained in Mexico?

Mexico has provided me with opportunities to explore my creativity. While here, I developed and released an e-book of travel tips and advice, exhibited photos in three gallery shows, and performed an original poem in Spanish at a recital. I've dabbled in drawing, ceramics, jewelry-making, and cooking classes. The insistence on perfection that's pervasive in the US doesn't exist here, and that's extremely liberating.

Mexico's slower pace has helped me unhook from some of the dysfunctional aspects of the American lifestyle that are rooted in capitalism. In Mexico, I can rest when I'm tired, and my worth is not determined by my productivity. I can be more present when I meet with others and enjoy the time we spend together because I'm not anxious, distracted, and rushing to accomplish the next item on my to-do list. In Mexico, businesses are often closed when they're supposed to be open and seemingly simple tasks may take hours to accomplish. Therefore, it's a wonderful place to practice non-attachment and patience.

I came to Mexico in 2020 with a desire to heal, and indeed that has been my focus for the past few years. On physical, mental, emotional, and spiritual levels, Mexico is a healthy place for me to be. It has provided a safe space for me to do all sorts of inner healing and personal growth. I doubt I would have been able to achieve as much intense transformation in another place. The correct people have crossed my path in serendipitous ways, and I also joined a *temazcal* (sweat lodge) circle that has been instrumental in helping me evolve.

The cost of living in Mexico is lower than the US, and substantially lower when it comes to things such as rent. In the US, there's a sense of always needing more money, whereas in Mexico the attitude is "we have everything we need." And a modest income in US dollars here fosters a feeling of abundance instead of struggle and lack.

In Mexico, I've found a sense of acceptance and belonging that eluded me in other countries. My own energy is part of the equation, though I also feel Mexicans are more open in general compared to other places where I've spent time. Being somewhere long enough to build a social network and participate in community has been rewarding.

My process for leaving the US and eventually settling in Mexico was not one of extensive, meticulous planning but more akin to following a trail of breadcrumbs. Making one decision, then another, and another, to see where it would lead. Admittedly, at times it has also felt like stepping off a cliff and hoping for a safety net below.

I took a break from my NYC advertising career in 2011 to travel in Southeast Asia and India. I wasn't sure how long I'd be away, but I fully expected to resume life as I knew it within a year. Thirteen years later, I haven't returned to the corporate world or to live in the US, and I have no plans to do so.

I'm often asked whether I'm bored after spending years in Mexico. Is it possible to be bored in such a large and diverse country? I liken my experience to peeling back layers of an onion. There are always more traditions and histories to understand, more regional foods to taste, more slang words to learn, more *pueblos* to visit.

It's taken me a long time to realize my definition of building a life is heavily weighted towards travel and movement. I don't expect that to change. However, now when I return home, I'm returning to Mexico, and that's a good feeling. *Mexico, te quiero mucho.*

⮑

*Ann Woodward has been location-independent and living outside the US since Oct. 2011. She has visited 82 countries (and counting!) but feels fortunate to hold permanent residency in Mexico. Ann believes travel can be a force for good, and she supports community-based tourism initiatives. She is an organizer of the Chacala Bird Festival in Nayarit, which promotes nature conservation and sustainable tourism. Ann grew up on a farm outside Savannah, Georgia. After graduating from the University of Georgia's Grady College of Journalism and Mass Communication, she worked in New York City advertising agencies for 17 years. Follow her adventures on Instagram @eastvillagenomad and read her blog EastVillageNomad.com.*

# 21. A Good Move

Ruth Thompson Artis

Mazatlán, Sinaloa

Travel and adventure always had an appeal for me, and I never lost interest in wondering, "What's over there?" When I retired after more than two decades of a career in the federal government in the Southeastern US, I felt that I finally had the opportunity to explore more of life.

Through the years, my two sons were always up for travel adventures during school holidays and summers, and our excursions spanned from road trips to family reunions to exploring East Coast seashores. Our landmark adventure was spending one whole summer traversing the entire continental US via Amtrak, disembarking and touring at selected destinations along the way.

Travel felt wonderfully liberating and exciting. I had always been a rather high-energy person and curious about the world. I wanted to instill imagination and curiosity in my children, and the spirit that their aspirations could be limitless as they became aware of the world around them.

Later in life I became the sole caregiver for a parent with Alzheimer's disease for several years until their passing. During this time my marriage also ended. I realized I needed to find a new direction as I'd lost touch with many of my friends and activities during those caregiving years. I felt out of touch with life and mentally and physically drained. I was unsure of the next path in my life. Fortunately, both sons were doing well, engaged in their pursuits out of state in college and extracurricular activities.

At some point I ran across information about teaching English abroad. I discovered a local university offered an eight-week

189

concentrated study program culminating with TESOL (Teaching English as a Second Language) certification which qualifies individuals, as long as they're native English speakers and have a college degree, to teach just about anywhere in the world.

I enrolled in the program and discovered a full class of formerly mid-level professionals who had found themselves displaced by the recent economic implosion of 2008, or were, like me, just ready for a change. The program course was not difficult and was actually more like a refresher course in English grammar; most instruction covered basics for beginners or refined grammar and language skills for those more advanced.

The university also offered recruitment and placement assistance after completing certification. I threw my net out to different language schools abroad, which proliferated in Europe, the Middle East, and Asia. Most schools were accredited and processed all licenses, permits, and visas that were required. In most cases, contracts were established at a higher rate for foreign instructors than for locals, and modern, furnished apartments were provided in popular areas. Most terms were nine months, with round-trip transportation included.

Within a few weeks, I began receiving offers. I narrowed my choices to positions in Ankara, Turkey and Zhanjiang, China.

My sons, who apparently inherited my wanderlust, were eager and excited for me. My close friends and associates, however, even though they were aware of my zest for adventure and my inquisitive nature, were dumbfounded and perplexed that I would consider leaving my comfortable, known world for such a venture. Most had apprehension about such a leap into the unknown.

After researching both offers and locations, I decided on Zhanjiang, largely because of its relative safety and proximity to other ports-of-call in Asia. I completed the preparations for my passport and visa, and I essentially had five months to make arrangements. I ran an ad to rent the first floor of my home, and luckily found a mature, pleasant woman who mostly spent weekends in the mountains north of the city with her aging parents but worked in the city and wanted an affordable place in the city to stay during the week. We remain in touch to this day. I maintained the basement apartment for my comings and goings while in the US.

Zhanjiang was a bustling modern metropolis not unlike any mid-size American city with traffic congestion and crowds, but very, very little crime or violence—one of the primary reasons I chose China over more lucrative assignments in the Middle East or even Europe. Cantonese was spoken and English was uncommon, but it was a commodity many middle-class Chinese aspired to master in order to take advantage of enterprise with their expanding economy. Consequently, language schools flourished.

I taught mostly at private elementary schools, but on occasion I had adult or business classes in the evenings. I had an average of three, 45-minute classes a day and two business or adult evening classes each week. My teacher salary was modest, but I essentially had no expenses except for groceries, and I actually was able to squire funds away and build a savings account.

I met several other teachers from the US, Canada, and Britain, and we made lasting friendships through our mutual shared experience. It was not a strenuous schedule, and I had plenty of time to explore the city, which had numerous parks, gardens, and picturesque locations, with plenty of inexpensive public transportation available.

College-educated young women were assigned to me as "assistants" and accompanied me to all classes. Most of them were fascinated with meeting me and full of questions about my life and living in America. We did shopping trips and dinners, and a few invited me to meet their families for dinner parties and holidays.

Most Chinese in Zhanjiang had never met an African American and were curious and surprised to see me strolling through the city streets. A few were not shy about asking to take photos with me. Once, a senior lady, dressed in the traditional Mao Tse Tung-era garb of loose, cropped black pants, sandals, and square buttoned jacket, gave me a "thumbs up" as she passed by and I jovially gave her one back. I was not uncomfortable with the celebrity status and actually found it amusing.

I traveled to Beijing, Hong Kong, and Bangkok on breaks and some holidays, and was awed and amazed by the history, beauty, and size of the region. I literally could not get enough of the depth of history, creativity, and accomplishment on display here on the other side of the world.

Between assignments, after saving a few more coins, every chance I had I was on a bus or plane exploring. The history in Beijing and Hong Kong was awe-inspiring, and the sheer beauty of the beaches of Thailand was mesmerizing. My only sibling, an older brother, retired and single, came to visit for several months and was so enamored of the region that he remains in Asia to this day, living in Thailand.

After my third year in Asia, I'd planned to sign another contract and was visiting the US on a summer break. On a chance perusing of an online dating app, I met the love of my life, Will, a widower with adult children. Gadabout that I was, I was attracted to Will's calm, steady nature. I decided not to renew my contract, and after a whirlwind courtship, we married the next year. I settled into happy domesticity with Will, who was a few years away from retirement and trying to decide how to spend his golden years.

My new husband was impressed and encouraged by my adventurous life, and I enthusiastically convinced him to plan pockets of time to travel and explore in the years preceding his retirement. We started our life together taking one trip after another, covering lots of ground and creating sublime memories. We did everything from exploring the Valley of Fire in the American Midwest, to climbing glaciers in Alaska, to sailing the sapphire blue waters of the Aegean Sea in Santorini, and many other spots in between.

While at home we spent weekends discovering and hiking some of the gorgeous, wooded trails of the Georgia mountains. We camped and navigated the white-water currents in Oconee, Georgia. We were also active in several collaborative efforts for the disadvantaged in our city, volunteering with various meal programs and participating with voter registration campaigns and other city-sponsored volunteer efforts.

However, over time we'd both become disillusioned and frustrated with the antics of American politics. The apparent lack of interest of the richest country in the world to improve the lives of its ordinary people, seniors, and veterans, the failure to provide quality education for all of its young people, and failure to stem the rampant domestic terror of mass shootings and gun violence was disheartening and demoralizing. In addition, there was the continuing issue of racial disparity, discontent, and separatism that underscores the problems of American society.

On a personal level, as a member of a racial minority in America, I can attest to the fact that racism is not only prevalent in the US, but alive and well. Ugly sentiments about anyone who is different are freely voiced, especially now with the newly elected president and the nationalistic spirit of this administration.

As Black Americans, my husband and I couldn't ignore the injustices and inconsistencies of politics, media, and policing that are undeniably part of life for many people of color in the US. Often racism is not overt but manifested as a disadvantageous bias to a person of color. The experience of encountering bias, discrimination, or outright racism in housing, policing, or employment is an unfortunate reality of being a minority in America.

It can be daunting to try and keep an open mind and positive spirit as you go about your daily life. And I have to say, it's easy (or perhaps the norm) for a person of color to have their interpersonal guard up before going out for the day, never knowing what to expect.

In general, there's a disconnection, and unfortunately a lack of community, in American culture. Will sold his large suburban home when we married, and we decided my small bungalow in a lovely older neighborhood which was convenient to town would be sufficient for us. However, the area was being re-discovered by a younger generation of professionals who were starting their families and building larger, more expansive, stylish new homes. These newcomers were nice enough, but we rarely interacted with one another except for the occasional wave and small talk about lawns and the weather. Everyone mostly stayed to themselves.

Both my husband and I had adult children and relatives who lived variously in state, out-of-state, or out of the country, who were busy with their lives and building their careers. We chatted, Face-Timed, or arranged visits as frequently as schedules would allow.

As a consequence of marrying later in life, Will and I had fewer shared friends and acquaintances, but we found ourselves building associations more on the activities we both enjoyed, i.e., the track club, hiking groups, rafting groups, etc., essentially activities that could be replicated elsewhere. We mused about trying a new way of life and after many conversations and reflections, decided to explore living out of the country for a breath of fresh air and adventure.

We decided that Mexico would be our destination, primarily because of its relative proximity to the US, the fact that it was drivable (albeit an adventurous full day-and-a-half drive), and the cost of living would be within our retirement budget. Neither of us had much of a handle on Spanish, but we figured we'd fumble through with Google Translate and quick practice sessions with Duolingo. We were not naïve about what to expect in Mexico; the country has its own set of problems, and we tried to familiarize ourselves with what we might expect.

We researched YouTube and International Living articles and film clips, and quickly discovered that once you repeat an internet search once or twice, you're rewarded with an algorithm of copious referrals and suggestions, which in a few cases, were of locations and cities we'd never heard of. All of this worked for the good, however, because that's how we discovered Mazatlán.

Through the years we had vacationed in the tourist towns of Cancún, Playa de Carmen, Puerto Vallarta, and Cabo, but Mazatlán was different in that it's an actual working city on the Pacific coast and a kingpin of the shrimping industry. It appealed to us because it wasn't just a tourist town, but had a real mixture of locals, history, and beauty, and felt more "authentically" Mexican. Historically popular with Canadians and movie stars, Mazatlán also had gorgeous beaches and a delicious food culture. During the '50s Hollywood developed a Western studio in nearby Durango, and stars like John Wayne, John Barrymore, and Rita Hayworth vacationed in Mazatlán to enjoy the sea and sun while on break from filming.

Once we decided our direction, we opted to rent our house instead of selling it or leaving it unoccupied, just in case our move to Mexico didn't work out. Our house was a small ranch that happened to be located in an area that was growing in popularity. We discarded, donated, and eventually made decisions on what to take, what to save, and what to leave behind. We basically took only what we could pack into our Mazda SUV with our two dogs. A few large items we decided to temporarily put in storage.

We selected a local property management company to handle the rental, oversight, and transactions on the property for a reasonable fee. We were fortunate in that we were able to rent our house for not only enough to cover our mortgage, taxes, and insurance, but to also cover our rental in Mexico!

Family and friends were a mix of amazed, fearful, excited, and apprehensive about our venture. Our drive from Atlanta was … an adventure. We drove only during daylight. Hampton Inn was our choice for an overnight stop as they accepted pets. We crossed into Mexico at Columbia, about a 40-minute drive north of Laredo, Texas. Two border guards at the Columbia checkpoint asked to search our car, which was stuffed with our belongings. One guard asked my husband to open the carrier on top. Before he could unlock it, the other guard asked him to open the hatch. As soon as he did, items came tumbling out. Both guards smiled, petted the dogs, and waved us through.

We rented Airbnbs for our first few weeks in Mazatlán, which were inexpensive and relatively easy to find. Before we arrived, we searched for and contacted some rental agents online, looking for a more permanent rental. We were a bit uneasy about finding a suitable rental easily because we discovered most landlords do not permit pets. Implausible as it seems, we found our rental in Mazatlán via a Facebook post. The home we found was a three-bedroom, two-bath house with a two-car garage, and a lovely courtyard for under $700 dollars a month. It was in a lovely neighborhood just three blocks from the beach and the owner had no problem accepting pets. Needless to say, we were delighted.

In many ways we found Mazatlán not such a difficult transition from the US, as it was "sophisticated" enough to have a well-stocked Walmart, Sam's Club, and Home Depot. Best of all is the abundance of fresh produce at neighborhood *fruterías*. Several awesome restaurants, such as the upscale Agatha and San Juan Lenaro, and the more casual, open-air Las Brochetas, have become our favorites.

My husband has taken up bicycling again and joined a couple of other expats who ride the oceanfront malecón several times a week. For a break in their 10-mile ride, they stop for breakfast in the Olas Altas area, where the restaurateurs remember and greet them. Besides the fact that they're regular customers, they're quite distinctive as senior African Americans.

Within our first year, we met several American expats that have become our community. We have shared experiences, built bonds, and become friends. We have occasional dinners together, have gone on scenic catamaran rides, shared birthday celebrations, and organized meet-ups for various professional sports events. We've also established friendships with Mazatlecos who've lived in the US, speak fluent English, and have extended themselves to us

We've found the Mazatlecos to be pleasant, endearing people. We've met many of our neighbors, established relations with local shopkeepers and drivers we hire occasionally, and are recognized and welcomed by proprietors of restaurants we regularly frequent.

We have certainly found the pace of life in Mazatlán calming. Seldom is anyone in a hurry, it seems, about anything. So much is taken in stride. Transactions of any type are usually completed with a *gracias* and a smile, and rarely do you see tempers flaring. Children and teenagers seem well-behaved, tolerant, and polite, and there are very few pouty faces of children or teenagers accompanying their parents on late-night strolls on the malecón.

Of course we've had to make adjustments, mostly related to the climate. Being this far south and close to the Tropic of Cancer, the heat and humidity were more than we were accustomed to in the southeastern US. We quickly learned to limit our excursions, whether shopping, strolling, or sightseeing, to either early morning or after sunset.

We also had to adjust how we looked at things. Irregular and unsafe construction procedures, like dead electrical wires dangling from old or unused electrical boxes, random holes or gaps in bricks or sidewalks, or sewer water bubbling from clogged drains in many streets after heavy rains are common. Traffic and pedestrian guidelines are significantly lax and it's still amazing to us how few accidents occur in high-traffic areas,

However, we found ourselves falling for the lifestyle, peace, serenity, calm, and stress-free life of Mazatlán. Of course, because we're retirees with stable incomes living in an economy where the cost of living is significantly less than in the US, it's easily sustainable for us. Mazatlán will continue to be our home for the foreseeable future.

Truthfully, we don't see ourselves moving back to the United States. Of course, we'll visit, schedule for special occasions, and maintain contacts, but Will and I both agree that we actually don't miss very much about living in the US. This was a good move.

⌒

*Ruth Thompson Artis is a native Washingtonian, born and raised in Washington, DC. Retiring after a federal career in both DC and Atlanta, Ruth embarked on a few years stint of teaching ESL in China. The experience fueled her desire for more travel outside of the US. With an appetite for exploration of other lands and cultures, Ruth and husband Will turned their sights to Mexico in 2022 and settled in Mazatlán.*

*Living in Mexico has been an adventure, a learning experience, and an attitude adjustment, which has broadened their lives immensely. Ruth and her husband have been captivated with the essential beauty of Mazatlán and the warmth of its residents. She is learning Spanish and also enjoys distance walking or biking on cool mornings as well as cross-circuit training.*

# 22. The Perpetual Motion of Re-Inventing Oneself

Teri Salahi

San Blas, Nayarit

My biological father flew me into the airstrip of San Blas, Nayarit, in spring break 1979. I was 15 years old. San Blas is a small fishing village on the west coast of Nayarit. It's easy to walk everywhere on cobblestone streets; to the beaches of Las Islitas by day; to the vibrant plaza in at night for social visits and a *paleta* (ice cream). What a vacation! I was introduced to the simple charm of a Mexican village and loved it.

I returned to my home in Texas where I'd always lived with my mother and second father. A "Leave-It-To-Beaver" life. My half-brother and I had parents who were interested and interactive with our lives and our friends. I was a straight-A student, without opening a book. Freshman year in high school went by; I participated in all available sports and took every advanced course I could, yet I was still intellectually bored.

In 1979, six weeks into my sophomore year, I made a choice that would change my life forever: I decided to live with my biological father in Mexico. I flew to El Paso to meet him, and we drove to San Blas. There he left me to live while he worked in the state of Michoacan. A 16-year-old, living in a simple *pueblo* where everyone knows everybody, and kids are free to go about as they want safely. It was a complete 180 from my previous life.

I befriended a local family with 11 kids; four of them were around my age. Their family was so welcoming, and their mother was a bundle of unconditional love. They accepted me and I became part of their family as their *gringa* 12th sibling. What was one more mouth to feed? Subconsciously I'm sure I also gravitated toward them as a sort of protection, as I was alone in a foreign country where I spoke almost nothing of the language. Not that I ever felt afraid—my experience was quite the opposite.

I learned to do my part, helping with the cooking, cleaning, and ironing. I washed my own clothes on a rub board just as my Mexican sisters did. Their house was filled with music that their father would play. I did what their kids did, running errands, going to the daily market, and riding to Tepic, the capital city about an hour away, for supplies. There were family outings at the river, evenings out with the girls, dancing at the local *discoteca* on the weekends, plaza time, card games late into the night during rainy season, and plenty of beach time with the girls and the family.

At that time, telegrams were the most effective means of communication into and out of San Blas. Every month or so, my father would send a telegram for me to meet him, usually in Guadalajara, about a five-hour bus ride away. The bus drivers always made me sit in the front seat so they could keep an eye on me. It was the perfect vantage point. Over time I memorized the route and seasonal changes, specifically burn season, with its distinctive sights and smells from sugar cane fields being burned before harvest. Often my dad and I would spend our time driving to archeological sites, his passion. I enjoyed being with him but can't say the archeology stuff appealed to me as a teenager. All I wanted was to be back in San Blas, where I could be a kid with my friends.

After about two years, my father unexpectedly told me I was going back to Texas. He dropped me off at my mother's front door in Austin and I was left to repair and reinvent my life in the USA.

I focused on building a life in the States the way we're programmed to do and did "the American thing." I got a job in insurance and my career soared. I worked during the day, attended university at night. I got married and divorced, bought houses, cars, and stuff.

I kept in touch with my Mexican family for about a year, with letters back and forth, but when I got married communication faded away. I held the beautiful childhood memories of my time in

San Blas as my most cherished experience of a lifetime, in a kind of Pandora's box of hope, not to be opened.

In my forties, I traveled by myself in an unorthodox style. I sailed throughout the southeast Caribbean on a masted sailing ship out of Grenada, went to a small island in Honduras to work to be a Divemaster, and took a trip to Peru, where I went by motorized canoe three days deep into the Manu National Forest of the Amazonia, coming out of the jungle experience the grandeur of Machu Picchu. I kept meticulous notes of the weird and wonderful things I saw in a little notebook, which I wrote into stories at night. Over time, my storytelling improved. My readers were hooked, living vicariously through the interesting, unexpected twists and turns I had on these "adventure vacations."

Although proud of my personal successes, in 2011 I recognized that I was restless and no longer content. I was fed up with corporate America. I'd spent 40 years trying to stuff my widespread wings into a small square box. My soul was broken and I was lost; alone and lonely within myself. I knew I needed to change something. I quit my fourth-floor office-with-a-window corporate job. Beyond that, I had no idea what to do next.

I was born, raised, and lived in Austin, Texas my entire life, other than the two years I'd spent in San Blas. I'd never wanted to return to Mexico, afraid to open my Pandora's box and contaminate the beautiful memories. Yet suddenly, I wanted to try to recreate and write about what I considered the greatest experience of my life. I pulled out all my letters, telegrams, and photos from that time, put them in postmark order, and began to piece together a timeline. After 30 years of silence, I searched the internet for some sign of my Mexican family.

I found my Mexican sister on Facebook, and she was loving and curious. She and her family had wondered what happened to me, and we tried to catch up as best we could. Her ailing father was asking for me, and she begged me to visit. I resisted. I felt ashamed that I'd abandoned them for so long with no contact, and at the same time didn't want to open old wounds of my parents which I'd worked so hard to repair. I also didn't want to test my memories, which I'd been guarding for so long. But in the end, I chose to bravely and gracefully face my fears, and in December 2011, I flew to Puerto Vallarta, where my Mexican sisters welcomed me and were my caretakers as I returned to visit San Blas.

I no longer knew Spanish (Tex-Mex doesn't count) and was totally dependent on Google Translate, which I learned is only about 50% accurate. During the two-week visit, I saw all 11 siblings, their mother, and their father. I was amazed when people I'd met 30 years before recognized me on the street in San Blas. It was an overwhelming and surreal experience. We were all adults; they were all married with kids. I felt a deep sense of comfort and peace, and one night, sitting in the plaza trying to digest all that was happening, I realized why my father had left me there while he went away to work. He knew the townspeople of San Blas were truly kindhearted and that it would be safe for me.

For the next six years, I returned to San Blas twice a year for two-week visits. I stayed with various members of my Mexican family, rode a bicycle to the beach each sunrise and watched brilliant sunsets with the iconic lighthouse in the distance. When I emailed friends back home, they remarked on how different I sounded; there was a tranquility in me they'd never seen when I was in the States. As I returned to San Blas again and again, that stuck in my mind.

Somewhere around the end of 2016, I decided my next trip to Mexico would be a reconnaissance visit to learn what my options were: rent, buy, build. San Blas is a small fishing village, with dirt and cobblestone streets, full of cows, animals, children, dogs, motorbikes, and bicycles. Could I find something where me and the loves of my life, my two delicate foo-foo dogs, could live comfortably?

At the beginning of 2017, I did just that. I visited all my contacts, asked a zillion questions, looked at options, and somehow, some way, it just happened. The house next door to a friend might be for sale; my friend would make inquiries about it. From that day forward, everything fell easily into place, which supposedly means it's meant to be.

By August, I was closing the sale of my house in the States and selling off everything, and then, within two days, I closed on my new Mexican house. I stayed with my parents temporarily while I put some remaining pieces in order for moving. The San Blas house needed things like air conditioning; immigration paperwork for my Mexican residency and for my furry kid's importation had to be started in the USA.

Finally, on Nov. 17, 2017, I loaded myself, my kids, and four suitcases on a plane and headed for Puerto Vallarta. It was the hardest thing I'd ever done in my life, but I knew it was right. I rented a car and drove us to San Blas. As I unpacked and organized our space, I told the kids the hard part was over. We'd made it.

It took me about a week and an "Aha!" moment to realize I was wrong about the hard part being over. In reality, the hard part was just beginning. I had to completely build a new life from scratch in a foreign country, where I didn't know the language, culture, or laws. I knew nothing about how to live, survive, and thrive here. Yes, I did choose to move to a *pueblo* where I had a history, and with that, a network of acquaintances. Nevertheless, the thought of re-inventing my life at 54 overwhelmed me and I was in shock for days.

There was a long list of things to be done: Go to immigration and start the second half of the residency process. Identify all monthly and annual bills, get them put in my name, and figure out how best to pay them. Find and purchase a vehicle that had plates from my now home state of Nayarit. Get a Mexican cell phone number and service. All of this seemed simple enough, but clearly, it was not. I had to find these places, figure out the processes, and navigate the city of Tepic—all with only about 20% Spanish language skills.

In Mexico, the amount of actual paperwork required, along with multiple copies, is incredible. My experience is that procedures are done one slow step at a time until they're completed. The "next step" remains a mystery until the next visit, and many times it's a sidestep that could have been completed concurrently during the previous visit. It's just how their process works and it's best to follow it with a kind smile, one baby step at a time, until the end is finally reached. It took five visits to immigration before I had my Permanent Resident "green card" in hand.

For each initial *trámite* (loosely translated as a piece of business or a process), you must physically go to the office and wait in line, all the while hoping you have all the paperwork needed to do what you're trying to do. Standing in long lines for a long time is normal and another part of the process that requires patience. I've become accustomed to it, and it doesn't bother me anymore; I just plan for it. Waiting in lines also offers the chance to say hello, mingle with other residents, and improve my language skills.

Buying a vehicle was a must; I needed my own wheels. My Mexican friends recommended not purchasing a vehicle from the coastal areas or *pueblos* with cobblestone streets because of wear and tear. I went to a big reputable used car dealership in Guadalajara. Vehicle purchases are interesting. There are no "titles" as we know them in the States. All vehicles carry their original paper invoice for life, with all endorsements of sales on the back. These will be registered with the state, but the documentation of ownership must be the original paper invoice, no matter how old, frail, and brown it may have become. I learned to store the paperwork in an airtight Ziploc bag, safe from a possible hurricane or flood.

The long and short of learning the language is to fake it till you make it. Overall, Mexicans are friendly people with kind hearts. If you try to speak what words you can of Spanish, they're proud to help you the rest of the way. You don't have to know every single word a person says—you only need to understand the subject and context. Pick out the words you know, follow the context, and only ask questions when it's needed to solidify the context. One of the easiest ways I learned and practiced Spanish at first was speaking with children when I was at the plaza in the evenings. They speak more simply, they're fascinating, they listen intently, and they'll correct you with zero judgment.

In many ways, Mexicans have a formal, polite culture, and friends, family, and helping others always come first. Greetings like, "How are you?" "How's your day?" or "How's the family?" are always prerequisites to begin any conversation. If they're smiling, smile. If they're humble, be humble. If they laugh, softly smile along with them. A kind greeting and a smile given to everyone you pass along the street works wonders. Over time more understanding will come.

I learn new words according to what I'm involved in. My first project was to tear down the uninhabitable front room and rebuild an apartment and carport from the ground up. That year, my new Spanish words were all about construction and concrete as I watched in amazement what was involved in building a concrete house in a rural Mexican town.

Next, I established some basic medical providers, and my Spanish expanded as needed, by subject and illness. As far as doctors, it's much the same as the States: it's hit or miss if you like them. My experience here has been that they're all notably educated—most have done internships in the US or Europe—and there are many accredited hospitals. Appointments can be scheduled within 1-2 days any day of the week, including half-days on Saturdays. And doctors take as long as is needed; there's no hurry-up, 15-minute window.

The simplest way to describe medical costs in Mexico is that they're about the same as a co-pay in the States. I pay for my regular medical costs out-of-pocket, and I purchased a Mexican health insurance plan for the unforeseen major accident or illness. I can go to the pharmacy and pick up daily medications I need anytime and buy as much as I want.

What a blessing to have a simple, self-serving system without bureaucracy! I love that I can go to the diagnostics clinic on my own and request, for example, my mammogram, bone density scan, and blood work. In about three hours I can return and pick up the results without a doctor's authorization. Then I make an appointment with my doctor, bring the results, and it's all handled in one doctor's visit. Very efficient.

I'm inspired by living in this small, historical fishing village. There are three beaches near me that are usually empty except on weekends. I can ride my bike, walk on the beach, sit at a palapa and absorb the power and Zen of Mother Ocean while enjoying a fresh seafood meal. San Blas flanks an awesomely green and beautiful jungle mountain chain where mango, papaya, and limes are grown. It has history, ruins, pyramids, and jungle waterboat rides to a spring-fed pool where you can swim. Our mangroves are a world-renowned site for bird migration and there's a community of jaguars that live in and about the mangroves and jungle. A new toll road from San Blas to Tepic was recently completed, and it's one of the most beautiful drives there is! I especially love coming out of the tunnel and descending to the flat lands of the coast and Matanchén Bay, with the view all the way to San Blas point.

I wanted to integrate into the genuine local community of Mexicans. There's something in their lifestyle that's calm and content, regardless of their challenges. I know and greet all my neighbors every day. I buy my staples from locally owned stores. I befriended the woman who owns a corner store, Doña A; a beautiful lady with a beautiful soul. I used to help out in the evenings, weighing customers' ham or eggs, handling the money, stocking the drink refrigerators. I met so many locals this way. Doña A and I were genuinely interested in each other, although at first neither she nor I could understand the Spanish either of us spoke. We eventually developed a deep friendship.

After several months of volunteering at the store, I was surprised to find out that her son knew of me from my adolescent days. We started dating. He was a dapper, four-stripe Chief Mechanical Engineer of a large ocean fishing vessel. I'd been single and independent for 30 years; he's at sea for two months, on land for a couple weeks, and then the cycle repeats, with December off. Both being middle-aged adults, this "dating" routine was perfect for us. My Spanish was only about the 40% level, but we managed to communicate. We had a common history from my childhood years in San Blas, and I'd already earned the trust of his family from time spent helping with the store. One day, poof, we got married.

Within weeks, COVID hit—a surreal worldwide experience. G returned to sea; I moved into the apartment and remodeled the back house. That project was completed in six months; now what was I going to do? As I watched COVID unfolding online in my American hometown and around the world, I can honestly say I felt the safest exactly where I was, in a remote Mexican village on the ocean. But after a year of staying at home, the remodel project finished, I was restless. I decided if I had to continue this protocol, I needed to change my view, travel to a new location, and stay cooped up there.

I love to drive and absorb the beauty of the scenery around me. As I learned and adjusted to driving in México, I found it much safer than driving in the States. I've driven a hundred thousand kilometers throughout México, in towns, on highways, and on toll roads.

Usually I drive alone, and as a single foreign female, with a foo-foo dog as my companion, I have my driving rules. I keep my car meticulously maintained, and I only drive during daylight hours, with a general rule of driving five hours a day. It's been my experience that somewhere along the way I'll miss an exit or get confused with signage—something that adds an hour or two to the trip.

Part of my traveling goal is to re-visit all 32 Mexican states. The country has many beautiful historical cities, as well as the federally designated *Pueblos Magicos*, small towns or natural wonders worthy of a visit. I also wanted to go back to the archeological ruins I have photos of that I'd visited in my youth. One by one, I'm going to the same places and taking a current picture. Nostalgically comparing them is fascinating. In my older age, I've grown to like visiting these archeological treasures.

The first year I traveled to towns within a 150-mile radius of home, which was a comfort zone for me. It's amazing how many cities and cute towns one can experience just outside of where you live! I visited Mexcaltitán, Santa María del Oro, Mazatlán, Puerto Vallarta, Nuevo Nayarit, Mascota, San Sebastián del Oeste, Talpa de Allende, Bucerías, Sayulita, Amatlán de las Cañas, Tequila, Guadalajara, and then Manzanillo, where G's ship came into port.

As I increased my radius of travel, I visited cities, towns, and *Pueblos Magicos* in the states of Jalisco, Querétaro, Guanajuato, Hidalgo, Mexico City and back through Michoacan, to see the Monarch butterflies.

I'm now finishing my seventh year of living in México with a home in San Blas. The sudden death of my mother-in-law, my best friend, about three years ago hit me hard, especially with G out to sea. That accounts for part of my wandering travels these past years, trying to persevere through the pain of loss. Sadly, G converted back to the purest sense of being a *marinero* (seaman). He abandoned me and cut off contact without a word. But that's OK—I have no regrets, only beautiful memories.

I find myself once again working to reinvent my life. What

I know is that my soul lives in San Blas and I'm grateful that my life choices introduced me to and then inspired me to return. I'm sad to have left my aging parents in Austin, but we keep in touch multiple times a week and I visit them several times a year. We communicate easily and often on WhatsApp, and I share pictures and road links of where I am on adventure.

Here in San Blas, I have a good house, a dependable Mexican family and friends, and a warm community of local Mexican townspeople. They're my home base and my solid network, as I continue to live, learn, and grow.

I always have an eye on the horizon for my next travel adventure in my quest to explore Mexico. Hot on my list are Morelia, Michoacan, or Oaxaca, for the Day of the Dead celebrations. I've been told they have fascinatingly different cultures than the rest of Mexico. As I relax in San Blas through the tranquil summer months, I'm gearing up to expand my driving radius level a notch.

I think I returned to México in 2011 to close a circle of my youth in reuniting with my Mexican family after 30 years of silence. It nurtured my restless soul to be back there again, inspiring me to move my entire life; a brave, vulnerable, and daunting change. I reinvented my life with the colorful culture and the kindness of the people. It's a different way to live, one that values life, people, community, and simple living. I learned that circles do not close; life goes round and round like the earth around the sun, in perpetuity. For me, one's life journey is about going through experiences and reinventing yourself along the way.

Why do I stay here? Mexican culture is warm, friendly, and fed by human kindness. I'm comfortable and tranquil, and it's peaceful living here. I'm also continuously learning, keeping my mind active so I can reach out, experience, learn, accept, grow, and flourish in this beautiful country I call home, México.

⌒

*Teri Salahi has lived full-time in San Blas, Nayarit, Mexico, since 2017. A native of Austin, Texas, she had a career in insurance for 30+ years and also attended university classes at night for more than two decades to keep her mind growing. She has been a mother to four papillon dogs, the joys and companions of her life. In her younger years, Teri travelled extensively throughout the USA, then went off the beaten path to the Caribbean Island cultures of Grenada, St. Vincent, and the Grenadines, all the islands in between, Honduras, and then Peru, blogging her adventures along the way.*

*Later life brought a calling to return to Mexico, reinvent herself, and submerse herself in the Mexican culture, where she finds tranquility within. Teri now lives a soulful, peaceful life near Mother Ocean with San Blas as her home base, continuing to travel and re-visit all 32 beautiful states of Mexico with her furry little buddy, Oliver Joe. She believes that when you find your place where peace surrounds you, you should engage, expand, and experience it; you only live once.*

# 23. Tales of an Expat: Learning to Be at Home in the World

Raechel Bratnick

San Miguel de Allende, Guanajuato

It's nighttime as my driver stops on a cobblestone street in front of a closed door. As he unloads my suitcase, I ring the doorbell and hope I will be met by someone who speaks English. The driver and I wait. As I'm about to ring the bell again, a tiny grey-haired woman opens the door. She welcomes me into a garden, unimaginable from the street. Plants and trees burst from every direction. A tiny stream runs to a pool.

My life as an expat has begun, even though I don't know it. I think I'm just visiting San Miguel de Allende, Mexico, for a month-long retreat from the intensity of the last four years of my life in New Jersey.

In 2007, my husband, Michael, and I were living a relatively normal American life: marriage, two children, a home in the suburbs. We ran two businesses from our home offices. We vacationed at the beach or sometimes to Europe. We sent our children to international camps to give them an experience of the larger world beyond our white, middle-class suburb. Our youngest daughter had just graduated college. We expected to work for another five years, then retire in the US Already we were dreaming of finding an artistic, liberal community where we could write and make art and find ways to share our gifts.

Then life threw us a curve ball. We'd been home for a month after a blissful vacation when Michael seemed to have the flu. Then he looked jaundiced. Suddenly he was diagnosed with a rare cancer, with no cure or remission possible. Our dreams shattered. He was 65 and I was 64. Four months later I was a widow. Now the future was both wide open and narrower than I ever expected.

This was February 2008; within months, a global financial crisis, the most severe since the Great Depression, melted the stock market. I stumbled through grief and financial catastrophe. Everything I believed secure had disappeared. I felt an enormous sky overhead.

I would often read a quote Michael had tacked on his office bulletin board: "One doesn't discover new lands without consenting to lose sight of the shore for a long time." It became a lighthouse as I prepared to leave the American dream. My accomplishments were many: an advanced education, successful career life, marriage, home ownership, mothering. My children were in their mid-twenties, beginning to anchor themselves in the world. I was ready for an adventure by myself.

But I was also anxious and perplexed; how would I know where to go? A friend suggested San Miguel de Allende, Mexico, and my curiosity was sparked. I knew very little about Mexico and nothing about this city, so why not?

And now here I was staying for a month in San Miguel with no plans. I wanted to simply soak up the atmosphere. The first morning, with the sun flashing through the floor-to-ceiling windows, I looked out on a blank wall that was the color of the long wooden table in front of those windows. I saw a place to create art.

I was curious and hungry and ready to see this city. After breakfast at Café Rama, where I savored *huevos rancheros*, a refreshing green drink, and a dark coffee, I returned to my *casita*. A man with a paint brush was on a ladder in the garden, painting a mural of the Parroquia church.

This trip to San Miguel elicited two important dreams. In the first one I was volunteering to be an aerial artist, hanging 10 feet above the floor—even though I'm afraid of heights, I was willing to go beyond my fears. Then at the very end of the month I dreamed a straightforward message: "Go towards what it is you are afraid of. It is the remedy and pulls you to it." Now I understood that I was being propelled to leave the United States and move to Mexico, so I made plans to return the following August and experience daily life from a different side of the city. This time, I lived close to Fabrica la Aurora, a textile mill for 90 years which had been converted into galleries and art studios. After coffee under the trees at Geek and Coffee, I'd wander up towards the Jardin, stopping at the Mercado de Artisans, filled with handmade Mexican crafts.

I also joined a Facebook page for expats. There I learned that Mexico was redesigning its immigration process. The current process for becoming a permanent resident was still simple, and my monthly Social Security qualified me financially. This seemed more reasonable than leaving every few months to renew a tourist visa, even if this wasn't going to be my permanent home. By now I knew that I would move to Mexico as soon as my house was on the market. I found an immigration lawyer who spoke English to guide me through the process.

I put my house up for sale, flew to Mexico, and moved into a sublet in a *colonia* that was new to me. I was ready to start my life as an expat. Five days later my lawyer and I went to the Mexican immigration office, and a few hours later, I was a permanent resident of Mexico, which I still am today. Ten years later, the residency process is not as simple.

Living in a very quiet town in New Jersey for 30 years, I was ready for stimulation and difference. I was ready for the smiles of Mexican people. A few days before I left New Jersey, I was in the grocery store and noticed that no one smiled at each other. In Mexico, smiles appear on people's faces without expectations. Silently they say, "Happy to see you!" Their smiles evoke my smile.

As I was dismantling my life in New Jersey, I set an intention for simplicity. I wanted to be the kind of expat who lives lightly on the earth. I wanted to be available for adventure. I didn't want to be bogged down by possessions or pets or children. Of course, this was scary, as I was an American possessed by possessions. But I knew I needed a focus if I were going to adapt to another country.

Now I wandered during the day; evenings I scanned Facebook, looking for my next apartment, as my sublet was nearly up. And there it was: a one-bedroom apartment on the third floor of a small building in the same *colonia*. I called it "the penthouse" because of the floor-to-ceiling windows that looked out on a wide patio with a view of the mountains. Lightning storms were wondrous.

I gave up having a car, walking everywhere or taking a taxi at night. It was great exercise walking uphill to the center of the city, altitude 6,400 feet. For the six years after Michael died, I'd lived like a hermit: working, writing, grieving. Now I was learning how to be a social being. I continued working with my American clients, but here I had an endless sense that I was a tourist on vacation. I learned the way of the land: drink bottled water, disinfect all produce, don't flush paper in the toilet, heat the bedroom, turn off the gas heater, quickly hop into bed because there's no furnace or insulation. Expats are friendly; let yourself meet new people. Be surprised: one day a store is open, the next day not.

I soon realized that expats are a transitory population, which meant that I too had the freedom to leave. Friends asked me if San Miguel was forever: I always answered, "I don't know," because I didn't. I'm here for now. "Now" is my security.

Life continued to surprise me. Once my house sold, I was on my way back to Mexico with four large suitcases, the rest of my possessions in storage.

My neighbors greeted me with a glass of wine. They'd retired early to San Miguel after visiting several times and already they were building their own house nearby. Years later, we still enjoy sharing our adventures each time they return from their home in the States, especially after the pandemic, which upended everyone's lives.

Now that Mexico was going to be home, I began researching San Miguel's healthcare resources. Americans believe their healthcare is the best in the world so I was under the impression that healthcare in any country outside the US would be mediocre.

My first serious healthcare situation was not with my body, but with my eldest daughter's. Unexpectedly pregnant, she came to San Miguel to have her baby because of the strong midwifery program here. After a skilled emergency cesarean, I held my first grandchild, born in "my" city, the city of Michael the Archangel. My husband's name was Michael and now my grandson carries his name. I felt like the Universe was blessing me and my daughter with an unexpected continuation of love.

Then, another surprise: my daughter was accepted to graduate school in Tel Aviv, Israel. I was attached to my grandson, and since I hadn't put down deep roots in San Miguel, I made plans to leave with them. I packed, sold some things, and shipped a few boxes to the States. The next chapter of my expat life began.

Israel did not go as planned but became a steppingstone for living in a medieval hill town in southern Italy. An expat life often has unexpected course changes. It's a practice in pivoting and developing resilient skills while smiling.

A woman I'd met in San Miguel connected me with a friend in Italy who could legally rent me an apartment. After an email exchange, I flew to Bari on the Adriatic, spent a week in the countryside of Basilicata, and said "yes" to a life in a medieval walled town. I was in awe as we drove the winding roads west to Irsina. Wheat fields surrounded the plateau, a landscape like the Palouse hills in northern Idaho where I grew up. As a child I'd dreamed of ancient Europe. After a week in Irsina I said yes to this new plan.

Now my life centered around southern Italian culture: morning shopping, main meal and siesta in the afternoon when everything in town closes for four hours, evenings beginning with *la passeggiata* stroll, ending with pizza at 9 or 10 p.m, children included.

My apartment was hidden beneath the street and houses, carved into the old wall that had been built in the year 1000. Stone walls five feet thick and beautiful brick *boveda* ceilings created a feeling of time being suspended. It was a perfect place to complete my memoir of my husband's death and heal my grief.

Outside my front door was a large terrace that overlooked fields and hills below, where trees laden with figs looked down a steep path lined with olive trees. Here is where I'd hang my wet clothes to dry. Here is where I'd hear the baker's wife screaming at him. Here is where I'd gaze at the flat-topped mountain that changed colors with the sun's path.

My favorite time of the week was Sunday afternoon. As the locals enjoyed their siestas, I'd wander the labyrinth of cobblestone streets. I liked to visit the 13th century cathedral where Mantegna's stature of Saint Euphemia, her hand in a lion's mouth, reminded me of the Tarot card for "Strength," a good patron saint for a village that has endured for centuries.

Securing a visa or *permesso di soggiorno* for non-EU residents is time consuming and must be started in one's native country. I was fortunate to have friends in the US to stay with for the three months of that initial process. I flew to Italy to tackle the next 13 steps: getting the correct stamps on the application, paying fees, being seriously fingerprinted, plus making several trips to the immigration office in the stunning ancient city of Matera. To qualify for a visa in Italy, you have to show a monthly income that's three times what Mexico had required. At the end of it all, I had a visa for one year; similar steps would have to be repeated each year for five years until I was eligible for a permanent visa. (Three years later the pandemic would interrupt that process.)

For me, Italy was a world of solitude. Though Irsina has a population of 4,000, the majority of people lived outside the old wall where all the shops were. You enter the old city through a massive arch to a plaza with a few restaurants. From there, a maze of streets, with no cars, winds around and back and forth. Only the elderly stayed on in the old town, the buildings emptying as they died, until people from the British Isles, Belgium, and even South Africa began to buy and remodel the old stone houses. Most new owners bought them for holiday homes. In August of 2017 I was the first American seeking residency; that winter there were only 11 of us living there year-round. Now the village is populated with foreigners, including many Americans.

Life for me was a storybook. Entering the courtyard to my house, I walked down a series of steep stone stairs, past parakeets singing from their cages hanging on the wall, past a workshop filled with ancient tools and artifacts. The key to my house was made of steel, forged in a fire. When I asked the man in the hardware store if he could make a duplicate, he laughed. I was kidding, of course.

The door to my house was medieval, designed with a small window that could be opened to receive goods or talk to a visitor without actually opening it. To let someone into your house, you must trust them. First, the huge iron key opened a lock on the window.

I'd reach in and lift a wooden block from a steel bar that held the door shut, then swing open another wooden panel. Once inside, I'd put the block back in its holder, then carefully walk down the high steps to the kitchen below. I was home.

Daily needs were easy to satisfy here, even though most people didn't speak English and I had no Italian. But even if I had spoken some Italian, the people here spoke Irsenese, a dialect combination of Arabic, French Norman, old Spanish, and modern Italian that reflected their history.

My lack of even rudimentary Italian was tested when I was suddenly thrust into the Italian medical world. For several weeks, I'd been unable to sleep longer than 90 minutes at a time because of unrelenting nerve pain in my leg. Desperate to relive it, I found an acupuncturist through a clerk at the local pharmacy and hired Christa, a friend, to drive me to a town an hour away a few times a week until the pain calmed down.

A visiting specialist sent me to Matera for an MRI, which identified three herniated disks and scoliosis. Using a visiting ultrasound machine, he injected cortisone into the inflamed disc. All without English. (No wonder I was in pain: I'd been pounding the streets of Berlin, visiting my daughter and grandson, and walking all over Rome.)

Now I joined Italians at the physical therapy office just outside the old town, learning exercises from an Irsinese with no English. For six weeks we handed our phones back and forth navigating the Google translation app. Slowly but surely, my body healed. Throughout the process I leaned on my friend Ann from Ireland, who'd lived a long time in Irsina and spoke some Italian. She accompanied me on my first visit to each doctor; after that, I trusted the doctors and they trusted me. She also discovered a genius who custom designed orthotics for my flat feet.

In my search for a dentist who would do preventative teeth cleaning the way it was done every six months in the US, I found a reliable dentist who did three root canals as she repaired a dying tooth, all without an assistant, her tools immaculately sterilized and separately packaged in plastic bags. Once again, we communicated through smiles and limited English. At the end of it all she kept reducing her already modest fee. The tooth survived for a few years and finally a dentist in Massachusetts had to remove it and make a bridge, costing thousands.

In Irsina there are no receptionists or appointments; you just stop by your doctor's office, read the note on the door that says when they'll be open, then show up and wait your turn. No numbers—you simply notice who's ahead of you and wait. A visit to the doctor requires patience, so I usually took my Kindle to read, but everyone else took this time to visit with each other. I used to look up from my Kindle and watch their hands moving as they spoke.

One of the amazing parts of expat life is the unexpected: The first spring in Irsina, I heard that the town was planning their very first passion play which would involve the whole town. That night I joined the throng, following the unfolding of the story in the old town, winding our way along narrow streets from station to station, each scene in a different location. To add to the mystery, the night was foggy, the moon barely visible. We were back in time; we were outside of time.

Being in Italy made it easy for me to meet my daughter in Berlin and Dublin, where she lived for six months after her time in Israel. When she landed a job in Portland, Maine, I visited for holidays. I felt like a portable expat, able to transition from culture to culture. I continued to work remotely on Zoom and led in-person retreats in Italy, France, and Scotland. And then another surprise: A few days before another trip to Maine, my daughter got a new job in Sacramento, California. "Would I like to go on a road trip across the United States?" she asked. As her mother, it was natural for me to turn on a dime and help them get settled in a new city, a new job, and a new school. So off we went on another adventure.

Returning to Italy in mid-February 2020, I took the pulse of the country and realized the north was in a panic because of the pandemic. I was scheduled to give an in-person retreat in the States in April, so I began looking for a refuge in the US where I could stay for a few months. A friend offered her summer house on the Cape in Massachusetts. Resilience had become my middle name; repacking my suitcase, I flew to Logan airport. Four days later Italy closed its borders, but Irsina went even further. Everyone was locked in their houses except for one assigned morning a week to shop for food and pharmacy needs. No one was allowed to leave their houses, even for walks, for the next 10 months! By grace, I was on the beach in Wellfleet, Massachusetts, and not locked into a medieval cave.

As the pandemic upended life throughout the world, it cancelled my US retreat and I found myself converting to Zoom. But where to go next? My stay in Wellfleet was coming to an end as the summer season would start soon. I was lightly familiar with Massachusetts. Then I thought of Cheryl, whom I'd met in San Miguel. We'd struck up a conversation and kept in touch. I remembered that she lived in Northampton, Massachusetts, so I thought maybe this could be the next stop in my nomadic life.

Now instead of navigating the immigration department and a new language, I was buying a car virtually, complete with registration and delivery. When the car was delivered to Wellfleet, I was so frightened of the virus that I wouldn't even sit in it for a couple of days! Then I signed a lease online for an apartment and furnished it through shopping websites like Wayfair and Overstock. A friend of a friend of my daughter's recommended someone who unpacked and put together all my furniture before I arrived. A year later, my possessions arrived from Italy, after months in storage on a pier in Naples and months in a London pier. Ten tattered boxes but everything intact.

Living in an unfamiliar town in an unfamiliar state in the middle of a pandemic was as foreign as moving to a country without speaking the language. My expat life was on hiatus; there was no clear path back to Italy. Like so many people, I shopped online, drove to the store, opened the trunk, and waited for a masked clerk to load my groceries in the car.

Eighteen months later, not having made any friends in Northampton, I flew to San Miguel de Allende to visit my daughter, who'd fled California when work and school shut down and the air was filled with smoke from forest fires. This time, I looked around the city and thought, this is home. I'm not a tourist anymore. I want to live here as permanently as I'll live anywhere in the world. Even San Miguel's celebratory fireworks and rockets seemed to welcome me.

Now I live in an indigenous neighborhood overlooking the city. I have trusted drivers who ferry me down the steep cobblestone streets to shop, and excellent traditional and alternative health care practitioners to help care for the needs of my 81-year-old body. In my 10 years of expat life, I've learned how to navigate banking, health insurance, and mail, while still maintaining a presence in the US. I feel grounded.

With the pandemic, my Zoom life became a source of classes and connections. As I traversed loneliness, confusion, and uncertainty. I often think of Thich Nhat Hanh's book, "At Home in the World," which fell off the shelf in front of me in a bookstore in Ireland exactly when I was confused and uncertain about my future. Thich Nhat Hanh was ejected from his home country for 40 years because of his activism during the Vietnam War. He wrote about feeling lonely and disoriented without his root country beneath his feet. I knew that if he learned how to be at home in the world, so could I.

San Miguel has changed in the intervening years. At the end of the pandemic many new chefs opened restaurants and new galleries and shops opened too. But it's still a mecca of art, writers, music, and traditional Mexican festivals.

Once a friend asked me what I take with me to help me be at home wherever I am. I told her about the few small, light treasures that I always carry with me. In a foreshadowing moment, just before I left San Miguel for Europe, I bought an art piece from Susan Fiori called "Dream Rider," with a red-haired woman flying over mountains on a black raven. It has traveled everywhere with me, along with a Thich Nhat Hanh calligraphy "Go Like a River," and a detailed needlepoint of a mandala which my youngest daughter painstakingly stitched for me when I started my nomadic life. Today the mandala is finally framed and hanging on my living room wall, a talisman that reminds me I'm done wandering. I am an expat comfortably at home in San Miguel de Allende, Mexico.

‿

*Growing up in the 1950s in northern Idaho, Raechel Bratnick dreamed of living abroad. That dream finally came true in 2014 after careers in teaching, public relations, mothering, and psychotherapy. She has lived in Mexico and Europe while continuing to approach psychotherapy from a spiritual perspective through the lenses of Buddhism, Kabbalah, the Tao te Ching and Eva Pierrakos' Pathwork. She is a dream adept and author of "Awakening the Dreamer." After the death of her husband and spiritual teaching partner, she published her memoir, "The Likelihood of Dawn: An Intimate Journey Within and Beyond Grief," a finalist in the 2020 Next Generation Indie Book Awards. Wherever she is living, she enjoys creating ink and watercolor drawings and writing. www.raechelbratnick.com*

# 24. All in Due Time

## Tim Leffel

## Guanajuato City, Guanajuato

When I've hit the wall from working, I'll head out the door and take a long walk in my adopted city in Mexico. If I head uphill, I eventually get to a shady park with flagstone walkways and landscaped gardens, then a man-made lake where people are paddling around in rowboats or eating at a waterfront restaurant, the lake framed by mountains.

If I go downhill, I pass buildings that have stood for hundreds of years, mixed in with grand ones that came in the early 20th century, like the Teatro Juarez, a beautiful theater that stages concerts. I grab an ice cream or a cold beer, maybe buy something from people selling fruit, vegetables, or nuts on the sidewalk. I come home through another park and climb 37 stairs back up to my house on a pedestrian-only street on the hillside.

I've been living in Guanajuato, at 6,500 feet in altitude, full-time since late 2018. Before that we came for a year, went back to the States for two, returned for two years, then went back for my daughter to finish high school in the USA. She wanted to go to a school that looked like the ones on the Disney Channel shows, complete with lockers, a cafeteria, and groups of geeks and freaks who were shunned by the mean girls.

All this started when I was on a travel writing assignment in Mexico that brought me to Mexico City, San Miguel de Allende, and Guanajuato. We'd been to coastal Mexico on vacations and had a little beach house on the Gulf Coast near Merida that was a getaway place from our then-home of landlocked Nashville. None of us had spent any time in the central highlands though, where many of the historic silver mining cities were clustered in Spanish Colonial times.

My wife and I had lived in Turkey and South Korea in our childless days when we were backpacking the world and we often talked about living abroad again, this time with our daughter. We looked at Argentina, Nicaragua, Guatemala, and other spots, but Mexico remained at the top of the list because of its closeness and its air connectivity. It didn't hurt that it also had better food than the rest.

"I found the place!"

That's the e-mail I sent to my wife within the first 24 hours of getting to Guanajuato.

"What are you talking about?" she asked. "You just got there!"

"I know, but this is the one."

I sent photos and talked about how different it was from most other colonial cities set out in a grid. Curvy pedestrian streets all over, colorful houses clinging to steep hillsides, sunny weather all year, and a tiny fraction of the foreigners that had so visibly taken over San Miguel de Allende.

I was reviewing hotels for a trade publication, so I saw nearly every neighborhood in one go, finding something delightful and interesting in every one. By the time I got on a plane and headed home, I was making plans for a trial run the next summer break.

## Trying Guanajuato on for Size

The following June when school ended, we went on what looked like a long vacation to our daughter, but was really a "feel it out" trip for my wife. We enrolled in Spanish lessons, rented an apartment for three weeks in the historic center, and did all the routine things a resident would do. We went grocery shopping, visited the butcher and the baker, and had lunch at Hidalgo Market. My wife checked out schools and I checked out bus schedules to see what our options were for exploring from there.

"Yes, let's do it!" was the verdict after we found a Waldorf school for a year of elementary school and discovered that the local airport and bus stations could get us almost anywhere in Mexico and beyond.

We had a lot to plan for in the coming year because at the same time, my wife made it clear that she didn't want to return to Nashville when we were done with this year abroad. She wanted to get closer to her mother and sister in Florida and leave the winter grayness for good. It would be sun all year from now on, whether in Mexico or the USA. So that meant selling off or storing everything we owned and putting our house on the market before we left.

As anyone who has had to prep a child for an upcoming move knows, the conversation with our daughter was wrenching. Not only were we leaving the only house she had ever known and the only city she had lived in for 10 years, we also weren't coming back to it or her friends. We were making a clean break. We knew she would adapt quickly to two new homes—Guanajuato and Tampa Bay—but that didn't make the talks any easier.

We also had terrible timing, it turns out, when it came to selling our house. We moved to Mexico in 2010, just as the Bush-era financial crisis was hitting full stride and the housing market was imploding. Our historic East Nashville neighborhood, the hot place to move to that was on the upswing, was suddenly filled with "For Sale" signs on every block. Banks were the ones negotiating the deals on some of them and their biggest priority was a quick sale, not the final price.

So for much of our first year in Mexico we were paying rent and a mortgage until a deal finally came through. It helped that our rent in Guanajuato was only $800 dollars per month including utilities, with four bedrooms and two baths, plus a shared roof terrace looking out at the mountains and sunsets.

The main problem with the rental apartment was that it was at nearly the highest point in the city. Fine if we got there in a taxi, but a major hike if we didn't. It was especially tough the one night we arrived back from a vacation on New Year's Eve, when there seemed to be 100 people wanting a cab for every one ride that was available. Giving up after half an hour of vain attempts, we trekked up the mountain with all our luggage in tow.

We enjoyed living there as much as we thought we would, so we started making plans for returning. We'd go back to the USA for two years, then return after that for who knows how long.

## Wait, we bought a house?

As our year-long trip to Mexico came to an end and our house in Nashville went into contract, on a lark we started looking around at houses just to see what prices were like. The first couple of rounds showed us how affordable real estate was in Guanajuato, but nothing that we saw really grabbed us. The houses were too far from the center, too chock-a-block in the layout from six rounds of construction over the years, or we didn't like the neighborhood.

When we entered the house we eventually bought, though, it was a whole different story. The layout was open and airy, the rooms filled with natural light. Some of them had a terrific view, especially the sunroom that had windows running the length on three sides. From the living room and bedroom we could see El Pipila lit up at night, the giant statue that's perched over the observation area where the best-known image of the city is photographed every day. It was close to a big local market and a park, and near a bus stop that took people to the rest of the city. A walk to the middle of the historic district was only 15 minutes at a leisurely pace.

The house had four bedrooms, two bathrooms, and plenty of space, with no structural work needed and a functional move-in condition, apart from a tired-looking kitchen with particle board cabinets that were showing their years. The price was under a million, but that was in pesos. They were asking the equivalent of $85,000 dollars.

"Hmmm, maybe we should buy this place," my wife muttered in a low voice as we finished the tour.

"I think you might be right," I answered.

After we left, we talked it over a bit and came back to the real estate agent with a proposition: we would pay them their full asking price, which was fair, but we needed to split it into two payments. We would pay half upon completion of the contract, and the second half later when we got paid for our other house in the States and could take possession. That way the owner could stay on for a while and take her time packing up, since we weren't going to be there to move in anyway.

It was a novel approach, but it served both our needs, and we signed the deal. Two years later we returned and started making it our only permanent home.

## An Introduction to Mexican Time

After we wired the second payment and the house was all ours, we had two big jobs to farm out. The floor tile was just plain ugly and looked about as Mexican as a US interstate rest stop, so the first thing we wanted to do was lay down more appropriate saltillo ceramic tiles.

The other big project was to redo the kitchen. The house did not date back to colonial times—only a few decades actually—but we both wanted a colorful Mexican tile kitchen, so we hired an architect/contractor to make that happen. We ordered Talavera tiles, custom wood cabinets, and a new island for extra counter space in the middle.

The set-up was easy, the execution not so much. I naively thought it would be a great idea to have the tile work done well before the kitchen work and our arrival, with nobody in the house. Unfortunately, that meant nobody in the house to see what was getting done—or more accurately, not getting done. It took constant badgering before even one room would be finished and we were weeks behind schedule when it was time for the kitchen crew to get started. This meant two sets of competing workmen getting in each others' way.

I was in and out when we finally got on track, so a few things did not turn out quite as planned. The tile guy's work was not up to the usual standards, with a few shortcuts we've been dealing with ever since, but the custom cabinet work was top-notch and the total tab for the kitchen renovation was around $10,000 dollars, including appliances.

Since we are halfway up a mountain on a pedestrian-only street—the most common kind in Guanajuato—I was a bit worried that we'd have trouble getting bulky items delivered. Apparently they're used to it, though. Our first few weeks in the house saw a parade of grunting men bringing heavy items through the door: stove, refrigerator, beds, propane tanks, bookshelves, and more.

Everything didn't all come at once though, and a local carpenter made much of the furniture, so for the first few weeks our house was laughably bare. I'd gotten two beds and mattresses delivered before we moved in, so the three of us had places to sleep at least, but there was no living room furniture and no dining room table. When it was time to eat a meal, we had two stools to scoot up to the island in the kitchen. Two of us would sit down and the other would stand up. When I needed to get some work done on my laptop at home, it was literally on my lap.

When you buy a house in Mexico, it's usually fully furnished or absolutely stripped bare. Ours was the latter: We had to buy lamps to even have some light outside of the new kitchen. We scouted out light fixtures and put those on the handyman's list so that we could utilize the bare wires extending from the ceiling.

Poco a poco, little by little, we filled the rooms, complementing the utility items with beautiful handicrafts from Mexico. Over time we added masks from throughout Latin America, alebrijes from Oaxaca, and catrina figures from Michoacán. A few rugs from our earlier travels in Morocco and India brought back memories of other adventures. We made do with Mexico's commercial furniture choices and relied on the skilled local carpenters for anything that could be made from wood.

We had one more construction project in the early days, though. When we got ready to buy a TV, we discovered that the entire house's electrical system was running on a single circuit, with one breaker in the box. We had to have the house rewired, splitting it into multiple circuits, so we wouldn't blow up the new TV or our computers when the microwave went on.

On trips back to the USA, we'd go up with nearly empty suitcases and come back with them stuffed to the max. Each time the house became a little more ours and we could supplement for items that were hard to find in Mexico. (This was before Amazon arrived; it's much easier now.)

Our daughter Alina, in middle school at this point, was enrolled in "the most expensive private school in Guanajuato," which set us back about $300 dollars a month. While it was prestigious, it was all in Spanish, so she became fluent in a hurry with the help of her friends and her teachers. That made up for what felt like an incredibly lax curriculum, with more holidays and performance practice days than time spent actually learning anything.

We took it all in stride though, remembering that the US obsession with "teaching to the test" isn't ideal either, and at least she was getting some interesting cultural education and gaining language skills. We got her a math tutor for her weakest subject and enrolled her in a Florida online English literature course so she'd be ready for a US return, but otherwise we figured she'd catch up later when back in her home country.

At first I would ride in a taxi with my daughter to her school and come back on the public bus, eating up a good hour or more from my morning. Eventually she decided that Dad didn't need to come along anymore, taking a step toward becoming a more independent teenager. I would flag down a taxi and send her off, then she would ride the bus with a few friends after school to return.

Those two full years in Mexico as a family went by in a flash. When we had a school break, we often traveled within the country, going to Real de Catorce, Oaxaca, Puebla, Zihuatanejo, Puerto Escondido, Morelia, and Patzcuaro. We attended school events with drawn-out speeches, went to concerts at the Cervantino Festival, and kept earning money in dollars to spend in pesos.

We took advantage of the arbitrage to get some dental work done at one-fifth the price, even more if we factored in the up-selling we could avoid. ("You could put her in braces if you want," the dentist said, "But I'd advise trying this spacer for six months first to see if she really needs them.") In the end she didn't need them, but that wouldn't have stopped a US orthodontist with grad school bills to pay from ordering them up anyway.

We also got full-body checkups from the dermatologist, new prescription glasses for Donna, and had some other routine checkups done, all at prices that were less than a typical co-pay where we came from. With all the walking and less stress, my blood pressure and standing heartbeat both dropped to their lowest levels in a decade.

With utility bills that were next to nothing in the "eternal spring" climate and property taxes of under $250 dollars per year, the main stress was thinking about how we were going to adjust when facing American prices again, an inevitability since we were headed back to Tampa for grades 10 to 12 of high school.

## Looking Forward to Leaving Again

While we had plenty of good times back in Tampa Bay and enjoyed all the USA's convenience and ease, the sticker shock never really wore off. Whereas the three of us were averaging expenses of $2,000 dollars a month in Mexico without being at all frugal with entertainment and eating out, back in the States we were paying more than that just for rent. In Guanajuato we didn't need a car, and when we did need a ride, taxis were a few dollars. In Tampa, just sharing one car between us was costing more than $600 dollars a month.

Utilities were a few hundred more, health insurance was eating up another $800 dollars per month, and groceries were easily triple the price of what we had been spending in Mexico. Going out to eat went from something we did routinely without a thought to something we needed to budget for and do sparingly. While we would go out to cultural performances and concerts for $6 to $10 dollars each in Mexico and visit museums for $2 dollars, in the USA it felt like everything was a splurge.

One of the worst adjustments we faced was having to clean our own house again. When you're used to a housekeeper coming in once or twice a week to sweep, mop, and tidy up, you forget what a pain it is to scrub toilets and dust down everything. A top-to-bottom house cleaning in Mexico would cost me what I earn in about 20 minutes in a normal week. If I wanted that same kind of work done in Tampa, it would cost me three hours of my wages instead. So we would buckle down and get it done ourselves when the place got too filthy to bear.

On top of all the money stress, the cultural workaholic stress and political stress were weighing on us as well. While the Mexicans we interacted with were often smiling and in no hurry, most of our fellow Americans were pressed for time and regularly worried about something. While Mexican conversations revolved around family, friends, and fun, the conversations in the USA were often more about work, money, or politics, with a lot of negative undertones. Everyone was seemingly in a battle to see who could appear to be more busy, that busyness somehow being a badge of honor.

The 24-hour cable news seemed to always focus on who was winning or losing on the political football field and what issue of the day was stoking the most anger. The news networks could then go fan the flames so the angriest people would keep tuning in.

When our daughter graduated from high school and got accepted into her college of choice, the bags were already half packed in our mind. As soon as she went off to college, we were off to Mexico again, this time for good. We were not putting anything into storage like we did before, apart from a few boxes that would go in my mother-in-law's garage.

I laid all my tools out on a tarp and put them on Craigslist with a listing that said, "All or nothing, here's the price." We tossed out bulky mementos we had held onto for a decade or two, sold off everything of value we weren't taking with us, and turned in the car we had leased for a set three-year period. We donated to the Salvation Army and gave our daughter the most robust set of kitchen and dining items that any middle-class kid going off to college has probably ever experienced.

This time we weren't making a temporary move. We had a house waiting for us in a home we couldn't wait to get back to, in Mexico. Sure, we'd still have a permanent address for taxes, banking, and voting, but really we were cutting the rope for good this time.

## A Permanent Base in Mexico

Now that we're empty nesters, we both travel quite a bit these days, but we tell everyone our home base is in Mexico. We moved back in late 2018 and haven't regretted it once.

We're back to $1.50 pints of fresh juice, bargain buckets of beer, and symphony performances for the price of a Big Mac. When we return to the USA on business or to see relatives, we shake our heads over the prices. We gladly spend money on what we've missed, but we have to be 10 times more careful about how often we whip out our wallets.

When the stressful Covid pandemic times hit and many businesses had to shutter their doors for a while, our income from our travel publishing pursuits took a nosedive. If we had been living in Tampa then, with our high fixed expenses, it might have done us in. Living in a paid-for house in Mexico though, it was a time to work less, cook more, and enjoy the increased downtime. Since we weren't going out or traveling for months on end, our expenses dropped down to under $800 dollars per month for two. The biggest thing to worry about was whether the beer supply was going to run out when the breweries were deemed "unessential services." (Says who?!)

When I masked up and went out for a walk then, it was nice to stroll past buildings that were older than anything located between St. Augustine and Quebec. I was thankful to be walking on streets where people walked in the 1500s instead of looking out at a parade of strip malls and parking lots. I appreciated the fact that most of the restaurants were already offering outdoor dining: we eat outside all year.

Not everything in our corner of Mexico is ideal, of course. We've got some trashy next-door neighbors that collect more junk than Sanford & Son. The high tolerance of noise among Mexicans is truly astounding: fireworks, mariachi bands, loud stereos, and military parade bands are sometimes all firing off at once, each trying to top the other in volume. Sometimes the parties don't start until the wee hours—including on Christmas Eve—and only wind down when the sun comes up. Then the morning Saint Day cannon sounds take over.

As anyone who has lived in Latin America for some time can attest, the fluid sense of time cannot be fought, only accepted. Almost everything that needs to get done will get done eventually, but it usually won't happen as quickly as we want. That contractor might show up at 10 when he said he would, but it's far more likely that he'll show up at noon. Or 2 p.m. Or maybe the next day.

The work itself is seldom sloppy, however, and when someone is working, they're usually giving it their all. They just know when to turn it off and go have some fun instead. Work to live; not the other way around.

As someone who likes to work hard and then play hard, these days I identify more with the Mexican attitude and the one in the land of my birth feels more foreign. It is far easier to live in the moment and enjoy it when you're not constantly pursuing money or status. I'm a lot healthier too. I eat more fruit and vegetables, I get more exercise without trying, and it's dramatically cheaper to get preventative medical care than it is under the broken for-profit health care system up north. The daily sun is great for the mood and the sound of laughter all around makes me smile.

Mexico feels like home now and when I sit in my house that we decorated, looking out at the colorful houses and mountains in a climate that doesn't require air conditioning or central heating, it's easy to be content.

⌒

*Tim Leffel is a travel writer and publisher based in Guanajuato, Mexico. He is the author of the popular living abroad book, "A Better Life for Half the Price," and founder of the Cheapest Destinations Blog, which launched in 2003. He and his wife Donna both work from home. See more of his work at TimLeffel.com.*

Photo by Matt Mawson

# About the Author

Janet Blaser is an author, writer, and consultant who has lived in Mexico since 2006. A former journalist in California, her work now focuses on expat living. She has been a writer and storyteller her entire life, and has been fortunate to write about great food, amazing places, fascinating people, and unique events. Janet is a regular contributor to CNBC's "Make It," International Living magazine, and various other publications.

Her first book, *Why We Left: An Anthology of American Women Expats*, is an Amazon bestseller. She's currently working on a series of *Going Expat Guides* about Mexico, Italy, Portugal, and Costa Rica. Janet also offers individualized Expat Consultations via Zoom to encourage and assist folks wanting to move to Mexico.

A writer by nature, Janet also likes to surf, garden, read, cook, and, at times, rabble-rouse. She counts among her many blessings three wonderful adult children as well as a trio of delightful grandchildren. The easiest way to learn more about expat life and see Janet's extensive body of work is to Google her name. Stay connected by following @TheJanetBlaser or @GoingExpatGuides on Facebook and Instagram or visiting JanetBlaser.com.

Made in the USA
Monee, IL
06 July 2025

20588323R00142